THE OLD COUNTRY STORE

The

Old Country Store

BY

GERALD CARSON

ILLUSTRATED

ADAM SMITH ON TRADERS: 'They have frequently more acuteness of understanding than the greater part of country gentlemen.'

New York · OXFORD UNIVERSITY PRESS
1954

CONTENTS

FOREWORD

The contributions to American life made by the country doctor, the village lawyer, and the editor of the rural newspaper have been frequently and generously recognized. Yet it must be acknowledged that though a four-corners might become a hamlet, a hamlet a village, without benefit of medical or legal services, or the clank of a flat-bed press, it could never hope to be more than a wide place in the road without a general store.

'A store is badly wanted,' Dr. Hiram Rutherford, a pioneer physician in eastern Illinois, wrote in 1841 to a country dealer of his acquaintance back 'home' in Pennsylvania. 'People have to go twenty-five miles, and then not get what they wanted, perhaps.'

In the days when men lived separate and solitary lives, it was the country store that tied the scattered farms into a community. The store was what made a neighborhood and gave it its central nervous system and a conscience. It also put some fun into life.

The owner of the store was invariably an important personality, a community leader ex officio, a culture hero, too. Around him gathered tales and incidents, one of the few instances of the businessman appearing as a character in folklore.

For nearly a hundred and fifty years after the Revolution, the country store rendered a great variety of services not otherwise available in an unspecialized society. The successful storekeeper's ability to adjust nimbly to changing circumstances in times of war, financial panic, and depression, to make a profit in an orthodox manner at one time, and then at another to take a long chance, is a prime instance of American flexibility and durability, free enterprise in a very pure form. To develop fully his local opportunities, the country trader became at an early date a commodity speculator and practitioner of that form of applied psychology the specialists now call social engineering; that is, the gentle art of How To Use What You Want To Get What I Want.

The Yankee peddler had his roots in Europe. The city merchant and the shopkeeper had their analogues in older lands. But the general store was an American origination, something new under the sun, improvised to meet the raw conditions of a new continent.

An English historian, Mr. A. L. Rowse, throws out an idea applicable to the old general stores and their merchandise when he says that history is everywhere, even in the nib of his pen, which he got free from a bank. The pen point holds within itself the whole history of the Industrial Revolution. It could provide the text for a dissertation on metallurgy, shipping, paper, or the British postal system. It could easily lead on to a study of the commercial geography of the world.

The daybook of a general store is no less suggestive than a British pen nib. It affords documentary and contemporary materials for the investigation of such diverse themes as American agriculture, costume, merchandising, advertising, popular taste in literature, textiles, the temperance movement, humor, frontier medicine, firearms, diet, education, arts and crafts, transportation, or the development of lighting from Betty lamp to rural electrification. Though nineteenth-century country ways of life now seem as remote as life in a medieval barony, yet there are still millions of men and women living today who remember well, if not the golden age of the country store, at least its afterglow.

The country store contributes a definite flavor and personality to our American past: 'Particularly if you came from the smaller towns and villages — farming areas of our country — you have memories that are priceless,' President Eisenhower told a meeting of retail merchants in 1953. 'They so often centered around the retail store, the open cracker barrel, the prune barrel, the pickle jug or keg. Places where things were sold and people gathered because they needed them. They were the social centers of our time . . . Our memories today . . . center around that time, that place, those connections, those contacts.'

Rich opportunities still exist for the study of general stores regionally, the stores the Adirondackers knew, the down-east Yankee, the corn-and-hog farmer of the plains states. In coves, hollows, and necks, along creeks, at little 'points' and 'centers' all over the United States, the country merchants once had their old stands, each with an individuality of its own, varying according to its local situation and economy, yet all essentially the same — unity within diversity.

Materials for a study of the general store are widely scattered but, fortunately, extensive. The text of this book is based on unpublished journals and ledgers and other store records; on contemporary printed sources, almanacs, diaries, newspapers, trade journals, mail-order catalogues, trade cards, and odds and ends of advertising ephemera; on local histories, publications of historical and folklore societies, and the research of some modern authorities on business history. Many personal communications, which are acknowledged elsewhere, added a touch of realism and vivacity all their own; these were provided by friends and total strangers whose memories served them well.

Old customs in capitalization and spelling have been retained in quoted material for emphasis and atmosphere. Punctuation has been modernized occasionally, or supplied in places where there was none. Notes on sources and authorities will be found at the back of the book.

The geographical limits generally observed throughout the book consider the country store as it evolved in the northeastern and north central states, though an item of general significance, an anecdote or authentic bit of atmosphere was not refused admittance because it had a southern accent or had to travel east to cross the Mississippi River. In regard to time, the account begins around 1790 with the establishment of firm fiscal policies in the central government and ends with the development, state by state, of a network of all-weather roads soon after World War I.

The use of the past tense in discussing the country store may cause some raised eyebrows. Thousands of stores exist today, of course, with a sign above the door which says 'General Store.' They are, however, with a few notable exceptions, convenience or 'fill in' stores for small purchases, the forgotten items — a box of corn flakes, a tin of tobacco, a summer vacationist's post cards.

The purpose here is evocative, to bring to the reader's nose the celebrated country store smell, to present to his eyes the interior as it appeared to generations now gone. The store is a stage well filled with a colorful throng of those who inherited, for their time, the earth, the sun and seasons, the mud, the frosts, the smell of June hay, the joys and the pains of the flesh and the spirit; who had jurisdiction, during their brief generation, of the world and its contents; or, as Thomas Don-

gan, colonial governor of New York, said in granting a pat-
ent, they were in charge of 'all Woods Underwoods Waters
Runns Streams Ponds Creeks Meadows Marches fishing
Hawking Hunting and fowling and all other Liberties and
Previledges Heridaments and Appurtenences' of the good
earth on which they flourished.

As the reader enters and glances around this volume, he
will, it is hoped, say to himself, more or less: 'So this is exactly
the way it was down at the country store!' Exactly? Well, exactly — or something similar.

G. C.

Millerton, New York
January 1954

ACKNOWLEDGMENTS

IT IS IMPOSSIBLE to explain here the kind and quality of each grant-in-aid from friends, librarians, bibliographers, storekeepers, descendants, and strangers generally. There is one kind of help representing many hours, much thought and labor. Another kind consists of a brief but inspired suggestion. Each has its place. Any failure to acknowledge assistance which has been so generously given indicates an unsystematic, but not an ungrateful, author.

Of critical importance, each in its own different way, were the contributions of Clarence S. Brigham; Earnest Elmo Calkins; Lee E. Grove of Oxford University Press, who has been everything to the book which a gifted editor can be; Mrs. Helen B. Green, Thomas F. Haines, Professor Warner G. Rice, and Colton Storm.

Among the many hands which helped to shape the book were those of Henry Abt, Professor Robert J. Allen, Dr. F. Clever Bald, Leon C. Baldwin, Miss Dorothy C. Barck and all of her staff who serve the Reading Room of The New-York Historical Society.

Also Fred H. Barnes, Edward Battey, William F. Berghold, Hal and Barbara Borland, Wallace K. Boyer, John D. Briscoe, Evans Clark, Carl Carmer, James C. Colvin, the staff of the Columbia University Library, Sidney O. Cowles, Earl Cushman, Miss Helen Daringer, Leon W. Dean, Mrs. Alice W. Dickson, James Taylor Dunn, Mr. and Mrs. George T. Eager, Mr. and Mrs. Paul Eager, Norman M. Enman, and Miss Clara E. Follette.

Grateful acknowledgment is made to Roy A. Foulke, Allyn Fuller, Mr. and Mrs. E. H. Gay, Miss Pearl Hagens, and Bill Hall, a Yankee storekeeper in the old tradition. Also Fred Haviland, and the staff of the Historical Society of Pennsylvania, Mrs. Gladys R. Holton, Icho Iben, Miss Edna L. Jacobsen, Dr. Louis C. Jones, Mark W. Kiley, Sidney Kocin, Mrs. Louise E. Koier, Mrs. Richard Krebs, Mrs. Marjorie Kroehler, Joseph Wood Krutch, Mrs. Bella C. Landauer, Rev. S. S. Lappin, Donald M. Le Hockey, Dr. Clifford L. Lord, Robert W. Lovett, Dr. Blake McKelvey, and David W. Mearns.

George L. Moore shared his enthusiasm for country stores with me, and Edward B. Morrison his MS. account books in the New York Public Library. The staffs of various departmental rooms at New York Public, such as rooms 300, 308, and 328, opened up their resources with unfailing good humor, speed, and intelligence. I also wish to thank Leonard Panaggio, Dr. Harry E. Pratt, Mr. and Mrs. Stuart Peabody, Dr. A. W. Peach, Clay Perry, Rev. W. R. Phinney, Mrs. Blanche Purl, and Peter G. Rapp for the lift they gave me along my way.

I am grateful to Fred Reinhart, Mrs. Carroll Rheinstrom, Miss Ethel Richmond, Lawrence B. Romaine, inspired rare-book finder; also Mrs. Roy Ruhnka for some especially fine anecdotes, the staff of the Scoville Library, Salisbury, Connecticut, Donald Sears, Sherwood Schank, Mr. and Mrs. J. Kellogg-Smith, Clarence Stotts, Mrs. Horace Stump, Forest H. Sweet, W. Stephen Thomas, Mason Tolman, William D. Toohey, Jared Van Wagenen, Jr., the Vassar College Library, Sidney Wade, Dr. Louis A. Warren, Louis N. Wiggins, Mrs. Clarence S. Williamson, Ray Winans, Willis Kingsley Wing, and Arlington Yutzler.

G. C.

PART ONE

1791 – 1861

*'There is much to be learned
in a country store.'*
— P. T. BARNUM

A CHANCE TO GROW UP WITH THE COUNTRY

WHEN A MAN with a touch of silver in his hair speaks today of the general store, it is usually to reach back in affectionate memory to a particular store, the one where his father and mother, grandfather and grandmother, did their 'trading.'

Or perhaps he himself as a little tyke enjoyed exciting privileges in the store because grandpa was the storekeeper, remembered as a big, booming man, with the 'knack' of the merchant. The store at the dusty crossroads became a boy's window on the world, with the thrifty shoppers from hill and valley farms to give it warmth and neighborliness, the candy agent from Milwaukee (or whatever the nearest jobbing center might be) to add a touch of sophistication with his city ways, and the voluntarily unemployed, arranged around the store stove like a Greek chorus, ready to comment on each episode in the day's drama.

And so it is remembered and passed along, how in a Vermont store there was a 'setter' beside the stove who watched impassively as the proprietor wielded the turkey-wing duster, scattered the floor-sweep, and pushed the push broom.

'Where's Eddie — is he sick?' inquired the merchant's guest, solicitously.

'No. He's through.'

A pause for further reflection; and then: 'Got anybody in mind to fill the vacancy?'

The storekeeper went on with his dusting.

'Nope,' he said briefly over his shoulder. 'Eddie didn't leave no vacancy.'

A little fenced-off corner of the main room, faced with pigeonhole boxes, provided the facilities of the United States postal system. A wall telephone linked the store intimately with the great world beyond — except that the batteries were always going dead because, it was said, Grandma Crumbaker sat in her kitchen from dawn to dark with the receiver strapped to her ear.

Nineteen hundred, perhaps back to the middle 'nineties; and random memories drift past, of the country merchant's great leather-bound ledgers, of father's hunting case watch with the stag on the front, of that funny paper-covered book about Uncle Jeremiah's visit to the Chicago World's Fair. There was the stereopticon, too, pyrography, and the shirt-waist girl; and memories of Christmas at the old store counters, candy in wooden pails and Keen Kutter skates piled with the toy swords, drums, and magic lanterns.

That's about as far back as living memory goes, except for the indestructible few. Yet it is but a moment, a pin point in time, as compared with the long life of the country store. A hundred years and more before the opening of the present century, young men with little taste for the flail and winnowing basket were drawn to the game of barter and sale. For they saw that the storekeeper was a man of capital, 'a kind of community king,' whose work seemed to young farm eyes a mere recreation, 'buying and tying and counting the money.'

From earliest times men without the character and apti-
tudes of the trader drifted in and out of the attractive occupation of rural merchant; and often found it advisable, before
they were shut of it, to light out for Texas. There was always
more, a good deal more, to keeping store than having a capital
of $500, living off the store stock, teaching a Sunday school
class, and wearing a coat.

A trader keeping a general store, who had had the good
fortune to survive the War of the Revolution, might have felt
reasonably safe about his political liberties after the surrender of Lord Cornwallis at Yorktown in October 1781. About
his material well-being — the value of his ledger accounts, of
the bills and notes in his strongbox, of his stock of goods, his
oxen, sheep, and barns — that remained a matter clouded
with anxiety and uncertainty for a considerable time after the
victory was won.

Some ten turbulent years were to pass before a man who
'kept store' in any settled part of northern or eastern United
States could view the future of storekeeping with any confidence. Behind him lay the ruinous years of war and inflation.
During this time the state governments and the Congress of
the Confederation seemed to have made every possible financial mistake that would tend to make goods dear and destroy
the public faith in the money they issued. The pockets of the
ordinary citizen and the tills of the merchants were crammed
with paper money, the purchasing power of which diminished
to almost nothing. Refined sugar, in the cone shape of colonial
days, went to 7 shillings per pound, hay to $9 per hundred,
lime to $30 a hogshead. A clock cost £21, milk 15 shillings a
quart, potatoes 96 shillings a bushel, pork 60 shillings per

pound, rum 45 shillings per pint, corn $40 per bushel. If a man wanted to buy a cow it took at one time around $1200 to interest the seller.

It is not surprising, in these circumstances, that the country people turned to other mediums of exchange which represented real values. Small cubes of indigo would pass in a day when every house had a fireplace, and every fireplace had beside it a dye pot or indigo tub. Unofficial values were recognized in a bushel of salt, required in vast quantities in the days before refrigeration for pickling and preserving beef, pork, and fish. In western Pennsylvania a gallon of whiskey could be exchanged for 'European goods,' meaning glassware, hardware, dress goods, bar iron, thread, powder and shot; or for 'West India' goods — salt, molasses, sugar, tea, coffee, spices, rum, and various vegetable dyes. Often in the border counties imported goods were not to be had at any price.

The economic difficulties connected with the Revolution were a matter of recent and bitter personal experience. But any trader could have heard from his father or grandsire, as a racial memory, equally dark tales of wild inflation during the interminable French wars and how in those times, too, the money got poorer and poorer, the debtors more and more reluctant to pay.

> *The country maids with sauce to market come,*
> *And carry loads of tattered money home.*

The dread of a worthless currency was a deep and wasting worry. Once the disease got the upper hand, the cure seemed even worse; for when the necessary steps were proposed for redeeming the paper, a new difficulty arose. Instead of poor money, there would be none, with the hard money, what there was of it, draining out of the country to pay for exchange.

The doggerel writers sang a sad goodby to the departing coins:

> *To foreign lands they'll be convey'd*
> *Then what's our fate — the silver gone,*
> *The paper burnt — and we undone.*

During the Confederation, that loose association of friendly but sovereign states, while the ideas of delegated powers and a strong central government were germinating, the plague of paper money continued without relief. No one knew whether the national debt would be paid or repudiated. Such hard money as there was came from England, Spain, France, and Germany. It did not stay long. While it was here, it carried different values in different states. A man of large affairs might be paying bills in Spanish dollars worth 6 shillings in New England, 8 shillings in New York, 7 shillings 6 pence from New Jersey to Maryland, and 4 shillings 8 pence in South Carolina and Georgia. Adding to the confusion, counterfeiters were industriously occupied in turning French sous into Spanish moidores, an ingenious alchemy by which copper became gold, and was worth 36 shillings. Coppers washed with silver passed off as English sixpences. The British, delighted to compound American difficulties, manufactured counterfeits of their own English ha'pennies on a large scale in Birmingham and exported them to the United States in casks marked as 'hardware.'

Nor was the imitation of the paper money of the several states beyond the talents of our own native rascals who operated covert engraving shops and presses. The ethics of the keeper of a general store in matters of money and coinage was unvarnished self-preservation. When tainted money appeared in the day's cash the first rule of the country was — get rid of it quickly. Usually the junior clerk was the agent appointed to pass it out again so that if the gesture was discovered the responsibility would be diluted.

It was no time for a country merchant to relax when he saw a debtor count out gold coins of high face value and reputable origin, joes, half-joes, doubloons, Spanish pistoles, English and French guineas. They had been sheared and clipped so long and so severely that gold coin was acceptable only by actual weight. George Washington himself said that unless the United States soon had a coinage of its own or could find some way to stop the cutting and clipping of dollars and pistareens, a man would have to travel with a pair of scales in his pocket, or run the risk of receiving gold at a fourth less by weight than by count.

There was a problem of another kind which might have persuaded a storekeeper of the 1780's that he was in the wrong line of work. The young country, bursting at the seams, with few manufactures of its own, and few imports for nearly ten troubled years, acted with the pull of a powerful magnet on the markets of the old countries once trade was resumed. The American market was soon flooded with merchandise, and the storehouses of the importers were piled high with barrels and boxes as supply outran the ability to buy. Prices dropped and a chain reaction set in. The farmer could not settle up with his crossroads trader. The country dealer could not meet his obligations to the wholesaler and importer. The importer had to call for extensions from his correspondents overseas. Debtors everywhere could not pay. The courts could not enforce payment.

The turn for the better came with the adoption of the Constitution and the beginning of government under it in 1789. Here was assurance of a stable and responsible government on a federal basis. In 1790 Alexander Hamilton, as Secretary of the Treasury, presented a plan for the payment of the foreign and the domestic debt. There were also state debts, incurred in the same cause. These were also to be taken over by the Federal Government, a happy circumstance for the farmers and mercantile classes who held the paper. Congress adopted these measures and went on to pass a national coinage act based on the decimal system. The United States mint was projected and in operation within two years after 1790.

And so it came about that a man with a store on his mind had every reason to 'chirk up.' He could look around in the year 1791 and see peace, plenty, and a future as sound as wheat. The measures of the government were popular in the north and east where tradesmen and merchants, good Hamiltonians all, were now in a position to collect their debts and to be paid in sound money. Trade quickly responded. Packets were loaded down with freight. Loaded oxcarts and farm wagons appeared on the roads, for farmers were now eager to part with their produce. Commercial treaties were made. A patent office was established. The mails bulged. Courthouses were rising to serve new counties, canals dug, roads laid out. Schools, bridges, and docks were under construction. Powder mills became paper mills.

A Revolutionary gun factory at Sutton, Massachusetts, typical in its way, converted to the manufacture of scythes — 'of the best temper' says an old account — and their maker, Aaron Elliot, Jr., demonstrated his own product. On a wager he mowed an acre in less time than an expert required to rake it. The China trade was opening up. A new commerce with Russia brought in large quantities of iron in bars and rods. Jacob Perkins made a machine that would cut and head nails. Nathan Read learned how to make saleratus — our great-grandmothers' leavening for cake and biscuits — by subjecting pearl ash to the fumes of fermenting molasses, of which he, being a distiller, had plenty. 'Ingenious men' everywhere were improving stoves and fireplaces, the manufacture of 'cyder,' the draining of meadows, the preservation of peach trees from decay, finding better methods of rendering oil fit to be burned in the Argand lamp, and devising 'philosophical experiments that let light into the Nature of Things.'

A country storekeeper could look at the resources of his customers in the last decade of the eighteenth century with considerable optimism. America was at peace. Europe was involved in war and calling urgently for more and more food. Wheat prices were high, land values rising. Among the assets of his customers, in addition to farm crops, were the products extracted from forest and woodland — shingles, lumber, tanbark, cordwood, and potash. When the trees were cleared away for farm lots, the great burnings produced vast piles of ashes which were a cash commodity from New England to Ohio. They went to market through the country store in the form of crude potash or the more refined pearl ash or often simply as ashes. The potash trade was an important source of revenue to farmers on the fringe of the settlements. The 'black ash,' like the lighter pearl ash, was obtained by leaching lye from wood ashes and then evaporating the lye to a dry state. Not infrequently the storekeeper, being the local capitalist, undertook the potash business himself, mounting the big iron kettles and leach tubs near his store, and soliciting the farmers to bring him their ashes.

A crude form of potassium carbonate, potash was in active demand for making soap, for bleaching, and for fertilizers. Like whiskey, it had a high cash value in relation to its bulk, an important characteristic in an era when transportation ate up the value of heavy goods.

The sugar shippers of the West Indies wanted good American elm and red and white oak riven into staves for cooperage. Enormous quantities of young hickory, white oak, or 'hoop'

ash were cut and split vertically into hoop poles. What is a
hoop pole? Perhaps you have seen an old barrel, a really old
barrel, in an attic, at country store museums, at least in old
prints, bound not with metal hoops but with withes of split
saplings. Those are hoop poles, a commodity so prime that
Suffield, Connecticut, imposed a fine upon anyone who presumed to cut and carry away hoop poles from the commons.

Commission merchants and forwarders needed casks, barrels, hogsheads, tierces for wines, firkins for butter. They
shipped salt fish in cooperage; beef, pork, flour, biscuits,
crackers — hence the ubiquitous cracker barrel — rum, molasses, whale oil, tar, and pitch. The tanners needed the
hemlock bark of New England and New York. The hatters
called for furs. Shipbuilders were in the market for mast
trees, those great legendary white pines of the northeast,
often three feet in diameter and 120 feet tall, lifting their
crowns above eighty or a hundred feet of bare stick before
putting out the first limb. Never again would the British
Crown's surveyor put the mark of the broad arrow on the
great mast trees to reserve them for the use of the King's
Navy. Now republican oxen drew them to tidewater to be
stepped into the new hulls of a rising commercial navy. Tubs
were needed, too, and stock for pails, churns, baskets, sap
buckets, and all manner of noggins and scoops. Not to over-
draw the role of forest products, the point was this: the rural
merchant had to be ready to handle any product of farm or
craft produced among his customers, from a load of apples
to a piece of woven cloth, a pair of boots, or nails made slowly
by hand during a winter's evening around the fireplace.

The country trader liked the name of merchant. It lifted
him into the dominant class of a mercantile age. Actually, a
merchant was a large-scale importer and exporter, the nabob
of the times, with foreign connections and large capital, a

man who could ship a cargo of fish to Bilbao, invest there in
salt, wine, and handkerchiefs, buy olive oil in Lisbon, take on
raisins and almonds in Cadiz. He might direct his ship's return
by way of the West Indies for a cargo of coffee, sugar, and
molasses, the molasses to be distilled into rum at Salem or
Beverley, possibly at his own distillery.

These were great years for bewigged old New Yorkers with
Pearl Street connections, who gathered daily at the Merchant's Exchange in the Tontine Coffee House. Their incoming ships were filled with olives and dried fruits from the
Mediterranean, 'China goods' from the Orient. Outward
bound, they sent grain, breadstuffs, fish, and salt provisions to
a Europe that Napoleon had made hungry. The merchant
was the capitalist in the last years of the eighteenth century
and the early years of the next. He was the banker, the ship-
owner, the initiator of 'ventures,' the proprietor of forges and
water mills, a leading speculator in such rudimentary manufacturing 'works' as then existed. It is not to be wondered at
that the owner of a small country store relished the name of
'merchant.' Though he did not send full-rigged ships around
the world, he too was an entrepreneur according to his location and means, making an occasional turn in spruce shingles
or salt pork or Kentucky jeans.

In the cities the functions of the wholesaler and retailer
were not differentiated. The merchant would have a store
where he sold at retail to the family trade. He would also advertise, in the commercial phraseology of the times, that 'a
liberal allowance will be made to those who buy to sell again,'
i.e. he was a jobber too. His storehouse was certainly not a
country store — it was located in Boston, New York, Philadelphia, Baltimore, or some other coastal city — but the stock
of goods was as 'general' as that of any country store. Shortly
before the Revolution there were forty-four general stores in

Trade card of a Boston wholesaler who sent his 'West India goods' out to his country customers in a covered wagon.

New York City. Their advertisements, in the customary form of the day, a simple list or printed inventory, ran from beef and butter to shoes and satins.

Ten Eyck and Seaman advertised flour, rum, molasses, tea, pepper, coffee, chocolate, allspice, ginger, snuff, copperas, indigo, brimstone, lump, loaf, and Muscovado sugar, and 'choice Teneriffe Wines by the Pipe, Quarter cask or five gallons.' Goods that did not find a ready market were sold on consignment, sent out on trading voyages, or put up for sale at the auctions. 'Dry goods' meant most merchandise that was not weighed or poured. 'Produce' meant foodstuffs that would keep and could be shipped long distances: flour, pickled pork, smoked shoulders in bags, dried fruits and vegetables. 'Groceries' were the luxuries of diet from the West Indies and southern Europe. The settler of the American interior did not see much of them. Citron, spices, and raisins were groceries; so was wine, which was drunk in quantities that seem incredible

to us today. Indeed, the earliest meaning of a grocery store
is a groggery or saloon; which makes it clear what the Hud-
son (New York) *Balance* meant when it said 'there are 174
licensed groceries in the city of Albany.'

Sometimes the merchants owned the merchandise they
handled. There were also agency and commission relations, in
which instances they acted for a principal but did not take
title. It was to these large wholesale dealers that the country
storekeeper forwarded the butter, the honey, the live goose
feathers of his little trading area. He took the middleman's
risk, paid the tremendously high cost of transportation, extended long credit in some kind of compromise between his
heart and head, according to his nature. He also charged high
prices for his goods.

Through all the years of its long life, there was little system
or order in the country store. A great deal of time was wasted
in looking for articles that were not in place, or had no place.
Often the customer could find what he wanted more successfully than the merchant himself — an early version of self-
service. Flies swarmed around the molasses barrel and there
was never a mosquito bar to keep them off. There was tea in
chests, packed in lead foil and straw matting with strange
markings; rice and coffee spilling out on the floor where a bag
showed a rent; rum and brandy; harness and whale oil. The
air was thick with an all-embracing odor, an aroma composed
of dry herbs and wet dogs, of strong tobacco, green hides, and
raw humanity. This redolence was to become famous in the
annals of the country store as the assortment of goods grew
wider and the smells more complex.

The storehouse was usually dark and dim, with no windows
along the sides. This provided a maximum of shelf space from
front to back. There was a suspicion that the trader liked the

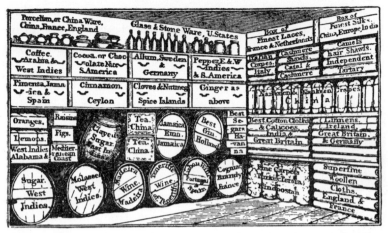

Emma Willard used the places of origin of country store merchandise to teach geography to her young ladies in the 1820's. Her quaint 'cut' gives a survey of goods that went to make up a general stock.

twilight so as to discourage exhaustive scrutiny of his goods. Most country merchants had an assistant or junior clerk. Though his salary was small, the clerk was often a luxury. He ate up quantities of groceries and candy, and always seemed to be tired.

The clerk in a country store was expected to open up the store soon after dawn, dust the assortment, build a fire, sprinkle the floor from the barrel of rain water that stood out back under the eaves, and sweep out. He wore a pencil over his ear, and waited on marriageable young women with more alacrity than on haggling old granddames. In regard to his duties, he needed constant encouragement, unless or until he too, in the course of events, became a storekeeper himself, in which case he came to share traditional views on store clerks.

In pleasant weather, two wooden trestles were put out in front, and boards were laid over them to improvise an open-air display and advertisement. Frying pans and sadirons were

arranged with cedar-wood pails or a bit of yellow queen's
ware. Fresh meat occasionally hung from a hook in the morning sun, an appetizing sight to folk jaded by the eternal diet
of salt provisions.

The last decade of the eighteenth century offered many
eligible situations in merchandising for a young man with a
taste for trading, who liked the idea of white hands, a well-
tied cravat, and hard money. It was a near tragedy for
Ephraim Hart when Samuel McBride stole the 1800 Spanish
milled dollars that Ephraim had saved up to take to New
York to buy goods. This is not the place to tell of how Mc-
Bride hid in a hollow stump, how he got stuck there, and how
he finally wriggled out — into the arms of his captors. The
point is, rather, who else but a merchant, in 1801, would ever
have seen that much good money?

A young trader starting in for himself would need, first of
all, simple honesty, and no touch of quackery in setting forth
his bargains, such as the practice of wetting sound goods 'that
they may be sold as damaged.' As a country merchant he
would require all of the knowledge he could accumulate on
markets, grades or qualities, the kind of goods his customers
wanted today and the kind they would be calling for tomorrow. The station of merchant called for some money, but not
much, since all business was conducted on long credits. It was
also helpful for a storekeeper to have a good temper, ready
address, a thorough knowledge of human nature, a slight
knowledge of commercial law, and a long patience. About the
latter, one early merchant compared retailing to the trials
which were put upon Job:

> *What a simple old fool was the Devil of yore,*
> *To vex poor Job's patience with itch and with blain;*
> *Had he set him to retailing goods in a store,*
> *He'd hit it — can't do it, and patience retain.*

The new stores which were opening up in the late 1790's would be no great shakes in the eyes of later generations, but they were adequate to their time and custom. A general store in settled country was likely to be an unpainted building of about 20 by 30 feet, with narrow doors and small-paned front windows, for display was not needed or thought of, and glass was expensive. The floor of the interior was soon darkened with the grime brought in by cowhide boots, with molasses drippings, and endless sprinklings and sweepings. The ceiling overhead was unplastered, black with smoke, festooned with merchandise hanging from iron hooks driven into the exposed beams. A little box of a counting room or office was set off for the trader to sit in when he was at his books. If his store was also the post office, that would exert a favorable influence on his business. If in due course the opening of roads and building of turnpikes brought a stage stop to his door he was twice favored.

One can picture a somnolent American village on a quiet August afternoon in early Federal times, the loafers draped comfortably along the old settle in front of the store, exchanging a 'chaw' of tobacco now and then, pulling on blackened pipes with stubby stems. The horses at the feed trough, contented after baiting, switch their tails at the lazy flies. A lone hen dusts herself in the middle of the roadway.

Suddenly all is action and animation. There is the sound of a horn, a clatter of hooves, and the stage rolls in under the store sign. The driver calls out a hoarse 'whoa,' reining in so hard that the lead horses rise on their haunches, as he flings the leather mail pouch toward the storekeeper's outstretched hand. A prance, a dash, and the coach is off for the next village. Before it is more than a few hoe handles down the road, there is a new liveliness around the store. Faces appear at parlor windows to make sure. Yes, the mail is in! There are let-

ters, papers with the latest intelligence. A little knot of customers appears on the store stoop to hear the news, to get a
hank of thread, or to replenish the meat tub with a slab of
mess pork. The very sight of store pretties was a refreshment,
a feast for the imagination of rustic customers, as the store
owner, with his natural salesman's instinct, reached into a
deep box and applied his flattery with subtlety: 'No one has
seen this pattern,' — *sotto voce* — 'you're the first.'

In the closing decade of the eighteenth century an energetic young merchant with a good stand might have dwelt on
the fact that the first census of the United States showed that
there were 3,929,214 American people to be clothed and
equipped, though this statistic, had he known it, would probably have seemed academic to a trader whose fortunes were
tied up with those of a particular four-corners. Yet it was an
underlying reason why, all in all, 1790 was a good time to be
alive. A country dealer with a brisk run of trade, who applied
the advice stamped on the Franklin penny — 'Mind Your
Business' — had a good chance to grow up with the country.

HOW TO LIVE WITHOUT MONEY

OLIVE BUTLAND ran up a bill of $2.33 at Michael Wise's store in Kennebunk, Maine. She needed tea, yarn, a skein of thread, some calico, a bit of butter for her bread. She settled her account by doing some weaving for Wise up to the amount of $2; and by cash, 33 cents.

A. H. French rode in to the Lyman Scott store at Atlas, Illinois, on his fall trading expedition. He bought some linsey, a spelling book, bed cord, a lard keg, indigo for his dye pot, iron dogs and a spider for his fireplace, an almanac for the year 1838. He cleared his debt by bringing in wheat, making some sacks — most general store owners were grain dealers, too, in grain country — by sawing out boards, and working on a piece of land that Scott wanted cleared.

John Burlend, an English yeoman come to thrive in the western world, got his first taste of prairie trade in the early nineteenth century when he made and sold three hundred

19

pounds of maple sugar. 'We disposed of the greater part of it to a storekeeper named Mr. Varley, at the rate of seven or eight cents per pound. It must not be understood that we got money for it. Business is seldom transacted after that manner in Illinois,' wrote his wife Rebecca, in explaining western trading methods as seen through Yorkshire eyes. Her husband received in the trade some corn for seed, meal to eat, 'a little coffee, two or three hoes, and a Yankee axe.'

John Mayhew wanted a spinning wheel and some potatoes. He was out of funds, but that did not prove to be an inconvenience in a barter economy. He financed his purchases with 'country pay,' butter, a sheep, three rag coverlets, three pieces of yarn-dyed striped cloth. Ashall Hall wanted a halter and some eatin' tobacco. He got up what silver coin he could, paid the difference in veal and cherry boards. And so it went, cordwood paying for pants cloth, wool or corn for vest patterns. Posts and rails bought matches and 'fruit cans' for home preserving. By drawing logs off the mountain a farmer provided himself with camphene for his lamp, for it was pleasant to have a light after dark. He could turn cider apples, through the thaumaturgy of the trading system, into a tasty salted codfish or some Yankee notions for his wife.

'Mr. Walker, Sir,' wrote the selectman of Lenox, Massachusetts, hurriedly on a scrap of paper, to George Walker, general merchant: 'Richard Hale has lost his wife. I wish you would let him have the necessary articles to make her grave clothes and charge to the town. Let prudence and economy mark your selection.'

In a later similar store 'order' the selectman authorized Walker to provide Hale with a pair of thick shoes 'and some crape to put on his hat.' The town of Lenox undoubtedly settled in cash for the indigent Hale; but that was unusual. The tally for each trade was calculated in pounds, shillings, and pence, or in dollars and cents; but that was just for convenience in keeping the running accounts. When Simon Reynolds needed a new scythe he traded labor for the scythe and got an order on the store: 'You may let Simon Reynolds select a [good] scythe and charge it to me.'

These store orders were a useful device, improvised out of a need. Torn from the back of a book, a child's writing tablet, the corner of an old almanac, no larger than necessary for the message, paper being as scarce as it was, they were not only letters of instruction but equally letters of credit for the settlement of all sorts of local obligations.

'What store do you want your order on?' the farmer asked the hired man when the time came to settle up. The order was as good as a modern check. It would get a man the scythe he wanted, a good one.

The great problem of trade was the difficulty in reaching the markets. Except for localities touched by navigable waters, production for sale was severely restricted by the problems of transportation. Bulky commodities could be moved profitably no more than ten to twenty miles by land. The emphasis was put on produce the value of which was high in relation to weight; butter, maple sugar, potash, livestock which drovers herded along on its own four feet, salted meats, and whiskey. Even in these instances the cost of moving the goods was a heavy charge to the producer. The country trader stood at the crossroads in a literal sense, and figuratively too. He was the key figure in our first system of distribution, operating the two-way flow by which rural America was supplied with the necessities of life, and taking in return as a discharge of the debts of pioneers and villagers whatever they had to sell.

The barter trade, running throughout the long history of the country store, reflects the various stages of the rural economy faithfully, and the variations from one region to another. In eastern Massachusetts payment might be made in shoes. Maple sugar was a prime item along the ranges of the sugar maple; in the Middle West, pork for barreling. Progress moved from east to west. A mature state such as Connecticut was largely converted to a money-and-factory economy while an Illinois storekeeper was still writing down in his journal the receipt of the pelt of 'an old she-bear' as acceptable payment for salt and shot. As industry moved from the cottage to the mill, as farming became more specialized, and the supply of money expanded the basis of trade shifted from commodities to cash. The chickens and the eggs, however, continued to go to market locally for generations, a tidy side line providing the farm wife with her 'pin money.'

In the states carved out of the old Northwest Territory,

FRESH GOODS.

The Subscribers respectfully give notice, that they are supplied from the markets, with a full assortment of FRESH GOODS, for

SPRING AND SUMMER TRADE;

Comprising every variety usually called for in a country store, including DRUGS, MEDICINES, GROCERIES, &c.; all of which are offered for sale on terms to suit purchasers, FOR CASH, APPROVED CREDIT, OR ALMOST ANY KIND OF COUNTRY PRODUCE. The patronage of our old customers and the public is solicited, with the assurance that they will find bargains decidedly to their advantage, as WE ARE DETERMINED NOT TO BE UNDERSOLD, under any circumstances whatever.

Briggs & Pierce.

Rochester,   18

The chief preoccupation of a country trader used to be how to acquire a stock of goods. His news, deemed worthy of a handbill, was that his effort had been successful.

the western merchant located on or near a river had a ware-house behind his store or at the nearest 'landing.' He bought the crops in the fall and stored them until the steamboat came again in the spring, carrying the produce off to river cities, and bringing back the substantials of life that were not pro-duced near by. The country merchant was in the agreeable position of being the farmers' preferred creditor. Other obli-gations were taken care of after the customer was all even at the store. If the harvest was poor and the farmer could not bring in enough produce to settle his account, he paid what he could and the debit was turned into a note and ran on at interest.

The country trader was no less concerned with his buying than his selling. The two-way trade meant a double profit, and the only way he could move his stock of goods, as he well knew, was to deal in the wool, shingles, or hides which came in from the back country. Usually he could use labor too. There was a hayfield that needed mowing. The debtor could draw a load of stone for him, raise a barn, or build a chest to clear his obligation off the store's ledger.

It has often been overlooked that the general storekeeper made an important contribution to the beginnings of Amer-ican manufacturing. As a small capitalist, standing between the artisan and the full-scale factory, the merchant fre-quently started up a forge, a grist mill, yarn factory, fulling mill, or, as has already been mentioned, an ashery. In some instances, the country trader placed factory-made yarn or leather, straw, or palm leaves with outworkers who returned to him finished cloth, shoes, bonnets, and hats, for which the storekeeper then undertook to find a sale. These workers, like the farmers, took their pay in store goods, bartering their skills for provisions. Joseph and E. M. White, at Danbury, Connecticut, accepted 'Walnut, Oak or Maple wood, Wheat,

Rye, Corn, Oats, Buckwheat, Flax Seed, Hats, Saddles or Shoes, at their full value.' In Hingham, Massachusetts, the local commodity was cooperage, an extension of the tub and barrel trade with the fishermen of the coastal towns. At Amesbury in the same state a dealer put out carriage hardware and trimmings and took in finished carriages.

Sometimes the general store advertised for specific articles of local produce. A Connecticut storekeeper announced in the Middletown *Gazette* that he was in the market for 10 firkins of butter, 200 bushels of potatoes, 500 ropes of onions, and 10 three-year-old mules. Other stores published notices that they were in need of hay, rags, hides, beeswax, ashes, and cider apples; recalling the smile and the remark of old-time neighbors as they passed a well-fruited tree loaded down with cider apples: 'There'll be a good many songs on that tree.'

The country merchants 'bought everything that had a market value,' a former clerk remembered. 'Mr. Barber,' he said — that's the Jedediah Barber who kept a flourishing store in Homer, New York — 'knew the value of everything in the market, from the highest down to wood ashes. I am sure about wood ashes as I hauled many a bushel on a hand sled hoping to raise money enough to buy fire crackers for the Fourth of July or a pair of skates for Christmas.'

A country store proprietor located, say, in central New York, like Barber, though the principle applied equally to Pennsylvania or Ohio or wherever he was storing, before Civil War days, had to be quick on his feet. He needed some sixth sense to tell him that the time had come to load the pung with maple syrup and start it off for Albany behind Lady and Ginger, because the market was ripe for that class of goods, and not overstocked. At another time, a big canvas-covered wagon, or a two-wheeled tip cart, if the roads were in bad repair, might be loaded with eggs and dried apples and taken to

Syracuse, provided the dried apples appeared likely to bring three cents a pound and eggs were worth eight or ten cents.

It was the custom for the farm wives to make their butter a little at a time, as the sour cream accumulated, putting it down in tubs as it was made, layer upon layer, and keeping it as cool as possible in the cellar, until it was delivered to the store. By that time the first churning may well have attained a considerable age and strength. The store owner usually explored the butter with a butter borer, plunging it deep into the tub, giving it a circular twist, and deftly removing the core, which revealed all the strata. He then applied a sound organoleptic test — a brisk lick of the tongue and a cautious sniff. He replaced the column of butter, withdrew the tester, and smoothed over the top with his thumb. A farm wife in checkered gingham and sunbonnet once brought six hens in a crate and a tub of butter to her store and 'traded it out.' In her order was an item for butter. Since her own butter was still on the counter, the clerk absently started to reach for it when she halted him sharply: 'Oh, I don't want any of that. I want some good butter.' In cases where the lady had produce to sell, but no purchases on her mind that day, the old stores often gave her tokens, which conserved cash and insured her return on another day.

The episode of the lady farmer who did not want any of her own butter suggests that the barter trade was conducted on the level of the commercial morality of the times, which was not always high. A trade was often a contest of wits between the dealer and his customers. When the farmer took eggs to the store, the general idea was to let the store find out which ones were fresh. This was before state candling laws. The merchant guessed and hoped. One description of egg was known as 'kept.' A kept egg was — well, one which should have been eaten or shipped off a long time ago, but wasn't.

Before the invention of the egg case, with its flats and fillers, packing the eggs was an arduous task. Eggs, the white, the brown, the large and small, fresh or not, bantam or duck, were counted and packed small end down in straw, oats, salt, or sawdust, then wired up, labeled, hauled to the depot, and put on the train for the city commission houses without grading though possibly with a little prayer.

A lady who is still a very young grandmother remembers the 'guess' era in Illinois. One bright summer day she dropped off her eggs at the country store on her way to her club meeting, intending to return to do her shopping later. A careless clerk left the eggs in the sun. When she came back in the late afternoon several chickens had hatched out.

Many a man who has run a store can testify that he has seen the farmers' eggs turn into chickens shortly after they became the store's property. Eggs that were a little rough to the touch, with a powdery shell, were apt to be all right. The ones to watch out for were the smooth, shiny ones. They had been sat on too many times. Sometimes the storekeeper tried putting them in a pail of water. If they floated it meant they were as useless as a rotted-off fence post. Often a man of sorrows, the country merchant knew from personal experience the background of such native American wisdom as: 'If you don't look out for yourself nobody else will,' and the secular beatitude 'Blessed are they who expect nothing, for they shall not be disappointed.' Over and over the storekeeper was on the short end of the deal; for the customer would give him the haha if he could.

When disease appeared among the chickens, at least this was the way it seemed to the man behind the counter, the farmers would rush them to the store so they could die on the merchant's hands. Sometimes the butter was so old there was nothing to do but dump it in a barrel and sell it to the soap-maker. The bacon was often strong, the lard likewise; but it was good enough to use in 'extending' the butter. Whiskey made locally, so it is said, could be diluted with water, with lye or tobacco juice added to give it a bite. Washing powder made the bead.

A man who owned an upbrush hill farm brought in a load of cordwood. The store owner looked it over and handed him up a nickel cigar.

'What's that for?' asked the farmer, pleased but astonished.

'You win the prize,' said the merchant.

'What prize?'

'The one we give for bringing in the orneriest, crookedest cord wood seen this year, and piled so loose a cat could crawl through it anywhere.'

Says a veteran observer of the old country game of trading: 'I have often heard farmers' wives say that a mouse drowned in the cream so they made it into butter and brought it to town to sell.' It took the chromo, one merchant wrote in his diary, when 'a farmer brought me a load of potatoes a while ago and half of them were frozen. Honest farmers? They are the damnedest lot of rascals out of States Prison.'

More accounts come down to us of roguery on the part of country store proprietors than of their customers, possibly because there are always more customers in the world than traders, and the majority makes the legends. Many stories about adulterated goods in the country store were told and retold around a neighborhood until they hardened into oral tradition; of how there was sand in the sugar, water in the rum, dust in the pepper, flour in the ginger, chicory in the coffee, and lard in the butter — though in the latter case it may have been the farmer's wife who put it there.

Drawing on youthful memories of what he observed as a country store clerk, in Bethel, Connecticut, P. T. Barnum gives an unflattering summary of the frauds practiced by both customer and trader.

'We are apt to believe that sharp trades, dishonest tricks and unprincipled deceptions, are confined to the city, and that the unsophisticated men and women of the country do every-thing "on the square," ' said the great showman. 'I believe this to be measurably true, but know that there are many ex-ceptions to this rule. Many is the time I cut open bundles of rags, brought to the store by country women in exchange for goods, and declared to be all linen and cotton, that contained quantities of worthless woollen trash in the interior, and some-times stones, gravel, ashes, etc. And sometimes, too, have I (contrary to our usual practise) measured the load of oats, corn or rye which our farmer-customer assured us contained a specified number of bushels, perhaps sixty, and found it four or five bushels short. Of course the astonished woman would impute the rag-swindle to a servant or neighbor who had made it up without her knowledge, and the man would charge carelessness upon his "help" who measured the grain, and by mistake "made a wrong count." These were exceptions to the general rule of honesty, but they occurred with suffi-cient frequency to make us watchful of our customers, and to teach me the truth of the adage, "There's cheating in all trades but ours." '

The practices of the store were no better. It was indeed a case of dog eat dog. Barnum goes on: 'Our cottons were sold for wool and cotton for silk and linen; in fact nearly every-thing was different from what it was represented . . . Our calicoes were all "fast colors" . . . our ground coffee was as good as burned peas, beans, and corn could make, and our gin-ger was tolerable, considering the price of corn meal.' Each party, under the horrendous code of this store, expected to be cheated at the slightest opportunity.

Allowance must be made for the fact that Barnum was certainly no man to hesitate at touching up a story; also for the additional circumstance that the sharp trades are the ones that are remembered, cussed over or laughed over, for years afterward. They are the stuff of which folklore is made. Department store executives find that 98 per cent of the people are honest. The other two per cent make the trouble. Around the general store it was the same way. And sometimes there were areas of doubt. 'Your weaving is bad,' reproved the storekeeper who supplied yarn to an outworker. 'The yarn was very rotten,' replied Sarah Ann Luther, tartly.

Farm produce came into the store in small lots. It was processed under home conditions, with primitive equipment. Standards existed only in such general terms as 'merchantable,' or 'workmanlike,' or 'shipping quality.' There was little inspection or grading, and no incentive to improve the quality since both the efficient and the poor producer were paid the same.

With little cash or credit available for 'boughten' goods, the ideal for managing a rural household economy was that succinctly stated by St. John de Crevecoeur, who wrote so attractively about, and also lived, the life of an American farmer. 'The philosopher's stone of an American farmer is to do everything within his own family,' wrote Crevecoeur, 'to trouble his neighbors by borrowing as little as possible; and to abstain from buying European commodities.'

A countryman was expected to be handy at all the trades. He could make a set of harness, whittle out an axe handle, construct a gate latch, and tap shoes too. His wife could spin, dye, weave, and cut out clothing, as well as dry apples and make soap. Most household articles were homemade contraptions. Meal for 'rye and Injun' was crushed in a mortar made from a hollow stump. The cheese ladder and dough trough were homemade contrivances. A good butter paddle could be shaped out of red cherry. Poplar was for making cradles. Maple was the bowl wood. Iron was used with great parsimony. The country stores stocked it in rods and bars, to be forged into tools and repair parts in the home shop. Flax was raised generally in the northeast. Every farm family knew how to ripple, scutch, swingle, brake, and spin; for linen was the great utility textile until it became possible to gin cotton.

It was an independent life, but lived on a low economic level, with ceaseless toil the price of liberty. The hope of gain lay in advancing land values. Rural folk did not accumulate worldly possessions at a rapid rate, as is evident from old wills, inventories of estates, and folk poetry:

> *A spinning wheel, 1 peck of meal*
> *A knife without a handle,*
> *A rusty lamp, 2 quarts of samp:*
> *And half a tallow candle.*

Our ancestors would not have understood the idea of obsolescence. They repaired, fixed, tinkered, turned over, patched, made do, and looked for their pleasures and palaces on the other side of the Jordan. One can imagine a country customer in the age of Jackson coming to the store from a remote corner of the township with a load of hemlock bark, exchanging jocular greetings with the relaxed gentlemen occupying the liars' bench on the store porch, before he proceeded with his business. The dress of the rural male in pioneer times, amounting almost to a uniform, was a blue hunting shirt, vest of striped linsey, the yarn dyed at home with alum, copperas, madder, walnut, or butternut bark, and pantaloons of coarse blue cloth dyed with indigo, a country store staple for generations. The farmer would be shod in boots or leggings and moccasins. His trading was a slow business. The dealer had to measure the bark to determine the quantity, examine it for condition. The price discussed and agreed on was set down on the credit side of the ledger. We do not have to imagine what the purchases were, for they still may be deciphered in old account books: salt, sugar, snuff, powder and shot, molasses by the jugful, and 'a looking glass to see your face.'

Each visit to the store stirred up again the ancient struggle between those things that were necessary and those that represented some heart's desire. A wife's eyes strayed longingly to a bolt of bright cloth and she came away dreaming of how her corner cupboard would look, pranked up with a queen's ware teapot. Children from back in the hills, shy as hermit thrushes, fingered a harmonica or exercised their salivary glands in front of the jars containing licorice, red hots, and lemon zanzibars. 'Waiting on trade' meant just that; patient and tactful waiting on the part of the merchant. Every shopper was a comparison shopper, comparing every item with every other and, if there was a competitor, also the prices quoted with those at the other store. A buyer did not lay out his money with a careless hand when the labor of a good man was worth a dollar by the day or fifteen dollars by the month.

The customer did not know what the price was until the merchant had peeked at the cost symbol, calculated on how he would come out with the load of bark, and reviewed the credit status of the customer. The country dealer's business philosophy in pricing his goods was that of a good monopolist: to get all he could.

A mountain man, buying a hat at barter, inquired the price of a hat as he saw a clerk removing it from a case of New York goods.

'Only five dollars,' said the merchant.

'Isn't that rather dear?'

'I never sold one for less,' explained the proprietor.

'He never sold one at all,' the clerk whispered to a by-stander. The hats were auction goods, cost a dollar each.

A trading expedition to the store was, from the customer's point of view, not only a serious business but high adventure as well, filled with expectancy and a delicious excitement. In addition to the attractions of the bazaar, there was neighborly 'visiting' to be done, and almost always a Saturday afternoon rumpus, at the very least a dog fight, somewhere in the vicinity of the store. If it was an election day, there would be beer, whiskey, and free cigars to be had out in the shed behind the store. Before the day was over there would certainly be an opportunity for any man who wished it to get into a fight, with seven or eight on a side; especially if the dusty wagon road passed between a Whig store and a Federalist, a Republican and a Democrat. A country family, creaking homeward in the twilight, still smelling the sizing on the calicoes and ging-hams, the mingling odors of whale oil or kerosene, onions, bourbon, and harness, could feel deep down that they had been 'Seeing the Elephant, seeing the world.'

On the whole, the dealer had the upper hand. The customer usually let his produce go at what the merchant said was the current price, for he had little recourse, and hoped through stiff bargaining to shave the price of the store goods he needed. The power of the merchant as 'middleman' often aroused mistrust and hostility as the years wore on. The attitudes of folk with limited education, poor access to market information, but lots of experience in trading, located far from population centers were traditionally hostile to the businessman. These convictions were deeply rooted, and had been there for a long time:

In the days of scoop-weigh-wrap-and-tie storekeeping, the main storeroom also served as an American equivalent of the English pub — a genial
setting for male companionship.

The miller he stole the corn
The weaver he stole the yarn.

In the later years of the nineteenth century similar feelings
are expressed about the store owner in a song which has been
traced as far back as the 'sixties, and may well have a longer
ancestry:

When the farmer comes to town,
With his wagon broken down,
O, the farmer is the man who feeds them all!
If you'll only look and see,
I think you will agree
That the farmer is the man who feeds them all.
The farmer is the man,
The farmer is the man,

Buys on credit till the fall:
Then they take him by the hand
And they lead him to the land,
And the merchant is the man who gets it all.

The happy farmer of Crevecoeur's 'Letters,' America's natural aristocrat, no longer ate off the top of the pot. In some way which he could feel but not understand, he had slipped from his high position in the scheme of things and become a 'rube,' a 'hayseed.' Used derisively by townies, these epithets were symptomatic of the shift of economic power from country to city, from agriculture to industry and Big Business. The farm family was used to the isolation of living alongside a grassy lane and fording the creek to get out to the wider world; but now the farmer felt a new kind of separateness, with new enemies hemming him in — the Trusts and the Money Interests. It rankled in his soul that when he sold his crops it was at wholesale prices, but when he came to buy factory goods it was strictly at retail, the merchandise passing through many hands, each of which exacted a profit for services which were not visible to the last man in line.

Aspersions on trade and traders are as old as the Greeks, or the Old Testament. In medieval England there was legislation against merchants as 'engrossers,' 'regrators,' and 'forestallers.' In the United States the overflowing barn and the conspicuously empty pocket put the drive into the Grange movement's opposition to middlemen. Mary Ellen Lease, 'the Kansas Pythoness,' toured the prairie states urging the farmers to 'raise less corn and more hell.' In this, the economic climate of the country districts in the 1870's, the mail-order catalogue business was introduced. At once, rural Americans came to feel that the catalogue man, Aaron Montgomery Ward, was on their side. Ward had once been a clerk in a St. Joseph, Michigan, general store at $50 a month and board.

He had traveled as a drummer for a St. Louis dry goods house. He understood perfectly the mental processes of the disenchanted folk on the outlying farms; and the goods they needed, too.

'Easy chair buying . . . as safe as it is easy,' was Ward's description of shopping around in their mammoth Wish Book, filled with 'an assortment of the latest fabrics ten times as large as all the stores in your small town combined. And from here it is not so much as a step into the huge Furniture Department . . . fifty acres of merchandise . . . the latest . . . the finest . . . no one to annoy you . . . no impatient clerks . . . no crowded aisles . . . no hurried decisions. The secret of our low prices is the cutting out of commissions to middlemen.' The sentimental tie between the agricultural population and their friends in Chicago lingered on into the chain store age, for even in our own day the redoubtable Gene Tallmadge found it profitable to remind his constituents that they 'had no friends except Jesus Christ, Sears, Roebuck and Gene Tallmadge.'

The catalogue houses exhorted with pious horror against the importer, the jobber, and especially the country merchant, all of whom dipped into the farmer's pocket for their 'middle profits.' 'Many an honest dealer has to charge you much more for goods than we do,' said Montgomery Ward & Company, 'simply because he has paid too much for them himself. Ignorance is less provoking than dishonesty, but it costs you just as much.' Sears, Roebuck & Company also conceded that the local man had to charge high prices, because of 'expenses necessarily large in proportion to the amount of business he does.'

Since the mail-order concerns sold for cash in advance only, and would not barter for live goose feathers or local eggs, the narrative of their lively vendetta with the country merchant

falls into the later years of the century and the early 1900's
when the currency dollar had superseded the commodity dollar. Meanwhile the general store continued to show its capacity to adjust and prosper under changing conditions.
Through all the fluctuations of money and credit, through
panics and wars, fat years and lean ones, the old country store
stood its ground. It knew only one rival, and that a not very
serious one, familiar, picturesque, and persistent — the wan-
dering peddler with a hearse-shaped cart or with a pack on
his back.

THE THRIVINGEST PEOPLE IN THE WORLD

A MAN WHO KEPT a country store any time between 1790 and 1860 had plenty of problems to occupy his mind, but competition was not usually one of them. Among his chief difficulties were acquiring a stock of goods, transporting them, disposing of the country pay that came into his store, and raising the cash necessary to meet his obligations. Trading areas were established by the distance a farm family could travel by horseback, oxcart, or wagon. A circle with a five-mile radius would represent a fair estimate of the amount of geography in which a country dealer could take a serious commercial interest. In the absence of a large town or city near by, the storekeeper got nearly all of the local run of trade; nearly all, but not quite all. No spot was too remote for the pack peddler.

A group of men in an Oregon saloon got to bragging about where they came from. A silent man, smoking his pipe by the fire, heard it all; then finally spoke.

'And *I* was born in the garden-spot of America.'

'Where is that?' they asked.

'Skowhegan, Maine,' replied the peddler, 'Kin I sell you a razor strop?'

We have contemporary testimony that it was scarcely possible to step out along a traveled highway from spring to fall in the first half of the last century, without running into a man carrying a tin trunk, or perhaps a pack wrapped in black oilcloth. He would be a young man, canted forward under a hundred-pound load, with a sharp eye out for a trade that might reduce his burden. This was the Yankee peddler, so-called, and though he might be a Connecticut man or a Vermonter, he could easily be a Jew from Germany, an Armenian, or Syrian, or for that matter, a Murphy or Cosgrove.

The peddlers were out in force as soon as the ice disappeared from the dog pan. Though his expeditions, or depredations, in the deep South have been chronicled in the most detail, the pack peddler was equally 'all over the place' in the eastern and north central states. Nor did he always require dry ground under foot, or mild temperatures. If the peddler was a 'carting gentleman' he went right on touring in the wintertime, traveling any road that would take a cart, gig, or old thorough-brace wagon. The peddler worked the canal boats. He 'ventured' in sloops through eastern coastal waters, with bayberry candles, Yankee rum, cheese, and codfish. He floated down western rivers on flatboats that served as stores, moving on to another landing place when trade languished.

If the pack peddler felt able to take a step up in the world, he bought a horse. Occasionally, very occasionally, a team of horses drew his bright red or blue wagon as it jangled over the rough roads with a rattle of tinware, the squeak of stiff leather springs, brooms sticking up behind like grotesque plumes, feathers, and bags of wool lashed onto the rear, growing bulkier with each day's trading. The cart was set high, so it could traverse the deeply rutted roads, with plenty of clearance for rocks, fords, stumps, and swampy places. The sides, hinged so that they could be dropped down, often bore a descriptive legend such as 'Enameled Ware.' Great double doors opened up the whole of the back. Many of the carts, as several generations recalled them, looked like the stagecoaches with oval bodies made familiar to the present generation by the movies, though they were lighter in draft. Some resembled a hearse. Others were half-wagon, half-carriage. Examples of these vehicles may be inspected in the transportation collections of the Farmers' Museum at Cooperstown, New York, at Old Sturbridge Village in Massachusetts, the Shelburne Mu-

The carting peddler on tour packed his stock with a marvelous ingenuity, calicoes among the pans, his cotton checks tucked under the tin cups. The longer the journey the greater the burden, for the peddler's small wares were gradually replaced by the produce of the countryside.

seum at Shelburne, Vermont, and in the great display at the Edison Institute, Greenfield Village, Dearborn, Michigan.

'Yankee' was sometimes a term of contempt or of fear, sometimes merely a descriptive expression used without prejudice, sometimes an affectionate and proud appellation, especially if self-applied. Much depended on who was doing the talking. In the West the Yankee was considered to be 'too quirky.' When used as a verb Yankee meant to cheat. In conjunction with 'peddler' the word was sufficient notice that a fraud was in the making. All of these connotations appear together in a newspaper piece published in the *Newark Daily Advertiser* before the Civil War — the heyday of peddling — and reprinted by the *Hartford Courant*, the venerable newspaper which still flourishes at the capital of the Yankee notion state:

'We may laugh at the Yankees as we will, but they are the most thriving people in the world, and "let those laugh that win" . . . It is unfair to judge of a race by the emigrant portion, who if the most adventurous are also the least steady; but even of this portion, including the whole procession of pedlars which annually stream southward, like emmets from an ant hill, there is something good to be said. Take your stick, and walk out on the highway: you will not have fairly warmed yourself with the exercise before a gaily painted equipage, snug and light, drawn by a sturdy pair of Vermont horses, will come in sight. The driver is a healthy, ruddy, happy-looking fellow, comfortably wrapped up, and with a shaggy buffalo skin gathered around his feet. You see at a glance that the master's eye has had its well-known effect on the cattle. When he alights to bait, you will easily get into conversation with him. His eye is even more inquisitive than his tongue, which is saying much; but beyond this he is not disrespectful. He has a book in his pocket, and has been taught to lay aside his cap in a Christian house. He does not drink, and he does not blaspheme, and he carries no bowie-knife . . . In a few months he will return to the banks of "the river," with money enough to stock his tiny farm. During his thousand miles of travel he will be sneered at, taxed for his license, hustled at court houses, brow-beaten at inns, blasphemed at barbecues, but never cheated, never beaten, never goaded into an assault, and never seduced from his main point.'

The peddler's little farmstead is described with the rich sentiment of a Currier and Ives print: It is 'surrounded by a stone fence, and has a small but comfortable house upon it. Trees are already planted both for fruit and shade. The winter's wood is all ready, and under cover, though it be summertime.' The young peddler is proud of his young wife who is 'as well read as the school mistress, while she can prepare the baked beans and Indian pudding for the Sabbath dinner as well as if she had never known a letter. Such are the couples — there are thousands of them — from whom proceed the universal nation of Yankees. Their sons will one day be in Oregon. Their daughters will be governesses here and there, and then marry legislators in those unnamed states which lie beyond Iowa.'

In 1850 there were 10,669 peddlers on the road in the United States; in 1860 there were 16,594. No wonder a Connecticut poet of the time wrote:

> *Why is the dust in such a rage?*
> *It is the yearly caravan*
> *Of peddlers, on their pilgrimage*
> *To southern marts; full of japan,*
> *And tin, and wooden furniture,*
> *That try to charm the passing eye;*
> *And spices which, I'm very sure,*
> *Ne'er saw the shores of Araby:*

Well skilled in that smooth eloquence
Are they, which steals away your pence.

New York state licensed 302 peddlers in 1841, of whom 227 traveled on foot, and paid twenty dollars a year for the privilege; 71 drove a single horse and one traveled by canal boat — for thirty dollars paid to the Secretary of State; and three opulent peddlers were drawn by a two-horse team, which cost them fifty dollars in license fees. Peddling dropped off to a low mark during the Civil War, made some recovery in the 1870's — New York licensed eighty in 1871 — and thereafter the decline was rapid as the railroads brought the expanding rural population nearer to markets and stores. How many persons peddled on a part-time basis or took the risk of selling goods without a license, there is of course no way of knowing. At any rate, with more and more country stores opening up, the peddlers' opportunities shrank, though some continued to make their rounds well into the twentieth century.

Much of the economic thinking of the middle 1800's still followed mercantilist lines. Trade barriers were set up by states, of which the licensing of peddlers is an instance. It was considered desirable to keep a firm hand on 'foreign goods,' which included merchandise brought in from outside the state by the peddler. Pennsylvania, Connecticut, Georgia, Tennessee, Illinois, and Ohio all required the peddler to take out a license which specified that the migratory salesman could not dispose of his goods at auction under any circumstances. Pennsylvania, Georgia, and Tennessee added the provision that the license was available only to those who were 'disabled from procuring a livelihood by labour' due to age, the loss of an arm or leg, or other bodily infirmity.

Many other obstacles were thrown in the way of the peddler.

The language of the New York licensing statute was severe. A penalty of twenty-five dollars was 'incurred by every person found travelling and trading in foreign goods without a license, and $10 for refusing to produce a license when requested by any officer or citizen, and he may be apprehended and detained by any citizen and carried before a justice of the peace.' The Overseer of the Poor of each town was charged with enforcement. 'This notice is given that persons engaged or about to engage in the business of pedlars, may know the penalties to which they are exposed.' The names of the authorized peddlers were struck off on sheets and distributed to local authorities. The Secretary of State's office advised county clerks to circulate copies of the lists 'in such a way as will be likely to cause the same to be most generally known.' Appropriate agencies for this dissemination were suggested. The justices of the peace, who profited from the fines, comprised one such agency. Publishers of country newspapers, who of course received no advertising from peddlers, 'are sometimes willing to give publicity to the list of peddlers holding licenses as a matter of general interest to their readers.' Retail merchants were also suggested.

In plain words, the natural enemies of the peddler were alerted and set on his heels. We can imagine the virtuous zest of a country merchant in posting the list of peddlers on his post-office bulletin board, alongside of notices of reward for the capture of bank robbers and horse thieves.

An Illinois sheriff specialized in catching peddlers who lacked a license. One morning he hailed a Yankee.

'Got anything to sell?'

'Yes, for sartin — first rate, too, razors. Need two of that article, square, from the looks of your baird. Good blackin' make those old cowhide boots shine. Bottle of balm good for the hair, only a dollar.'

The sheriff bought the bottle. When the peddler asked him if he wanted anything else, he said he did.

'I want to see your license for peddling in Illinois.'

The peddler produced one, 'a document fixed up good and strong, in black and white.' The sheriff handed back the bottle, said he guessed he didn't need it after all, and offered to sell it again. After some treaty back and forth the peddler said:

'Seein' as its you, sheriff, I'll give you twenty-five cents for it ef you rely don't want it.'

So a sale was consummated at the discount, which gave the Yankee a clear three hundred per cent profit at the very least.

'Now,' said the peddler, "I've got a question or two to ask you. Hev *you* got a peddler's license? It's a clean case you've been tradin', hawkin' and peddlin' that balm on the highway.'

He complained to the authorities, and got the sheriff fined eight dollars. At least, that's the story. Whether true or apocryphal, it indicated that the peddler was a familiar institution and people rather liked to brag of his ingenuities.

The verse quoted earlier in this chapter, with its reference to spices not from Araby and the peddler's 'smooth eloquence,' though written in good humor, carries with it a hint of the peddler's reputation as a sharp, slashing trader, a 'cute one,' who was always making a snug trade with his rustic customers. It was believed, and the belief often repeated, that if he did not cheat them on his pins, needles, or tinware, then he would certainly do so in bartering for the feathers, skins, and wool which he accepted in lieu of money; and most probably he would take them over the jump both going and coming.

The peddler's cheats made folklore. His lies were not little ones, such as ordinary men told, but monumental, impudent, and imaginative. The truth about the peddler's methods probably occupies a middle ground. Those who dealt with the same customers year after year would find honesty the best policy. The peddler making a once-around tour, never to return again, might be sorely tempted to adopt a free and easy brand of commercial honesty, especially when far from home. Sometimes he sold goods for resale to other peddlers, to country merchants, or whomever wanted to trade. For instance, one kind of Yankee notion was a 'trading' watch. It had an imitation gold case of white metal, engraved in elaborate designs, and was equipped with works that worked, for a while. The peddler sold the watch for twelve dollars. Hotel keepers, livery-stable owners, and cattle buyers would take from two to a half dozen at a clip. What they did with them may not be on the peddler's soul, though he undoubtedly knew that the watches were thrown in on a low cash offer to push over a sale, a cow changing hands for, say, twenty dollars cash and the watch; the cash and the watch, at the long price, coming to thirty-two dollars, the value of the cow being sixty.

Timothy Flint, as respectable a New England clergyman as could be turned up anywhere in 1815, visited Ohio and heard everywhere 'stories about Yankee tricks, and Yankee finesse, and wooden nutmegs, and pit-coal indigo, and gin made by putting pine-tops in the whiskey . . . Wherever we stopped at night and requested lodgings, we were constantly asked if we were Yankees; and when we answered that we were, we constantly saw a lengthening of visage ensue.' 'Sam Slick,' the fictional clock peddler, described his methods of selling clocks as a combination of 'soft sawder and human natur' and proceeded to demonstrate how to flatter a Nova Scotia yeoman by calling him 'Squire' and complimenting him on his splendid farm; while conveying to his wife that he had only one clock left, and another woman wanted it. His most potent device, however — here was where he helped himself to a large slice of human nature — was to leave the clock behind him, knowing that a luxury once enjoyed is not likely to be given up without a struggle.

The peddler knew just when to lay out a tablecloth of linen for the farm lady to feast her eyes on, or when cotton would be better, just as he had some extrasensory perception of what neighborhood would be in need of clocks. One Yankee 'calculator' described the signs of a homestead that required a clock. If the house had glass windows, if the man of the house did not wear a cap but a hat, if he had boots on — the clock was as good as sold. If the wife appeared in calico and a checked apron, the peddler knew she had had a taste of buying from another traveling merchant and would be easily excited by a gaudy ribbon or a shining pair of scissors. The peddler understood bearings and distances as well as an engineer, could ford creeks and rivers, cross sloughs, mend a broken harness, shoe a horse, repair a watch. He 'never met a stranger, for he was intimately acquainted with a man as soon as he saw him.' Like his eastern counterpart, the western peddler was 'the beatingest fellow'; and often he was the same fellow. With an excellent memory and an ingratiating manner, apt in recalling who had been sick on his last trip, whose daughter was ready for long dresses, who would welcome advice — and who wouldn't — the loquacious peddler clipped the purses of the women with shining scissors or thread and ribbons and papers of pins which he drew from a well-packed coffeepot.

The writings of 'Sam Slick,' the old clockmaker from Slickville, may be dismissed as fiction and therefore incompetent evidence, though it might be urged that they present essential truth, as does a cartoon or genre painting. Here then is a majestic presence, no less a figure than that of President Dwight of Yale, a great traveler himself, who had met peddlers on Cape Cod, on Lake Erie, in Canada, as far west as St. Louis, and as far south as New Orleans. He described

Suffield, Connecticut, as a particular center for peddling, and pontificated:

'The consequences of this employment, and of all others like it, are generally malignant. Men, who begin life with bargaining for small ware, will almost invariably become sharpers. The commanding aim of every such man will soon be to make a good bargain; and he will speedily consider every gainful bargain as a good one. The tricks of fraud will assume, in his mind, the same place, which commercial skill and an honourable system of dealing hold in the mind of the merchant . . . I believe this unfortunate employment to have had an unhappy influence on both the morals, and manners, of the people.'

Whether or not peddling was the reason, Lewis Morris, Jr., of New York, held much the same opinion of Connecticut commercial morals. In his last will and testament, Morris desired that his son, Gouverneur, be given the best education that was to be had in Europe or America; but expressly forbade that the boy be educated in Connecticut, 'lest he should imbibe in his youth that low craft and cunning so incident to the people of that country.'

John Bernard, in one of those unflattering nineteenth-century English accounts of American life, also took a dim view of Connecticut, equating the arrival of a 'Connecticut chap' in the South with yellow fever as a calamity, and outranking taxation, locusts, and a wet spring. Yet with all the disapproval and fear the peddler inspired, he was at the same time recognized as a kind of natural symbol for the American aggressive spirit when applied to business. His tenacity, his defiance of fatigue, danger, and even murder — many stories come down the years of peddlers killed and robbed on lonely wooded roads — was accepted as a recognizable self-portrait of the commercial American. Solid services were rendered by thousands of wayfarers who ventured where stores were few, among a people scattered thinly over an unfriendly and half-conquered land.

In singular antithesis to the peddler as a sharper was the reputation his goods had of being cheap. This too was not wholly deserved. Peddling was an expensive way to get goods to the customers. The economics of peddling scarcely support the idea that it was a highly profitable occupation. How many calls could a peddler make in a day? Obviously not many. His business was mostly in small wares, and mostly with farm women who had little money or truck to trade with. The wagon peddler started out with a stock of merchandise worth from $300 to a top of $2000, and he turned his stock in a period of two to three months at a gross profit of 100 per cent, more or less. That was generally in line with what the country storekeeper made in selling a considerably larger volume of goods. There was a living in peddling for the man who had plenty of git-up-and-go. James Samson, who bought his goods at Albany and peddled along the Erie Canal, owned a house at Lockport free and clear, supported a wife and three children, and was worth $2000. Those peddlers who, like Jim Fiske, accumulated a fortune, did it by abandoning their itinerant way of life and applying their sharp minds to urban merchandising or new fields such as railroading, manufacturing, and finance.

Contemporary prints repeatedly show the whole family, the farmer, his wife, and all the children eagerly gathered around the visitor as he spreads out an astonishing quantity of wares nested in his pack. He bought the housewife's rags, weighing them out carefully on the old steelyard. Discarded horseshoes and other scrap iron which the boys had been collecting from around the barnyard went into the peddler's van. All was paid for either in cash or in goods, while the peddler kept up an enthralling commentary on his offerings, passed out the news and gossip, speaking generously and frequently of his calico, fine 'woosterds,' and remarkably cheap prices.

It requires an effort of the imagination now to understand what the visit of a peddler once meant to a farm family. The road or track wound its way through the great boles of the forest trees, just the width of one cart or wagon — with 'thank you ma'am's' for passing — a morass of mud most of the year, never level except when filled with snow. There were few enough passers-by at best. Perhaps that is why it seemed more pleasant and neighborly to build houses close to the 'street.' When weather choked the road off completely, the farm family looked out through spattered panes, seeing only the rain slanting across the dark trees, or the steady growth of wind-carved snowdrifts, sweeping up against the eaves.

For reading there was the Bible and the almanac, or school readers with literary selections; possibly a gift album or annual, or a handbook of advice for the farmer on how to cure glanders or instructing him in 'the management of cyder.' A wife could perform her domestic duties only by steady toil from earliest daylight to lamplight time. A man had a little more freedom. His work took him among other men. He could ride to the grist mill, or disappear with his gun. A woman had her home, her washboard, and her thoughts. Battered as we are today by mass communication, with more contacts and impressions than we can deal with adequately, we are unfamiliar with the effects of solitude and long hours of grinding toil. The monotony, the empty silences left the rough edges on character, making a woman as skittish as a woods creature. A man became a 'regular original.' The unstable slipped over into a world of fantasy, 'teched' in the head.

Imagine, then, the spring thaw setting in, the road weeping with snow water, and a plodding figure at the dooryard. It is the stocky form of a man who brings with him a flash of color and vivacity, a little taste of civilization ; a man with a ready tongue and a miniature store on his back. He made his trades right there, settled up, and never dunned his customers as the credit merchant did. His arrival was an event, not of the day, nor of the week, or month. It was a memory for the years, to be told and retold, the droll things he said and what was displayed when he unrolled his pack.

It is not strange that the peddler should have been fixed in the national memory as a sharp bargainer by these shy and lonely people. Tied to the farm, they would naturally look with a touch of suspicion at a man so worldly and so different, who had seen towns and even cities, and traveled hundreds of miles in a season. Or we may advance the scene to a later and more settled period, when the road was good enough for horse and wagon travel most of the time. A peddler's wagon would lumber into the barnyard, bristling with rakes and hoes, a wreath of tin dishes and milk pans arranged around its sides. The rear doors opened with a delicious jingling and rattling. There came a whiff of mingled smells, the sizing on cotton print goods, the smell of paint from the toys, sweetenin', and the all-pervasive horse odor.

Perhaps the spring purchases would include a pair of salt and pepper shakers, brightly decorated with flowers, fruits, vines in conventional patterns ; a cake stand called a 'Tazza,' very elegant, a pan for roasting green coffee beans at home. The housewife would bring out a tin teapot, pointing to a hole. Out came a kit of tinsmith's tools. The peddler lit his brazier, laid out his maul, hammer, soldering iron, pot mettle, and made the repair. He would stay for noon dinner, of course, leaving as pay a small pitcher with a gay stencil on its side.

The peddler had a knack of seeming to be everywhere, and

always at the right time. Once a year came the country fairs, with the people assembled off the farms in a mood for a frolic, to see the biggest pumpkin, eat gingerbread, and inspect the newest marvel of a horse-powered mower or thresher. The traveling 'doctor' would be on hand in full Indian costume, speaking eloquently against ill-health. There, too, would be the peddler, with his notions and his gift of gab.

If the militia mustered for a Training Day, the peddler would be on hand, declaring his views on light infantry tactics, circulating up and down the line of temporary booths and stands. From time to time he would compliment the captain on the brave appearance his men made as they performed the eighteen prescribed maneuvers in the manual of arms from the *present* to the *shoulder arms*. He would be loud in his admiration as the men in the company fixed and unfixed their bayonets, assuming that there were some militiamen present who possessed bayonets, and had remembered to bring them. Near by would be the sedentary merchant's permanent store. We can imagine the proprietor of a country store sourly watching the peddler go in and out of the tavern, 'working' the holiday crowd, jingling the coins in his pocket — the thrivingest fellow you ever saw.

Hawthorne sketched a peddler who auctioned a miscellany of small articles at a Williams College Commencement, of all places. 'There was a peddler there from New York state, who sold his wares by auction, and I could have stood and listened to him all day long. Sometimes he would put up a heterogeny of articles in a lot — as a paper of pins, a lead pencil, and a shaving-box — and knock them all down, perhaps for ninepence. Bunches of lead-pencils, steel-pens, pound-cakes of shaving-soap, gilt finger-rings, bracelets, clasps, and other jewelry, cards of pearl buttons, or steel, "there is some steel about them, gentlemen, but my brother stole 'em, and I bore him out in it," bundles of wooden combs, boxes of matches, suspenders, and in short, everything — dipping his hand down into his wares, with the promise of a wonderful lot, and producing, perhaps, a bottle of opodeldoc, and joining it with a lead-pencil — and when he had sold several things of the same kind, pretending huge surprise at finding "just one more," if the lads lingered; saying, "I could not afford to steal them for the price; for the remorse of conscience would be worth more," — all the time keeping an eye upon those who bought, calling for the pay, making change with silver or bills, and deciding on the goodness of banks; and saying to the boys, "Fall down, roll down, tumble down, only get down"; and uttering everything in the queer, humorous recitative in which he sold his articles.'

Writers found in the peddler a shrewd character through whom they could comment on manners, politics, and life generally. So Judge Thomas Chandler Haliburton created Sam Slick, the clock salesman. Seba Smith's Major Jack Dowling was the confidant of the President, a literary ancestor surely of Mr. Dooley of the early 1900's and of Will Rogers. 'Live Yankees,' said Josh Billings, 'are chuck full of karacter and sissing hot with enterprise and curiosity.'

Mr. Richardson Wright, in his attractive *Hawkers and Walkers in Early America*, unfortunately long out of print, evokes the colorful eccentrics who strolled the American highways before the age of steam. He portrays the peddler as disarming his customer with a burlesque recital of fraudulent goods as he opens the parley: 'Madam, are you in need of any pocket saw-mills? Horn gun flints? Basswood hams? White oak cheeses? Tin bungholes? Or calico hog troughs?' His pleasantries having cut the ground from under suspicion, he then got down to the business of finding out what the lady of the house was in a mood to buy.

Turning from the literature of humor and imaginary in-cident to the journal of James Guild of Tunbridge, Vermont, we find a real-life peddler no rascal, but a youth of sober sentiment. As he started on his first expedition, Guild confided to his diary, 'No one knows the feelings of my heart when parting with my little all for a trunk of goods and losing my caricter, if I had any, by being a pedler.'

Guild need not have exclaimed quite so vehemently about parting with his all, a note for seventy dollars, for it was un-collectable. Nor did everyone take as mean a view of peddling as did young Guild. A fellow-Vermonter, Oren Wiley, who manufactured tinware, set his brother up to peddle it, re-marking with better feeling than syntax: 'Whoever may think the office of a Tin Pedler a petty office will do well to make themselves experimentally acquainted with its duties before they decide.'

Despite a tendency toward posing and self-pity, Guild demonstrated that he could live well enough by his wits and industry. His pen was occasionally as vigorous as the artist's brush he finally learned to wield. On the way to Cazenovia, he passed through a part of New York state which was Dutch in manners and customs. He became curious to see a veritable Dutch girl, 'for I had often heard of them,' and found one in a setting similar to a painting of the Flemish school. She was rinsing clothes in a brook on a cold winter's day. Guild would watch her take up her basket of clothes and walk barefoot down to the stream and into it, standing in the icy water as she doused each garment. 'This I thought was more than Yankee Girls could do.' He told her so, and also that she was smarter than the Yankee girls.

'She would spat her feet and say, Oh Dutch Girls ant afraid of cold weather.'

From peddling Guild turned to tinkering, fortunetelling,

profile-cutting, became a writing master and invented, so he said, a system of writing. Graduating to miniature painting, he went to England to advance himself as a professional artist. We take leave of him in his journal, or rather he takes leave of the reader, at an exciting moment, far from his Vermont hills and the life of a tin peddler. He is sitting in a London life class, painting the nude human figure, the subject 'a young lady, stript to the beef and placed on a pedistal, and we twenty Artists round her drawing her beautiful figure, perfectly naked.'

Another authentic peddler differs from the Yankee 'calculator' of folklore, as he reveals himself in the diary of William C. Holbrook. Holbrook wholesaled tinware and matches to country merchants, with a side line in silverware and dry goods. Traveling in eastern New York and up and down Vermont in 1854, Holbrook was the employee of a 'Mr. Noyes,' probably Morillo Noyes, a master-peddler with twelve assistants, eighteen horses, and a warehouse in Burlington. A young widower and often lonely, Holbrook 'detested' liquor, stayed at temperance hotels whenever he could, labored not on the Sabbath, and made New Year's resolutions to be 'prolific of noble deeds.' As he sold his merchandise, Holbrook took in trade the rags the country dealers had collected, and pelts, fleece, socks, horn, and hair for mattresses. He was thus a part of the mechanism of the country store; a transitional type in that he was a peddler, yet he anticipated the modern traveling salesman. He took orders sometimes like a salesman and the goods were shipped via railroad freight. He received and paid out substantial amounts of cash in addition to the barter trade that he handled. He shipped money by express, and used the new electric telegraph.

Sometimes Holbrook recorded 'a hard trade'; sometimes 'a good trade.' He admits it when he 'got shaved.' There are dis-

couraging notes of 'traded none.' Graves and Root of Ben-
nington wanted $806.56 for their 1135 skins. Holbrook's
offer was $776.20, a difference of $30.36. That was the end
of it, too: 'could not get any nearer each other.' Let us hope
that it was not on that night that he 'received a lecture from
Mr. Noyes.'

Like the traveling man of a later day, Holbrook spent his
after-work hours with friends in similar lines of trade who fell
into his way — Hotchkiss, the tin man; a book agent; a peddler of cast-iron tombstones; his friend Lloyd, the Burlington
clock peddler. At A. L. Hyde's, in Wallingford, Vermont, he
and a Massachusetts peddler of Yankee notions were entertained during the evening by Hyde himself, who played the
violin, accompanied by his sister-in-law on the melodeon. On
one occasion, like a modern sales manager in search of good
human material, Holbrook went to interview a Thomas Taylor, 'a person who proposes to Peddle,' no doubt following the
advice of the New England philosopher who recommended
that a young man 'farm, teach, peddle' until he found his
talent.

Some peddlers were specialists, such as Fred Ellis, who
traveled through the Missouri mud behind a wiry team with
home remedies, extracts, and spices. Like many of his colleagues, he was a versatile fellow who could graft an apple
tree, sharpen scissors, half-sole shoes, call a square dance, or
hang wallpaper. Other specialized lines were Bibles and baskets. Peddlers of patent medicines were legion and closely
related to the itinerant doctors, such as the Indiana irregular
who doubled in brass as an 'eclectic physician and part-time
farmer.' Some dealt in heavier articles such as chairs, corn-
shellers, spinning wheels, and patent washing machines.
There were even peddlers who pulled after them a train of
wagons or sleighs, repaired and renovated from a stock of old

stray parts, 'Yankeed over' with shiny new paint — canny forerunners of the used-car merchandiser of today.

Sometimes the goods belonged to the peddler, as in the instance of the Ohio firm of tinsmiths, Haven & Wiley; Oren Wiley recorded in his journal that 'We purchased a pair [of] horses and [a] wagon and turned our attention a little to the peddling business.' At other times the peddler was in the employ of a wholesaler, as was Holbrook, or of a manufacturer trying to find a market for his product.

The Scovil Manufacturing Company of Waterbury, Connecticut, sent two peddlers into northern Ohio in 1828 to sell brass buttons, whip lashes, and thread. It was a pioneering venture. The men found they could not sell for cash but took whiskey and horses instead, an early experience in the vast extension of peddler-merchandising which carried the manufactures of Connecticut not only to Ohio but to every inhabited region of the United States — tinware from Berlin, pins and needles from the Naugatuck Valley, combs from Essex, 'gum elastic galluses' from Middletown, clocks from Plymouth Hollow, silk thread spooled at Willimantic, and 'genuine Spanish cigars' made by the senoritas of Windsor, known to connoisseurs as Long Nines and Windsor Particulars.

Hawthorne told of how he met up with one of these specialized peddlers near Northhampton, Massachusetts, a vendor of essences, aniseed, cloves, red-cedar, wormwood, opodeldoc, and hair oil. His cologne water was of local manufacture, but had a foreign label on it. The peddler told Hawthorne 'of the trials of temper to which pedlars are subjected, but said it was necessary to be forbearing, because the same road must be travelled again and again. The pedlars find satisfaction for all contumelies in making good bargains out of their customers.'

There were even women peddlers. Elizabeth Covey of Wilmington, Vermont, recalls that women with dark skins, wearing cheap jewelry, who were possibly Armenians, came through that part of Vermont, wearing small brightly fringed woolen head shawls, dresses of rusty black, green, or brown material with tight-fitting basques and full skirts of calico. Their articles of sale were necessarily small, though their packs seem to have weighed nearly 100 pounds at times, crammed with rolls of lace, doilies, pins, needles, thread, and cheap jewelry.

'The valise was wrapped in a square of black oilcloth and was fastened on the women's backs with leather straps. Like the men who wore packs, the women were always bent over under their heavy load . . . No one recalls that the peddlers ever molested or stole from the farmers who were their customers.' Armenian or Syrian women peddlers were also known and received with hospitality in Maine in the 'nineties. They wore a red handkerchief over black hair, gold earrings, and bright necklaces, 'a huge oil-cloth-covered pack on each hip fitted with embroideries and notions.' It should be mentioned that there were other wanderers who called at the farms strung along the country roads — cobblers, mantua-makers, spinners, tailors, silhouette-cutters; but these were craftsmen, not merchants. They dealt for the most part in 'bespoke work,' or, as we would say, made-to-order. And now and again the empty road was animated by the passing of a Mormon missionary or a dusty eccentric distributing tracts about rum, tobacco, or the Second Coming.

There must have been something in the bracing air of Vermont which led men to increase the scope of their ventures. Morillo Noyes not only sent out his own force of hired peddlers but advertised 'Particular attention given to furnishing peddlers' with silver spoons, dry goods, Boston Friction Matches, and notions. Henry W. Carter peddled goods to country stores in a big way, using gaudy wagons whose arrivals caused almost as much of a sensation as a menagerie. With headquarters at Chelsea, Vermont, later at Lebanon, New Hampshire, he called on a store about four times a year, between the rural merchant's visits to the Boston markets. The country dealers in outlying areas bought from the traveling wagons in amounts of from twenty-five to two hundred dollars in sure-fire staples. Known as 'the Merchant Prince,' Carter was in effect a jobber on wheels to the country trade; on wheels — or runners, since the byword in the northern hills was *sleighing by Thanksgiving*. Instead of using a span of horses to haul his merchandise, Carter, a showman to his finger tips, at one time had four resplendent wagons each drawn by four horses, and one other especially magnificent equipage which was drawn by six horses. The wagons were large and handsome, their running gear bright, their sides embellished with paintings sparkling under fresh varnish. The horses were beautifully matched and wore harness with silver mountings. A 'Carter team' standing in front of a store in northern New England was a good advertisement for the store — and for Carter.

Barnum tells how, in his country store days, he matched wits with a wagon peddler and did not come off second in the encounter.

'On one occasion a peddler called at our store with a large wagon filled with common green glass bottles of various sizes, holding from a half a pint to a gallon. My employers were both absent, and I bantered him to trade his whole load of bottles in exchange for goods. Thinking me a greenhorn, he accepted my proposition, and I managed to pay him off in unsaleable goods at exorbitant prices.'

Another tale is told in upper New York state of a peddler getting the short end of the deal. William Cook, called 'Wit'

IMPORTER AND WHOLESALE DEALER IN

British, French, German and American Fancy Goods,

Hosiery, Gloves, Watches, Silver Ware, Jewelry, &c.

Also, a great variety of Shell, Ivory and other Combs, Buttons of every description, Sewing Silk, Twist, Linen Thread, Spool Threads by the case, Suspenders, Brushes, Cutlery, Looking Glasses, &c.

TERMS, NET CASH.

So. Johnsbury Dec 21st 1868.

Mr O. B. Cartting

Bought of H. W. CARTER.

1 dz Cuff Buttons (Sets)	1.75	
1 "	2.00	
1 "	2.00	
3 " Comb Rings Sld 62¢	1.88	
1 " " "	75	
1 ℔ Pins En 150 No	3.00	
½ " Asstn Bufpny 9ea	1.50	
½ " Fancy " 9ea	1.50	
1 " Shawl Pins	50	
1 " Cushion	1.50	
1 dz Cartridges	1.00	
2 dz Thimbles 50	1.00	

Just before Christmas the hill towns of northern New England needed such seasonal items as cuff buttons, shawl pins, cartridges, and thimbles. Notice the proud picture of Carter's four-horse team and elegant wagon at the top of his bill head.

by his intimates, and still well remembered in Warren and
Essex counties, was tricked by a pack peddler 'in what was
thought to be an unethical manner.' Shortly after, Cook's cat
died. He skinned her and when the peddler called again he
asked:

'Do you buy mink skins?'

'Yes,' said the peddler, 'I'll give you ten dollars for one.'

The skin changed hands at once without examination, since
'Wit' had a reputation for honesty. Next day the peddler returned.

'Say,' he complained, 'That peltry you sold me wa'nt a
mink-skin. It was cat.'

'I didn't say it was mink-skin,' answered 'Wit,' virtuously.
'I just asked whether you bought mink-skins. Anybody will
tell you that my old cat that just died was named Mink. I
guess we're even.'

Morillo Noyes, less dainty in his taste than this New York
peddler, would accept a 'house cat, prime and good,' along
with deer skins and cowhides, though he drew the line at
weasels, woodchucks, and squirrels.

After the Civil War the peddler appeared in a new form, as
manufacturer's 'agent' for the endless stream of new inventions that appeared as the country improved its techniques for
mass production. The new breed of peddler was highly specialized. The canvassers made sales directly to the customers;
delivered the goods, collected the money, and departed for
parts unknown. Famous among all the manufacturers' representatives for their numbers and persistence were the agents
who popularized the sewing machine and sold the cash register idea to small retailers. Magazines and newspapers were
full of advertisements for agents. Men and women were
needed to sell patent wire clotheslines, parlor organs, washing
machines and wringers, parlor matches, stationery, new kinds

of kerosene lamps with patented chimneys or no chimneys, grinding apparatus for farms, and books, books, books.

By the 'eighties the old-fashioned peddlers were greatly reduced in numbers. Only fifteen held licenses in 1881 to follow their trade in New York state, while the 'agents' were numbered in the thousands. Peddling had always been a marginal occupation, something to do for a time, to get experience, a way to learn about human nature, meet people, see the country. The young, the adventurous, the ne'er-do-well, the defeated, the immigrant, or 'mover' drifted in and out of peddling. Anyone could get into the peddling way with a tiny investment.

When the Lincolns and the Hankses and the Johnstons got restless in southern Indiana and lit out for Illinois, Tom Lincoln's gangling boy, Abe, put his little capital of thirty dollars into pins and needles, knives and forks, buttons, thread, and other notions, and peddled along the way. We have already noticed how James Guild acquired his stock — by turning over a dubious note for $70. Jared Warner of Canfield, Ohio, set himself up as a wagon peddler at Pittsburgh at a cost of $324.71 for merchandise. His horse cost $45; his harness $14 and wagon $6. All he had to put up in cash was approximately $200, the rest being advanced on credit. A man with a sharp eye, such as Warner, traveling and trading as he went, jogging along at six to twenty miles each day, covered a lot of territory. In a single tour he would move over hundreds of miles of roads and cross several states, talking to all kinds and conditions of men, from the woodsy coon hunter to a lawyer on his way to being a judge. He had excellent opportunities to spy out the country.

For many young peddlers the way ahead in the world was to pitch on a promising spot and set up as a country storekeeper at a permanent stand. That is precisely what Jared did, what many another long-headed youth did, such as Dexter Knowlton. Knowlton left the old family farm in the hills of Chautauqua County, New York, for a peddling trip to the western prairies. At Freeport, Illinois, he exchanged his pack for the counter, ruler, and slate of the sedentary merchant. Within a few years he owned a private bank as well as a store, and sat as a director of the Galena and Chicago Union Railroad; and was nominated, though not elected, for governor of the state. In his last years, still bubbling with enterprise, Knowlton reappeared in New York state as a substantial capitalist, and purveyed Congress Water to the ailing who took the cure at Saratoga.

Carting gentleman, storekeeper, banker, politico, promoter, and entrepreneur — peddler's progress, indeed!

In becoming a merchant with a home, family, and stake in the community, the peddler acquired a new respectability and regard. He escaped from the physical discomfort and loneliness of his old calling; embraced the opportunity to settle down and become a sound judge of Monongahela rye and the burgoo pot; and if he had something of the promoter in his make-up, talked expansively of plats, additions, and town lots. As a merchant he saw more cash in a year than most of his customers would ever handle in a lifetime of planting and harvesting. With his own store, a likely son coming along, the country growing up, the ex-peddler found himself a man of consequence; his prayer for his son, as one merchant expressed it, 'that he become a good, honest man and grow up to love his country and keep out of the Democratic party.'

New vistas opened up before the peddler-turned-storekeeper. Almost anything could happen. He might become school trustee, captain of the militia, supervisor of the town, or even make the race for the lower house in the state legislature. It was a better life, if also a more complex one; but a man who had cut his eyeteeth selling from a peddler's pack, and thrived on it, could also surmount the trials and complexities of storekeeping, some of which are noticed in the next chapter.

HUMAN NATURE AND OTHER TRIALS

EARLY OBSERVERS have left us varying estimates of the attractions of country storekeeping. For most raw country boys the hope of becoming an apprentice, chore boy, or clerk, and eventually the proprietor of his own store, far outdistanced any other prospect they could reasonably compare with it in the first half of the nineteenth century. Asa Greene, who often reported direct observation under a light covering of humor and invention, sketched a precocious lad of upper New York state in the 1830's who quickly rejected farming and also the crafts. 'As to the mechanic arts,' said this thoughtful youth, 'I could not help seeing that those who followed them could never obtain a cordial admission into what was accounted good society; and I resolved not to be a mechanic.' He also noticed unfavorably the hard work incidental to these two occupations. How immeasurably more attractive it seemed, as he thought about it, to be 'merely standing behind the counter to measure tape, weigh tea, and wait upon the ladies. I saw that the clerks and shopboys had comparatively an easy time of it; and I fairly envied the dignity with which they moved about with a goose-quill behind their ears.'

Many were attracted who just did not have the calling of merchant in their bones. Young Abe Lincoln combined the optimism of the frontier, the expansiveness of the monopolist, with a genuine distaste for storekeeping. No wonder the little Berry-Lincoln store under the pleasant shade of the great buttonwood tree 'winked out,' with a stock of unwanted goods in its storeroom and an empty till. Honesty was not enough to make a merchant. It is a delicate irony of government and politics, that as Lincoln's financial woes gathered about him, he was elected to the state legislature and promptly appointed to the Committee on State Finances.

Barnum remarked that he had a 'settled aversion to manual labor' so that 'in sheer despair of making anything better of me, my father concluded to try me as a merchant.'

Indeed, bright youths generally, who liked the idea of wearing 'appearing out clothes' on weekdays as well as Sundays, and hoped to advance in the world, saw that the successful merchant was a man of influence and substance. At a later time the boy who obtained a post as store clerk came up against reality — long hours, a considerable amount of physical labor, the cussedness of customers, and the sedentary monotony of working on the ledger. Storekeeping indubitably had its tedious side. This comes through clearly in a little sign which Solomon Aines, a greatly tried man, hastily prepared one day and displayed in his store at Middlebury, Vermont. It read:

THIS STORE WILL BE CLOSED
FROM 8:45 TO 9:45
TOMORROW A.M.

AS I AM TO BE MARRIED AT THAT
HOUR, I SHALL NOT WANT TO STOP
AND COUNT EGGS OR WEIGH OUT
BIRD SEED.

Let us hope that Solomon did not marry a greasy cook. It sounds as though his threshold was low enough without any further testing. Perhaps he would have been happier on the land than in a store, agreeing with the editor of *Willard's Troy Almanac*, who threw out a strong hint about keeping store to his rural readers: 'Farmers' sons had better learn to hold the plow and feed the pigs, than to measure tape and count buttons.'

Unless a young man was well posted on the life he was about to enter he would have found clerking in a country store quite a disappoinment as an escape from heavy work. All through the nineteenth century, and well into the present one, store goods came in large packages that weighed up to two hundred pounds. It took a great deal of pushing, heaving, and grunting to handle the barrels of vinegar, flour, and whale oil. Molasses came in a hogshead, nails in kegs, each large package identified only by its geographical origin. All stock had to be placed or stored somewhere — in a back room, in the store itself, in the cellar, or raised above the first floor with a windlass. Later all merchandise had to be rolled out again to the farm wagons of the customers, or else scooped, poured, cut, weighed, and wrapped up by hand at the counters. The clerk cleaned out the fireplace or stove, mended the fire, swept out the store, took down and put up the heavy shutters, ground the coffee by hand, and not infrequently found himself with a lame back or a pulled ligament. If there was no clerk, the merchant made out as best he could, and nobody worried whether there was dust on the ribbon counter.

As he tended to trade, the country dealer was expected to show his 'popular talents' in being pleasant, accommodating, patient, and well spoken. He had to grant long credits, which took an abiding faith and steady nerves. The kind of man who would always be digging up his seeds to see how they were doing would have made a pindling sort of merchant.

Almost to the end of the last century a storekeeper was satisfied if his customers settled up once a year. 'Merchandise rates at about double the price it is with you. Groceries at about one-third higher,' Dr. Hiram Rutherford wrote from Independence, now Oakland, Illinois, to a merchant friend back east in Dauphin County, Pennsylvania. 'Much is done on the credit system but people settle every Christmas and give notes or mortgages or money if they have it.' The nearest store which the Doctor could reach at the time — the 1840's — was at Paris, eighteen miles away.

This is just a way of saying that the country trader underwrote the annual crops of his farmer-customers.

The country retailer in turn received similarly liberal terms from the wholesalers and importers who supplied him with goods. It was supposed that within twelve months after he received a shipment, he would accumulate enough money to pay his bills.

The country dealer's principal asset was the produce he collected through the barter trade. From northern New England a trader would send a huge, four-horse wagon trundling down to Boston loaded to its roof with butter, hops, maple sugar, and cheese, the merchant following later in his chaise. There would be a busy ten days in the city as produce was turned into 'iron mongery' from Birmingham, sugar, molasses, and rum — 'West India' goods, they were called in the commercial argot of the times — Irish linen, and 'factory' cloth. The retailer would stay in the city to see his wagon started off on its return journey, creaking with its burden of sadirons, frying pans, DuPont powder, buckshot, scythes, chests of Young Hyson tea, and the other items for which he had an active call.

The wholesalers were specialized to the extent of emphasizing related lines. And so, the country dealer filled in his hardware assortment from one jobber, dry goods from another, and so on. Appleton and Paige would sell him muslins, handkerchiefs, calico, plaids, and swansdown. Grant's Paper Hanging Warehouse had wallpaper. There were blue-edged plates at Norcross and Mellon's, and luster tea sets, imported glassware, mugs, sugar bowls, 'sallads and nappies.' Charles Davenport sold raisins from Malaga. Lane and Read dealt in knives and forks, Jews' harps, gilt buttons, tin teapots, and powder for making your own ink.

This, remember, was New England, a mature region, near the sources of supply. Such a variety of luxuries and imports did not penetrate in quantity into the vast western hinterland until the day of rail transportation, commercial agriculture, and national marketing. The squire or the judge of the older states could sip his Madeira and crack his walnuts over the mahogany, but the Westerner bought only what he could not make, raise, or do without — salt, tea, indigo, flints or caps, candle molds, bed cord, and drops for the 'eggers,' also known as the Ohio or Illinois shakes, depending on which state one wished to honor as the home of malaria.

West of the Appalachian Mountains the country trader faced an arduous and chancy business when he undertook to convert his farm crops into a credit balance at some distant city. 'In the fall, Father and his partner used to go into the tall timber, about a mile from the store, cut down logs, and have the carpenters build them . . . a scow or flatboat,' said Will Brown, son of storekeeper Daniel T., remembering the early days in Amesville, Ohio. 'This they stored with grain, bacon, wool, tobacco, dried fruits. They'd have oxen to load the boat, pulling their goods through the mire. There they waited for the spring freshet to raise the creek and float them into the Hocking River. Sometimes the water would come with a rush before Father was ready to go, before the boat was fully outfitted. I can remember the tense excitement of such days . . . It was a thrilling thing to see the boat swing off down the creek, knowing it would be carried into the stream of the Hocking, next into the flow of the Ohio, and finally into the channel of the Mississippi. Propelled by oars and poles, swinging and turning, it swept on its way, irresistibly, to far-away New Orleans.' Along the way the storekeepers would stop from time to time to do some trading. Grain and tobacco would find a market at Cincinnati. Bacon was wanted by the plantations along the river, and molasses was taken in return. At New Orleans they traded the molasses into sugar, white sugar in sugar-loaf form, each loaf weighing about six pounds, covered with purple paper. Thrifty women saved the paper to use in dyeing. When the north-bound cargo of sugar reached the mouth of the Hocking River, Father Dan'l hauled it sixteen miles overland to the store.

Before leaving New Orleans Dan'l would sell his boat. He took the cash returns from all his trades and turned them into Mexican silver dollars, packed in boxes. The boxes went into a small, black, horsehair trunk which Dan'l carried home with him on the steamboat. The profits would usually come to around $2000. This money was then taken to Pittsburgh or Philadelphia to be invested in hardware, dry goods, farming implements, all the merchandise needed for a general store, and was hauled west over the mountains in freighters. 'I re-

member how exciting it used to be when the freighters drove
in with their big wagons of goods,' the merchant's wife,
'Grandmother Brown,' remembered. ' "Pennsylvania schoon-
ers," we used to call them — immense wagons, each with six
horses, each with a canvass top hooped and drawn in with
ropes . . . It was an exciting business . . . seeing things
opened at the store when the boxes of muslins and delaines
were brought in.'

On his buying trips the country dealer had to steer his
way among many perils. If he did not make the right selections for his trade he would find out soon enough that he was
tied up in unsuitable merchandise and would certainly not
be able to meet his obligations when they fell due. 'A stock
well bought is half sold,' was an old saying of the jobbing
houses. Poor Richard said the same thing in more universal
terms: 'Nothing is cheap that is not wanted.' The customers
of the old general store did not expect to find each article
at various grades and prices. The volume of business would
not support more than one kind of axe, one kind of rake, one
quality of boot. But the dealer had to know how to make up
the right assortment in the right quantities. He had to buy
at the right prices. If he had the gambling fire in his veins
he might take a personal flier in the wholesale commodity
markets instead of disposing of his pork and wheat through
his regular commission merchant. Or, on the buying side, he
might elect to visit the importers' auctions where goods moved
swiftly to new owners, and money was made — and lost —
with peculiar speed.

As a further exercise in versatility, the owner of a store
had to know the exchange value of money, between East and
West, between one state and another, and he had to be able
to calculate in the money of several nations in addition to
our own, since foreign coinage circulated in the United States

up to the decade before the Civil War. Counterfeit bills and clipped coins dropped into the till with discouraging frequency, as well as questionable paper currency issued by wildcat banks. The 'red dog' notes had nothing behind them but the anguished howl of the man who got bit by a worthless bill. And so, the prudent merchant kept ready at hand his 'Bank-Note Reporter' or *Heath's Infallible Counterfeit Detector at Sight.*

With good luck and good judgment in all these matters, and if the market was favorable at the time of his purchase and the assortment arrived seasonably, without falling through the ice or getting blown up in a steamboat race, then the country merchant still had at least two more opportunities to become a ruined man. He could lose all his profit through being a poor trader. Or some impersonal stroke of ill fortune could suddenly depress the markets for produce so that his hay or meat, standing on some distant dock or warehouse floor, would not produce the funds to pay for the store goods he had already received. A country retailer might also elect the 'soft option' of living by his heart rather than his head, granting credit to customers who did not deserve it and so impairing his own. The files of jobbers were full of sad stories of small merchants ending in this wise: 'Bankrupt'; 'Uncollectable and closed files'; 'Bad check'; 'Debtor has not enough to cover legal exemptions'; 'Worthless — could not collect judgment if we got one'; 'Bankrupt, no dividends paid. Expenses more than assets.'

As an illustration of the marketing system in the first half of the nineteenth century: J. M. D. Burrows of Cincinnati moved to Davenport, Iowa, then in Wisconsin Territory, and decided to keep a store, hewing out the oak frame for a suitable building with his own hands. In March he made the long journey back to Cincinnati to buy a stock of goods. Business was good during the summer. In the fall Burrows returned to Cincinnati, paid for his spring goods, and bought a general line for winter. As an interesting side light on the business methods of the times, Burrows stopped off at Covington, Kentucky, and collected a thousand-dollar debt for a neighbor. His friend let him keep the money and use it in the business for a year, subject to a month's notice, without interest. Burrows never did have to pay back more than a nominal amount because the neighbor took it out in goods at the store.

The farmers of the area often brought their cash into the store and left it on deposit. Burrows used their money in his business without anyone's thinking it strange or irregular. Like Dan'l Brown of Ohio, Burrows often got his produce to market by building a boat, as in the spring of 1844, when he loaded a large flatboat with pork, bacon, lard, beans, oats, corn, and brooms and floated it all down the Mississippi. On another and less fortunate occasion — just to underline the highly speculative character of these ventures — Burrows sent 2500 bushels of potatoes down to New Orleans at a cost to him of fifty cents a bushel. When the potatoes left home the New Orleans price was two dollars. When they arrived at the New Orleans levee the city was gorged with willow hampers of potatoes from France. The Davenport merchant had to take eight cents for his potatoes and he did not get even that in hard money. Payment was made in coffee.

The system of storekeeper-marketing was undoubtedly slow and inefficient and disadvantageous to the farmer. The merchant paid him low prices. The producer could not hold his crops back. He had no capital, no other outlet, and was in debt. For his part, the retailer took the middleman's risks, which were considerable. He paid the high costs of transportation, and his speculative position in the commodity markets called for a strong stomach. The system worked. The crops

did get to market. Those country dealers who were well fitted
for the occupation almost invariably made money over the
term of a lifetime. Success has to be judged relative to the
times and opportunity. A thin population could only support
a little store; but the resourceful merchant showed his mettle
when business was slack. He might keep a tavern as well as a
store, probably under the same roof, taking out a license to
sell by the drink as well as by the gallon. That's what Sam
Hill, prosperous general merchant and postmaster at New
Salem, Illinois, did. Tradition has it that Hill lost the postmastership to Abe Lincoln because of that tavern license. The
women of New Salem objected to calling at the post office
while rustic toughs made merry at the bar, and Hill underes-
timated the power of the women.

Old records show that the country trader could cut hair,
dig a grave, take a hand at sawing out hemlock boards, or run
up a suit of clothes. In a society without stratification and
without specialists, the merchant did what he could put his
hand to profitably, without self-consciousness, without false
pride, and without hesitation: which may be a tract for our
times.

The old country dealer met each situation on its merits —
the light-fingered customer who lingered too long around the
counters, the lazy clerk who preferred to tend trade out on
the front porch, the sudden request for an advance of cash, an
awkward demand for credit, with a good-sized order hanging
in the balance. The merchant produced a barrel of flour or a
paper of tacks with equal cheer. Enough of a diplomat to get
out to the wagon of a substantial farmer before he drove
away, hand up a cigar, and ask about the crops, he also found
it necessary to know the law of Attachment and Execution,
and to be resolute in taking reluctant debtors to court.

The merchant's generosity was not considered by his customers to be torrential. When he got hold of a dollar, the money was often deemed to have been withdrawn from circulation. He did not lie, but was economical with the truth, a form of taciturnity that was tolerated since it was almost universally practiced by his customers. A Yankee drummer once said, with just what mixture of humor and seriousness it is hard to say, 'I never could see why it is necessary to tell a lie when the truth can be just as misleading.'

Yet such a country retailer as has been described, if he gave 'down weight' — meaning that he piled on the goods until the beam of the scale dipped below the horizontal — if he endowed his store with the kind of personality to make it the natural place for reporting the first robin or for exhibiting the tallest corn or the biggest pumpkin, could be reasonably sure of an expression of community esteem in his obituary: 'always cheerful, patiently waiting upon all classes and kinds of customers, and ready with a pleasant word for everybody.' 'Grocers are born and not made by education,' wrote one merchant-diarist. 'I could not have have got along any better if I had seven degrees from Dartmouth College.'

Each day of life behind the counter of a general store brought certain routine experiences which could be reliably predicted. At seven o'clock on a cold, dark, winter morning there would come a knocking and a banging by an early-bird customer, a forgetful lady who had failed to remember that it was her washday, and that she urgently needed one bar of soap. Each day there was a young mother who went about the store making a pile of her purchases, poking here and there — an early indication of the attractions of self-service — while her untended baby played upon the floor, sooner or later to start throwing the ground oyster shell into the calf meal, or the calf meal into the white beans, or the beans into the onion sets. Country stores seemed to attract dogs about whom lin-

gered the memory of an extinct skunk. It was an unusual day
when at least one dog did not find an open bucket of pure leaf
lard and get in a few good licks. An encounter between two
strange dogs was certain to result in a snarling, whirling mass
of hair and teeth, with yowls of rage and anguish pitched to
split an eardrum. Trade stopped. Customers sought refuge as
best they could, and the stock tumbled in all directions until
the store owner could usher the contestants out the door with
a hoe or axe handle.

A special cross to bear was the hearty joker. His purchases
were light but his conversational efforts extremely heavy.
'Cold enough for you?' he would ask; 'Got any white lamp
black?' Or he would note the fall of a box of shoes as the dealer
labored over a fussy child, with a sally, 'A drop in shoes, eh?'

There was an acidulous old lady who homed regularly on
each general store and the storekeeper dreaded to see her enter
the double doors, for he knew he was about to hear an essay
on the degenerate times. What a pity it is that children nowadays are not taught to obey their parents or to respect their
elders. People don't think of anything but gadding around.
The churches are empty since the preachers got away from
the good old-fashioned gospel sermons. Then there was a par-
ticularized account of the slouchy housekeeping of the young
woman her son had had the misfortune to marry.

After the 'nineties there came the further interruption of
the telephone, a voice asking whether the storekeeper was sure
he had mailed that letter to Chicago last Thursday. (He
was.) The circle of loungers around the stove was sometimes
a source of amusement even to a busy store owner, but he
needed a watchful eye and a firm hand in case the talk got too
rough or they treated themselves too generously to cheese and
soda crackers. A reasonable amount of cracker barrel hospitality was accepted as a part of the cost of doing business;

☞SMOKERS and CHEW-ERS will please spit on each other, and not on the stove or floor.

The motto reproduced above suggests that the country merchant did not always play willingly or graciously his unavoidable role as host. He knew from experience that his relaxed peers would eat his soda crackers, ogle his more comely customers, and might at any moment raise a sudden cheer for Major McKinley, a tiger for Colonel Bryan.

but there were limits. Free matches were a serious matter, too, for matches were expensive. 'One to a customer' was the rule. One store, Fisher's old stand and post office at Poestenkill, New York, had an ingenious homemade device for holding matches. Only one could be extracted from it at a time. Another store had a mechanical eagle filled with matches. When the head was pressed it bobbed up offering a single match in its beak.

Come wintertime, one customer out of three left the door open when entering or leaving, from seven a.m. to closing time. In the summer there were swarms of flies. The country dealer fought back with the best means he knew of, mechan-

ical flytraps and arsenic paper, but there was an old saying
often heard in general store circles that you could kill a fly,
but 'Ten flies come to one fly's funeral.'

The country merchant could not have survived without extending credit, and often extending credit was why he could
not survive. 'Uncle Jed' Barber, colorful proprietor of the
'Great Western' store at Homer, New York, once brought
forty-two actions against forty-two delinquent customers for
a total of $550.18. He thought it was good advertising for
reluctant payers to know that he would have the law on them
to enforce payment. Public sentiment usually upheld the merchant in a determined effort to collect his accounts. R. E.
Gould, the John Wanamaker of Livermore Falls, Maine,
recollected with pain the type of customer who would run up a
bill on the understanding that he would pay for it in thirty
days; and then, if he paid in a year, thought he was entitled
to a free cigar.

Sometimes a simple combination of tact and firmness saved
the retailer from a bad risk. The pleasant stranger comes in
for a pair of shoes. He is happy to find just what he wants.
The shoes are wrapped and there is a moment of hesitation.
As he reaches for the parcel it appears for the first time that
he does not have the money right there with him but will surely
have it Saturday night. The experienced store owner at this
point checks the gesture by which he was about to place the
shoes in the hands of the customer, and completes the motion
by putting the shoes on the back shelf, saying smoothly, 'Now
I'll tell you, I'll just lay these shoes up here for you, and you
can get them on Saturday when you come in with the money.'

One way of collecting a bad bill was demonstrated by D. A.
Knowlton, who ran a store at Freeport, Illinois, and was
known as a 'sharp collector.'

'One day,' Knowlton said, 'a man named Charlie Hall came

into my store with an order for goods, but he wanted more goods than the order called for. I said, "Charlie, I cannot trust you; and no is a word I can always say in business matters."

' "But," pleaded Hall, "let me have them, Mr. Knowlton, and I will pay you next week." I then made the following bargain with him: "If you do not pay me the balance as per agreement, I shall have the privelege of kicking you every time I see you till the debt is paid." For several weeks the countenance of Hall did not grace my store; but after a while he appeared and walked into my store. I said: "Charles, I would like to see you a moment outside"; and when out I gave him a very violent kick. Hall turned around and said, "Knowlton, what is that for?" "According to agreement," said I.

'The sequel to the case was that in a few days Hall brought in a load of corn to me, in payment of the debt, which I received and placed to his credit. I afterwards learned that he was trusted for the corn by a farmer in order to avoid any further endorsements of my contract. It is unnecessary to add that the farmer was never paid for the corn.'

Sometimes during more modern times, within the memory of people still living, when country stores were not quite as close to their customers as they had been, store owners tried collection letters. They would send out 'Sugar letter No. 1,' 'Sugar letter No. 2,' 'Sugar letter No. 3,' and then being out of patience and sugar they got off a 'plain' letter — 'We will send the law after you.' If that did not produce action the account was turned over to a lawyer for collection. That was not always entirely satisfactory. Sometimes it took longer to get the money from the lawyer than it took him to collect it.

The best collection letters were not the stereotyped ones, but those written to the circumstances. 'We were certainly fair enough when you needed that hay; do you remember that?' Or, 'We feel that we have done our part to be fair with

you and then you give us a check which is no good.' Sometimes
the debtor offered an explanation: 'I can't send only $10. We
have had a little trouble and had to get a new bull.' Notes
attached to some of the accounts tell their own story of the
comedy and tragedy of rural life: a Connecticut man owed
$1.32; the record says, 'Not collectible — ran away.' Other
addenda to closed accounts: 'Crazy,' 'Dead,' 'Outlawed and
he knows it,' 'Joined the Navy,' 'Just no damned good,' and
'in jail.' Surprisingly, this last man paid his bill in full by
small amounts after he got out of stir. A man owed eleven
dollars for paint. While in the store to argue about payment,
he stole a five-dollar watch. The merchant got the watch back,
but the paint bill was never paid.

Each country store operator could provide material for developing the theme of man's inhumanity to man. The story is
still told of George Clark ('Dry Goods, Fancy Goods, Groceries, Drugs, Medicines and Gents' Furnishings') who ran a
general store at Salisbury, Connecticut, a good citizen, and
treasurer and town clerk for some forty years. Clark had sold
goods on credit for all of a long life. Many had taken advantage of him. One man who had been running up a bill for
years, but forgetting to pay, came in one day and asked the
price of ham. George told him, but the customer thought the
price was too high. So he changed the subject and asked if
Mr. Clark could advance him ten dollars and 'just put it on
the books.' Clark gave him the money. Whereupon the customer went to James Woodruff's Ore Hill store and bought
his ham there, with Clark's ten dollars.

A man said he wanted to buy $50 worth of goods, a nice
order, but said he hesitated to buy because he had been swin-
dled by the unscrupulous merchants with whom he had dealt
previously. The dealer said he would fill the order on a money-
back-if-not-satisfied basis. He put up the order, and wrote

across the bottom of the bill 'Your money back if you want it,' and signed his name. Later the customer came in and asked for his money.

'What's the matter, weren't the goods all right?' asked the merchant.

'No, they weren't,' said the man.

'All right, bring them back,' said the retailer, and thought he had him there. The customer pointed to his receipted bill.

'It doesn't say anything there about having to bring the goods in.'

The merchant stood his ground and got sued. He knew he was in trouble when the plaintiff's lawyer appeared, the man who handled all the cheap cases in town. A judgment was found against the store and the owner paid.

Petty theft was an unending nuisance. The country merchant needed an eye trained for the abnormal, wide-peripheral vision, a sense of something occurring when his back was turned, a feeling for a casualness that was too elaborate, the customer who drifted along too many counters, who could not seem to find what he wanted. A good many tales of shoplifting have been preserved in most localities and some of them are authentic folklore. Country people had a great relish for stories of the trickster tricked, the thief caught, and applauded the ingenuity of the storekeeper when the victory was his. The law was seldom invoked. These matters were settled quietly at the crossroads, with public opinion as referee.

Hiram J. Bissell had a peephole cut in the wall of the partition between the front and back rooms of his store. When a customer came into the store and began to wander around, inquire the price of this, move on aimlessly to that, tossing each piece of goods aside to take up another, then Mr. Bissell would retire to the rear and keep an eye out while the clerk took care of the trade. One day a man came in who was known

as a 'Raggy,' so-called because he lived high up in the Mt.
Riga woods, along the state line between New York and Connecticut, and also because of his apparel and economic station
in life. Mr. Bissell promptly took up his post. Sure enough,
Danny, the 'Raggy,' went to the rear of the store, slipped off
his coat, picked up a whole fried codfish, and hung it down
his back on a piece of string. Putting on his coat again, he
headed for the front door. Bissell caught up with him and
started an amiable conversation. As Danny grew more and
more nervous Bissell grew more relaxed and anecdotal. Time
seemed to mean nothing to him. 'Raggy' was in a panic. Finally Bissell said sternly that he wanted to give Danny some
advice: if he wished to steal a codfish he should either wear a
longer coat or take a shorter fish, as the stolen cod was in plain
sight. There is some doubt whether the fish actually was
longer than the coat. At any rate, that was Bissell's Yankee
way of emphasizing the Eighth Commandment.

One cold day this same resourceful Bissell saw a customer
slip a pound of butter into his coat pocket. So Hiram backed
the culprit up against the radiator and held him firmly in a
spirited gab-fest until the miserable sinner was dripping with
melted butter. This is an old story. The Bissell version must
be a late variant, since there is a radiator involved in it. They
tell it differently in upstate New York. The boss had been
missing articles for some time. His suspicions finally settled
on a man who always came into the store early in the morning
when the clerk was just opening up and always wanted to buy
a little oil. While it was being drawn in the cellar he was free
to circulate around and make away with whatever suited his
fancy. The man was dressed in better style than was common,
and wore a tall plug hat of the period. After one of his appearances a roll of butter was missing. The merchant called
out to the customer that he must not go so fast, as he had a

good story for him. So, seating his victim beside the box stove that would take a full-length stick of cordwood, he opened the drafts wide, and stoked her up with four-foot oak and hickory, well seasoned and crammed with b.t.u's. The doomed prisoner and his beaver hat met a horrible fate.

Jacob Sheafe missed a barrel of pork from his store in Portsmouth, New Hampshire, a very respectable robbery, since the barrel and contents would be worth, well, in the range of ten to twelve dollars. A few days after the pork disappeared, a man said:

'Mr. Sheafe, did you ever find out who stole the pork?'

'Oh, yes,' said Sheafe, promptly.

'Indeed; who was it?'

'Nobody but you and I ever knew it was stolen, so pay for it at once, if you wish nobody else to know about it.'

Barber, a trader who has already been mentioned, always on the job, his great voice booming up and down the store, has also been made the central figure of the same story, told in very circumstantial detail; how there were a great many barrels of pork stacked behind the store in a long row on the south side of the street; how early one morning the proprietor found one barrel missing. He said nothing about it. But the thief's curiosity got the better of him. There was the same inquiry, and the crashing answer: 'No one knew of it but myself and the man who took it.'

A man with a cane appeared at the Colebrook general store, at Colebrook, Connecticut, and, as was later discovered, tapped the cash drawer by putting some kind of stickum on the end of the cane and *reaching*. The same story bobs up in Illinois. This time the cane was tipped with a sharpened nail. The old gentleman waved the cane in the air as he sauntered up and down the aisle to accustom the retailer to its gyrations. Then, at the right moment, without going behind the counter or making any suspicious movement, he would spear a plug of tobacco on the back-counter shelf with a lightning thrust, and come up with his favorite brand.

A man who was caught stealing dry goods from a Wisconsin store was indicted for grand larceny and held for trial. He pleaded that the goods were priced too high and ought to be charged in the indictment at cost, which would have brought the value under the amount necessary to hold him for grand larceny. The judge ruled that a man could not steal at cost, but only at the retail price. Sentence: two years.

The country customers found many ingenious ways other than outright theft to keep a merchant on his toes. 'Lan' (Orlando) Camp, from out in the bottomlands of the Mississippi River in Pike County, Illinois, hauled a wagon-load of turnips into the Haines-Rupert store in Rockport. 'I examined the turnips,' said Tom Haines, 'cutting several in two, and I saw that they were pithy and hollow. I reported the condition of the turnips and advised against buying them from "Lan" because the store would get stuck. Nevertheless, we did purchase the wagon load and had them unloaded in the back room. Of course, "Lan" immediately spread the story that he had gotten the best of the Haines store on the turnip deal. We knew the turnips were unsaleable; but the Camps were excellent customers, spending probably two or three thousand dollars a year. It was better to be laughed at over a deal of this kind to insure the continued patronage of the Camps. Next day we hauled the turnips to the town dump.'

If the customers had to be watched, so did the clerks. Not every crossroads store clerk was a potential Marshall Field. The new man was likely to be too good to be true for the first week; but staying power was what counted. A good deal of hazing went on when a new boy showed up. He was given the task of driving a nail into an iron post. His coat pocket was filled with lard or molasses. When he ogled a pretty girl customer, a way was found to tell him loudly that his wife wanted him to bring a pound of crackers home for supper. The boss had to keep an eye out for the clerk who hung too eagerly over the counter when comely misses came to buy hose or flannel but disappeared into the back room when old and cranky customers appeared.

Sometimes a smart clerk relieved his feelings with a pert answer. A young fellow who rejoiced in the nickname of Tubbydub, generally hard up and known to be poor pay, visited the Cross store at Gurleyville, Connecticut, on a rainy day, and started to paw over the whips. They hung from a swinging ring attached to the ceiling. The whip came free when given a brisk jerk. Tubbydub tried one after the other, taking each one down, stepping into the clear and giving it a good hard crack. The clerk, Wilbur Cross, watched the proceeding with a feeling of growing irritation, and finally spoke up.

'You know, Tubby, it don't do them whips any good to snap them like that?' remarked the future Yale professor of English and Governor of the state.

He then went on to ask why Tubbydub could not find a whip that suited him. The audience around the stove hunched forward expectantly, waiting for better things to come. Tubby complained peevishly that none of them whips was long enough to reach his hoss's ears. That was the opening.

'Well, I guess, Tubby, if you took one home on tick it would be long enough before you paid for it.'

In the years before society took care of those who were mentally unbalanced, the dimwits and numbskulls found their way to the country store, like all others in the community, and were often callously exploited by the 'setters' or the clerks.

Sometimes Mr. Smart was outsmarted and a tale was made of it. Sophronie, of Watertown, New York, who sometimes wore pants like a man and wove daisies into garlands for her hair, was known to be touched in her head and fair game. One day she entered a store and asked for blue calico.

The clerk, being out of blue, measured off red, wrapped it up, and handed the package to Sophronie.

'But I asked for blue,' she protested.

'That's all right, Sophie,' said the clerk, reassuringly, 'you can just imagine that it's blue.'

With no more comment, Sophronie picked up the bundle and started out the door.

'Hey,' called the clerk, 'you didn't pay for that calico.'

'That's all right,' said Sophronie, 'you can just imagine that I paid for it.'

The average country store clerk made an art of keeping just busy enough so he would not be set to doing any real work. He was clever at it in the same way as Chaucer's man-of-law:

> No-wher so bisy a man as he ther nas,
> And yet he semed bisier than he was.

The alert merchant accepted the fact that he had to get out on the floor and stir the boys up with a sharp stick, even the good workers. Old Barber had his own particular way of doing it. He went about his store secretly knocking over displays of goods just to keep his help busy. When there was nothing else to do, the clerk could always count eggs, sprout potatoes, or wield the feather duster; although, as one old timer put it, 'advertising seems to be kind o' takin' the place of dustin'.'

Plenty of country merchants revenged themselves for the larded butter and aged eggs they received from customers by overcharging for articles whose value was hard to check, sanding the sugar, and using one set of scales for the sale of goods and another for the purchase of produce. Sylvanus Cobb, Jr., a writer who manufactured melodrama and moralistic fiction in enormous quantities in the mid-years of the nineteenth century, often with shrewd bits of observation tucked in here and there, based one story on a country merchant and his clerk. The plot turned on the circumstance that the dealer falsely accused his bright clerk of theft because he feared him as a potential competitor. In the course of the story, the retailer, who sold 'auction-bought goods at alarmingly high prices,' gave his son a few tips on merchandising. Always add half a cent, after calculating the retail price, he told his son. 'When you come the half cents over them they think you are shaving closer down to cost.' 'Always take advantage of a customer when you can,' was another maxim, 'but be careful and keep the bright side out.' It was important to find talking points to beat the farmer down on his produce. 'We must live and thrive, you see,' explained the rascally pop to his apt pupil. The verities are satisfied when we learn that it was the no-good son who tapped his father's money drawer.

The Watkins & Owens store at Prospect, New York, has been reported as offering molasses at two prices, by inserting two spouts in the same barrel, with a wall between them to disguise the fact. R. E. Gould remembered selling three kinds of port wine — California port, Tarragona port, and Douro port. The price range was considerable — from twenty-five cents to a dollar a pint. The wines came down to Maine from a Boston wholesaler in three kegs. Finally that got to be too much trouble. They just ordered one barrel at twenty-seven cents a gallon wholesale, and used it to keep the three kegs full.

Pork sausage that had been on hand some time was inclined to collect mold and become a loss. The trick here was to take a piece of cheesecloth and rub off the mold. The overhaul was completed by dipping the cheesecloth in butter and wiping the sausages. This added luster, an air of fresh goods, and made the old pork appear more appetizing. A man comes in for a cap. 'Show Mr. Howe some of those fur caps, Joe,' calls the owner, referring to a slow-moving number of which only one is still sticking on the shelf. The cap is tried on. Unfortunately, it does not fit. Too small. The clerk dives down behind the counter and pulls until the sticker gives around the sweat-band. 'Try this one, Mr. Howe, it looks larger — I think you'll find it fits.' Yes, the cap is just right. 'A satisfied customer is our best advertisement,' grins the merchant as he kicks the empty box out of the aisle.

In each generation of the life of the country store, countless thousands of store owners were rigorously honest, as they led the life of early rising, long hours, ate cold lunches out of a tin pail, fought the battle of cash and credit, cheerfully snipped off a yard of passementerie, stood aside quietly and unobtrusively while a countryman and his wife moved slowly along the counters, every purchase the occasion for a long conference. Perhaps the neighbors were brought into the discussion and asked for their opinion. Perhaps the goods were carried up to the front door for closer inspection. A man making a purchase for a woman, say a shawl or some bolt cloth, would rub it on itself, hold it off at a distance to view the effect, rub it again reflectively with a heavy thumb. He would squint at it in the light, ask whether it would surely wash, and was it the fashion. A country wife would not hesitate to take half an hour to buy three yards of ribbon, seeking advice and suggestions from other customers along the way, while the merchant struggled to keep his good nature.

A customer asked T. C. Rainey of Arrow Rock, Missouri, how much coffee he sold for a dollar.

'I told him four pounds and he protested,' said Rainey.

'Why, Mr. ——— sells five pounds.'

'You are his customer; why don't you buy it there?'

'I have just come from there and he told me that was the way he sold it, but he is out.'

'Oh, ah, well, that is the way I sell it when I am out, but you see, I am not out.'

Many an artist's eye has delighted in the genre scene suggested by a busy store porch — the tired boy returned from fishing in the 'crick,' a child who has lost her shoe, the male buzz group, and the housewife with her egg basket who will demand from the storekeeper, as a traditional *douceur,* two darning needles for every double-yolk egg.

Often the country merchant was a man of perception and good heart, who would see a hard-working country wife inquiring for handsome fabrics he knew she could not afford to buy. She would stand and admire them, with her gnarled fingers fold the pretty patterns into pleats, and drape them over her plain dress while her face lighted up with pleasure at the sight of such lustrous materials. And many times the store owner, when not too busy, would display each fabric, rolling out the bolt just to see her draw her hands over a bright delaine or rich cassimere.

There were many who found a variety of compensations in keeping a store, as did Dan'l Brown. There is no doubt about Dan'l. He liked his store at Amesville. His wife always remembered how he felt about it: 'Dan'l had a full life in the store,' she said, 'with exciting trips South to New Orleans to sell produce and East to Philadelphia to buy goods. Dan'l always liked to keep a store . . . I think that one reason he liked being a merchant was because, in those days, the village store was a meeting place for everybody who came to town. People talked things over there. And Dan'l was always interested in politics. He liked to argue about public questions.'

There is no harm in supposing that Dan'l Brown also liked the clink of coin as he put the day's receipts in the old salamander safe. It would be surprising if he liked equally well the business of invoices, discounts, letter writing, and stock-taking, which often kept him at the store late at night. It's always more fun to pail the cow than to feed her. Yet a man in the country store line could not be all trader and no book-keeper, though he usually kept his books with a kind of dash and originality which has left us many a human-interest story along with the accounts of trade.

A LOOK AT THE BOOKS

THERE WERE a number of different ways in which a country merchant could keep his accounts in the days before cash registers, adding machines, loose-leaf binders, visible files, or the early ticket register system.

He could tally up chalk scores on the wall, possibly the simplest system of all. He could run up a column of figures on a shingle, the ancestor of the visible file. He might calculate by pictograph, like the New Hampshire Yankee who got confused about whether the customer owed him for a cheese or a grindstone because at the time the transaction was recorded, he forgot to draw a hole for the crank of the grindstone. But whether it was by single entry or double, by notched sticks, or by a stub pencil and scrap of paper fished from a vest pocket, the storekeeper could not escape the burden of keeping accounts of some kind; and the only good ones were those the merchant himself could understand.

James L. Bragg used to run a general store with a lumber yard in back of it. One day a farmer wanted some cedar shingles. The quantity Bragg had on hand, as it turned out, was just what the customer wanted. 'I'll take them all,' he said. But Bragg held back on the last bundle.

'I couldn't sell that one,' he explained. 'It's got my store accounts on it.'

The country trader usually kept his accounts in great folios, full-sized sheets of heavy, white 'wove' paper, folded once by the stationer to make four pages, bound in rough sheep, or in brown leather scarred by long handling, or in stiff marbled covers with strong hubs, American russia ends and bands, trimmed and stamped in gilt, and indexed with linen tabs. The paper was rough in surface where the fibers of linen or cotton had felted together, but it was as enduring as time itself. Each book was ruled according to its use, for cash, daybook, single or double entry, and could be had — the best there was — for about a dollar and a half. The paper was made of all-rag stock, which today has become mellow and creamy with age, the ink shading from a medium to a dark brown in a delightful blend of color, the very shape and form of the letters giving us the atmosphere of another age. Until steel pens were introduced, the merchant had to be skilled in the cutting, slitting, and pointing of goose quills. He had his round pounce box with a perforated top, containing ground pumice for preparing rough paper to take the ink, or for writing over erasures. His high slant-top desk was equipped with sand for blotting, his penknife at hand for shaping the quill pens. Perhaps he had his own recipe for making ink. Many were handed down for generations. Three pints of 'Excellent Black Ink' could be made from

3 oz. Aleppo Galls
3 oz. Copperas
1 oz. Gum Arabic
6 oz. Logwood

First you boiled the logwood and strained it through a cloth. Then mixed the whole. The ink would be better if the galls were steeped several days first, the copperas and other ingredients added afterward. An old writer says that the gall-nuts should be hard, solid, and hairy on the surface, the copperas of a sky-blue character, and the gum arabic clear, transparent.

The instincts of a good merchant are all toward waiting on customers and promoting trade. Yet hour after hour the country retailer toiled at his housekeeping, checking invoices, arranging stock, and plugging at his books; hard work — harder than pulling a cat out from under a barn. When he worked at night he held a candle between his eyes and his books, its rays glancing and twinkling as they struck the silver bows of his spectacles. When lamps replaced the candle, he bent under the yellow lamplight that showered down on his cubbyhole. Hour after hour he transcribed, posted, totaled, and sometimes rectified — 'by mistake added to other side.' There he collected his thoughts, wrote himself important memoranda, most likely in the back of the ledger — 'You must not trust Elisha Sweet' — and tended to his correspondence: 'I regret that my payments have been slow, but for your lenience you have my thanks.' Before the days of duplicating processes, the store proprietor copied off an important letter on brown butcher paper or the back of an old circular or broadside, and slipped it between the pages of his ledger.

Replenishing stock was a big job, especially in the early

days when goods arrived infrequently and had to last for a season. A hundred years ago the arrival of a shipment made an animated scene. Ox-teams and carts, horses and wagons, stopped to watch. Bystanders craned and poked at the boxes of dry goods, barrels of meat, crackers, and hardware. There would be thirty or forty packages of smaller size, West India goods, groceries, and medicines. Calomel was a staple in the western country where the 'shakes' descended on good and bad alike in a most unchristian manner. Since the dosage was as much calomel as would stay on the blade of a knife, the quantities used were enormous.

As the merchant opened his bales and marked the goods, he checked his invoice to see that he got what he paid for. He would find it a wise precaution to go even further, and count, measure, weigh, and gauge every shipment he received. As he arranged his assortment for display and sale, he put a mark on every article showing the cost and the selling price. The cost price represented — or at least it should have — the cost from the invoice, plus the expense of purchase, freight, the rate of exchange, and incidentals. It was expressed in a secret code which could be understood only by the dealer and his clerks. The selling price was stated in plain figures, but it was known to be a matter for negotiation. It was not uncommon for a merchant to have in his mind, if not on the ticket, four selling prices; one for the man who paid cash, one for the man who paid on payday, one for the man who had to be dunned before he paid, and one for the man who had to be sued for the bill.

In the days when the Middle West was opening up, a merchant along the Ohio or Mississippi rivers would have considered a markup of 50 per cent as low. A 75 per cent advance over the wholesale price was common, and the trader often spoke of making 'one per cent' which meant an article that cost a dollar sold for two dollars. It was a part of the psychology of selling to flatter the substantial man when he brought in his truck and began to look over the store's stock, and let him know slyly that the prices could be shaved for him. 'All like to be made conscious,' wrote a storekeeper of the 1830's, 'of the realization of the advantages which wealth is supposed to confer.' Credit buyers were less fussy about quality and price. Their urgent need was to get the goods. So it cost them about 25 per cent more to buy.

Among the witnesses to the arrival of a new season's goods would be some who had once been merchants or clerks. They sought with particular zeal to read behind the mystic symbols in order to decipher the marks and to find the true cost. They would know the principle involved, having marked many a package themselves. Frequently the code was based on the use of ten letters, no two alike, each letter representing a number from one to ten: such as Cumberland, Perth Amboy, or Republican:

1	2	3	4	5	6	7	8	9	0
C	u	m	b	e	r	l	a	n	d
P	e	r	t	h	A	m	b	o	y
R	e	p	u	b	l	i	c	a	n

'Blacksmith' or 'Clean Shirt' were also used: or a nine-letter word with X for zero. To make it a little harder, sometimes the actual cost figures were each raised by one digit, so that 10, 22, 45, or 115 became 21, 33, 56, and 226. Or letters could be selected at random, such as:

1	2	3	4	5	6	7	8	9	0
s	u	a	b	d	c	h	r	v	z

Some traders liked a mark derived from the game of tick-tack-toe:

$$\begin{array}{c|c|c} 1 & 2 & 3 \\ \hline 4 & 5 & 6 \\ \hline 7 & 8 & 9 \end{array}$$

The lines drawn around each number stood for the digit with an X for the zero. One dollar and fifty-nine cents would be:
⌋ ☐ ⌈

The clumsy clerk had to pause and study the hidden prices in order to conduct his negotiations with customers. Perhaps he would have to whisper with the store owner, muttering that the article 'cost 56.' The nimble clerk learned to read the prices as rapidly as if they were printed in plain figures. If he needed advice from his employer about how far down he could go to get a trade, he had the natural suavity to remark: 'It is number 56.'

The invoices of goods received were filed as an important record of the business. This was accomplished by running them on a piece of twine or spearing them on a wire. Such festoons, recording the arrival of consignments long since forgotten, may still be seen in a few places even today; one example is the old 'Clat' Adams store on the river front at Quincy, Illinois. When tickets were filled out for cash sales, these were also often strung on a twine, in the same order as the occurrence of the sale during the day, those for each day's business being separated from those of the day before and the day after by a piece of cardboard with the date marked on it. The cash was 'made up' in the evening and the money put in the old iron safe. One old trader kept his cash account by hanging up a pair of boots, one on either side of the fireplace. In one he put the money he received. Into the other went scraps of paper covering monies paid out. To strike a balance, he emptied his boots.

Most country merchants kept their books by the single-entry system, 'According to the practise of well-regulated Counting Houses,' as John H. Shea, Baltimore author of a popular accounting handbook, described it. Under this procedure, two books were required. The first one, variously called a waste book or daybook contained a running record of goods bought and sold, receipts in the form of cash or farm produce, every transaction in the order of its occurrence, all of the undigested affairs of the day. That may sound more massive than it actually was, since many store records show a dozen trades as the sum of the day's work. The waste book was often just a quire or two of the commonest paper, sewed together, very hastily and roughly, where a busy man could set down 'skaits,' 'Boise shoes,' 'trasis' (traces) or, desperately, 'Rec'd for *something*.'

A better form of first record, a bound book, cap folio size, bound in serviceable duck, ruled for a daybook, could be had for under fifty cents. From such a book a fair copy was made into the ledger, the chronological scribbles arranged as debit and credit items so as to reflect the standing of each customer. To cut down on the work, the items were not always copied off on the ledger. Sometimes only numbers were used, referring back to the page in the journal where the purchases were listed. One store proprietor with a small business eliminated the daybook entirely. He wrote the charges on a slate and posted them to the ledger at the end of the week. In one Illinois store where there was a tight rein on credit, the preferred classes were school teachers, railroad section hands, and Civil War pensioners, all persons whose income was in cash, regular and *known*. The chore boy, when he was not straightening crooked nails at the back step, untangling string and rolling it up for the 'string box,' was allowed to wait on trade in small items, keeping his own cashbook, a giveaway memo and account book issued by the benevolent **Dr. R. V. Pierce** of Buffalo, 'the people's medical servant.'

In the ledger the customer who received goods on tick was marked debtor. The jobber or the farmer who delivered anything into the store's stock was set down as a creditor. Frequently there would be an entry in both columns, the buyer of merchandise receiving credit for live chickens or shoeing the storekeeper's horse. In the ledger, the real book of doom, each customer was allotted two pages, the debtor page on the left, the creditor or contra page on the right side, both headed

Part of a ledger page, showing that Thomas Lincoln, shortly before his marriage, purchased (from Bleakley and Montgomery) at Elizabethtown, Kentucky, different cloths in varying yardages, buttons, tape, and '6 skanes thread.'

with his name, written in a plain, round hand, and entered in an index. Posting the ledger was an arduous task, to be put off as long as possible, like taking a bath.

The accounts were continuous, and settlement infrequent, though the almanacs advised settlement annually, around December or January. Robert B. Thomas, venerable proprietor of the *Farmer's Almanack*, favored December. 'There is little to be done this month,' he said, 'except to enjoy the fruit of your past labour; but in the first place make a settlement of accounts with all. I trust you have continually kept an account book; if not, obtain one immediately, and depend no longer on your memory, nor on promiscuous marks and scratches about the walls of your house.' A settlement was made in proper form when the storekeeper wrote in the creditor column of the ledger a statement, dated, to this effect: 'This day Ballanced all accompts Between Thos. Cobb and Nehemiah Dean as Witness my hand, Nehemiah Dean,' which, when translated, meant that Dean acknowledged in his official book that the balance had been paid.

Along about February came inventory time. Then every article had to be accounted for, if necessary taken down from its place, counted, and the quantity on hand and the wholesale price entered in an inventory book. The book also contained estimates of the value of the store fixtures, bills receivable, payables, and other general calculations which would set forth the net worth of the business. Some dealers, with the gifts of a Mark Cone, who spent a lifetime in the dim interior of his little store at Hartford, Vermont, always knew where everything was, how much was on hand, where and when the goods were bought, and how much they cost. 'He never took an inventory,' says his granddaughter. 'Cleaning store' was a twice-a-year performance. Beginning at the front on one side, every shelf had to be cleared, starting at the top, wiped

with a cloth, wet or dry, whichever was appropriate, and replaced.

The authors of books on accounting recommended the use
of other kinds of records such as a Borrow and Loan and a
Cash Book; but most country dealers were not up to that
much paper work. They had gone their distance when they
jotted down each occurrence in the daybook, and along with
it, any other pertinent information that seemed important,
such as the date on which they put in their vegetable garden,
when the mare should foal, or a copy of the forms of commercial law which might be useful to a man who was often called
upon to prepare a lease or draw up a short-form will.

Whether the country merchant had ever carried his accounting studies far enough to hear of Lucas De Bargo
Paciolus, the fifteenth-century Venetian who is honored as the
patron saint of all accountants, is doubtful; but some preparation for the high stool and pen was necessary. The equipment of one young clerk in the early 1800's was that in arithmetic he had gone through Erastus Root, Jonathan Grout,
and Nathan Daboll from beginning to end. He had an easy
acquaintance with decimal fractions, read 'tolerably,' knew
the rule of three, and understood 'single and double fellow-
ship.' He could write a fair hand and his grammar was 'pass-
able.' He was also considered to be sharp at a bargain.

We can get some idea of what was considered suitable
preparation for keeping a store's books from the public notice of a Professor R. Megonegal, proprietor of a Philadelphia Seminary, who advertised for students who wished to
learn pen writing and bookkeeping. The other advertisements
with which the Professor's is associated are worth a moment's
attention as an evocation of the commercial atmosphere of the
second quarter of the nineteenth century. James Todd, attorney, advertised that he could help collect debts and settle

claims in the southern and western states as he had formed extensive correspondence with gentlemen of the bar in those regions. Schlesinger & Co. sold Dutch madder. Exchange brokers advertised for doubloons, Napoleons, sovereigns, and 'Fips' — five pence, otherwise known as the fipenny bit or Spanish half-real. Coffin & Landell had received fifty barrels of spermaceti fall oil which was 'in order to send to the country.' Fryer & Anderson addressed the country merchants on the subject of imported dry goods. Virginia Osnaburgs, a kind of coarse linen cloth, were advertised; Ohio and Herkimer County cheese, and Washington Irving's new book, *Astoria*. Corsets were offered in the most fashionable French shapes 'which are admirably arranged so as to improve the figure.' Auctioneers beckoned with evening sales of scissors, Britannia mettle, tea- and coffeepots, shoe blacking, shoe knives, coffee mills, gig whips, 'Russia quills,' and the new steel pens. A lad was wanted, about fifteen years of age, who wrote a good hand, as an apprentice in a dry goods commission house.

We can imagine a likely youth, on his way to find Mr. Megonegal and his Seminary, deaf to the tumble and bustle that was Philadelphia, the grinding of the drays on the cobblestone pavements, or the passing of a splendid omnibus such as the 'Stephen Decatur.' He would not hear the street cries of the vendors, since his thoughts were all of his future mercantile career; nor hear those of the sandman, either — 'Sand your kitchens, sand your floors, want an-y sand?' — nor the words and vocals of the charcoal man:

> *Charcoal by the bushel,*
> *Charcoal by the peck*
> *Charcoal by the frying pan*
> *Or any way you lek.*

Rather, his eager thoughts would be on the Seminary, open from sunrise to 10 p.m., though he might learn with regret when he arrived there that 'Ladies write in separate rooms.' At any rate, bookkeeping was 'taught in a superior Mercantile manner, in half the time . . . far superior to the Italian plan . . . a new and infallible rule for Dr. and Cr. upon Double Entry, and a new Journal form, with positive success to the learner in from Ten to Twenty lessons, with Bills of Exchange, and all auxilliary Books and Drafts, with Bottomry and Respondentia Bonds . . . a superior style of runninghand, round, text or leger-hand, combined with expedition and legibility, expressly for Mercantile, business and Ladies' letter hand.'

Instruction was based on copybooks, the left-hand pages illustrated with copper-plate engraved models of 'the flourishing alphebet,' the Engrossing hand, the Court hand, the running Chancery hand, the Round hand, and the 'running Mercantile hand.' On the right side of the book the scholar practiced. He started with words such as *command, mind,* and *manners* which very seldom require lifting the pen; this for freedom and speed. Later he practiced on *philosophy,* because forming the letters that go above and below the line gave him the mechanical control of his fingers necessary to a good flowing business hand. He also practiced making 'offhand Capitals' on a slate or scrap of paper, to save expense; sitting in such a way so as to face the desk and paper squarely, keeping calm, and balancing the whole hand on the little finger. The pen 'should not be grasped hard, as it will necessarily create a tremor and weariness.'

The goal was worth the effort in an age when the ability to write a good hand, with elegantly formed letters, was considered a polite accomplishment as well as a practical necessity. Sometimes a clerk with more of the artist in him than the

The ability to write a good running mercantile hand was not only of practical advantage in a business way but a status symbol as well.

trader, fell in love with calligraphy, as did Platt Rogers Spencer, who founded the Spencerian system of writing, 'a sloping, semi-angular style, rapid and legible,' with curves neatly shaded and capitals embellished with mazy whorls. Spencer's copybook appeared in 1855 and for a generation his textbooks dominated the public schools and business colleges; 'the curse of my youth,' recalls Earnest Calkins, advertising expert and historian of many phases of business, who as a youth could *not* make graceful doves on the wing holding scrolls in their bills.

The future merchant must have often dawdled over his exercise book as Fred Hall did when he went to bookkeeping school at Birmingham, Connecticut; he started with a prim and proper inventory, 'I Commence Business with the Following effects,' consisting of goods and notes held, cash owed, store expenses to be accounted for, and so forth. Fred wrote down firmly the Rule for Journalizing: 'Make what cash you value Dr. and what Produces value Cr.'; but he also enjoyed writing his name over and over — narcissism embellished with flourishes and doodlings. Underneath his name on the flyleaf of his exercise book a feminine hand has written, 'I wonder which Fred likes the best [sic], Derby or Long Island?' Then comes an apparent *non sequitur:* 'I wonder where Mary Clemens is.' Again, a question and an answer, both in the same hand, so it is a soliloquy of some ninety years ago: 'I don't think much of Fred, do you?' And the response, 'No, I don't.'

Inside the back cover of Hall's exercise book is a limerick, still in the hand of the fair intruder, to the general effect that Fred had quite a hand with the girls, and that his fondness for a girl in Patchogue, named *Hattie,* had made all the girls quite *wrathy.* Whether he ever completed his course, or what evidence of his proficiency he carried away with him, we cannot know now. The Professor usually issued a certificate, decorated with pen writing at its fanciest, with swirls, thick-and-thin shadings, the proportions and spacings of the letters, the evenness of the lines, demonstrating that the master was indeed accomplished in the art he taught.

William M. Haines, who became a widely known merchant of Pike County, Illinois, received such a certificate from Jonathan Jones in St. Louis, 18 March 1864. It stated that William M. Haines 'has this day completed under my instruction a full course of Double Entry Bookkeeping embracing Mercantile, Manufacturing, and Steamboat Bookkeeping, Individual Company and Compound Company, with Forms adapted to the Wholesale, Retail, Banking and Commission Business, etc., etc., together with Accounts Current, Account Sales, and a Complete system of Commercial Correspondence, and that he is in every respect worthy of public confidence as a Practical Accountant, and as such I do most cheerfully commend him to the favorable consideration of those who may wish to employ a Competent Bookkeeper.'

A young trader just setting up for himself would round out

his equipment nicely if he had a book of stereotyped letter forms which would enable him to write plain or elegant letters, and provide him with the forms of mortgages, deeds, bonds, and powers of attorney, in case he lacked stationers' blanks. Such a book could be had in the 1850's on Market Street in Philadelphia, or in Pearl Street, New York's crookedest but most important mercantile thoroughfare. A country merchant, wishing to avoid affectation and write in 'the language of the present times' might consult his letter-writing book, and address a jobbing house as follows:

'GENTLEMEN: I hope it will not be a disagreeable surprise to see below an order on my account.

'I am not in the least doubtful of your serving me on the best terms; that is, so as to enable me to sell as cheap as others. And whenever you have occasion for money, your demand shall either be paid, or you may draw on me for the amount. Pray be careful in choosing my goods, and expeditious in forwarding them, which will tend to increase your correspondence with,

> *Gentlemen,*
> *Your most obedient servant.*'

Once in business, with a store building, an assortment of goods worth in the neighborhood of $5000, a 'good run of trade' as the commercial phrase had it, there was nothing quite like a sturdy stand-up desk and an imposing set of books to suggest the substantial character of the enterprise. The ledger would usually be posted by the owner himself, though Wilbur Cross, when scarcely in his teens, and without benefit of a professor's certificate, was permitted to work at the books in the general store where he helped out from time to time, 'sitting in glory on a high stool before a high desk.'

Morrill & Shaw, of Jackson, Michigan, sought a young

man, in 1853, 'to oversee their Store & keep their [sic] Books with the privilege of some time to take out of door exercise each day until I am able to attend close to business . . . they keep their Books by double entry . . . I can do it very well by Single entry; and understand the theory of Double Entry also but want the practise.'

The daybook was in active use by all who waited on trade. 'I strutted behind the counter with a pen back of my ear, was wonderfully polite to the ladies, assumed a wise look when entering charges upon the day-book,' P. T. Barnum said; and for once we can believe him.

Generally speaking, the calligraphy of the 1790's and early 1800's was graceful and well drawn, with good quill-work and carefully formed letters in a shaded, flowing style, as taught by Mr. Megonegal of Philadelphia, or Henry Dean of Salem, author of 'Dean's Analytical Guide to the Art of Penmanship.' The writing got progressively worse as the decades advanced, until we can only wonder what the end would have been had longhand records continued. When the account book was new and the merchant acutely aware of the expense of having it, the writing would start out bravely, in 'a superior style.' As the novelty wore off the script became a scribble.

George Scriba, who moved an incredible quantity of goods from New York to his store on Oneida Lake, headed his book with mingled piety and learning, 'Nomine Dei, 1794.' John Garrison, who kept store at East Schodack, New York, limned carefully in purple ink on the verso of the front cover, 'Book Bought Mar. 11, 1870,' but from 12 March on the book is filled with hurried pencil scrawls, and when it was full he kept right on going until the flyleaf and the inside of the back cover, too, were choked with interlineations, cipherings, calculations, random memoranda, dates, notes of settlement, and lists of goods that should be reordered — Nervine, sal soda, slippery elm, and paper collars.

Paper was such a scarce article a hundred years ago that household accounts were written on whatever scrap came to hand, and every scrap was used. Letter paper was an infrequent purchase, and sold by the sheet, costing 7½ cents a sheet in 1853. Country newspapers constantly implored housewives to save their rags, and even undertook to collect them for the paper mills. Farmers and mechanics kept their tallies on the margins of the family almanac, writing all around the pages. The old store account books, with their tempting expanse of white paper, often had a surprising subsequent history. The store might burn, the trader die, but the old ledgers lived on. A later generation took up where the earlier one left off. Thus journals became ledgers and ledgers journals; an inventory of the store's stock suddenly runs into the business affairs of a lumbering operation, a blacksmith, or a tavern.

The spelling found throughout the account books of general stores shows fewer departures from established usage than the spelling in wills, personal letters, and diaries, but from time to time the merchants displayed originality of orthography. We can still catch accents from the past which are of considerable linguistic interest: '3 yds. Pantz cloth'; 'pr. overhalls'; '1 qt. Molassez.' Come Thanksgiving time, 'punquins' changed hands. One daybook lists the sale of 'Button Moles,' 'panterloons,' and vest 'patrons.' A wagon needed 'exeltrees.' A woman worked off part of her bill 'by weavering 29 yards of Damask.' A man did the same by 'dragin [cultivating?] turnips.' Bacon was 'bakin' in West Virginia.

The clerks were admonished constantly by their anxious employers to write down in the daybook all goods — everything — that went out of the store, 'even if the house is on

fire.' But they never did it. There were always costly leaks in
the country store business, more the result of human forget-
fulness and lax methods than of outright dishonesty.

The 1880's saw the beginning of the end for the old methods of bookkeeping. The first cash register ever used in a general merchandise store was installed at Coalton, Ohio, where
the clerk, young, hustling John H. Patterson, learned that
the new-fangled machine — 'an Ohio idea,' Patterson later
called it, proudly — cost about twenty dollars to manufacture but could be sold for around a hundred. He decided that
such a business had a rosy future, and acquired the strug-
gling little Ritty cash register plant in Dayton. Soon he was
on his way to becoming the head of the vast National Cash
Register Company, and great apostle of modern salesmanship, preaching the gospel of Making Proper Financial Records.

The registers recorded all transactions that occurred between store clerks and customers. They saved time, labor, and
bookkeeping. They even produced morality by removing the
temptation for clerks to 'go south.' They appealed to the eye
with a shiny nickeled beauty, to the ear with a pleasant 'bong'
when the lever was pressed. Like the automobile, they had an
audiovisual, mechanical charm. The retailer also netted a
psychic profit when he bought his register. It showed the
world that he was up to date. It was the Latest Thing.

By 1906 the National Cash Register was making over 400
different sizes and styles of registers selling for from $20 to
$820, the registers constantly performing more and more
operations. This led to rapid obsolescence and the exchange of
older models for newer and higher-priced registers. Sucker
lists were assembled in the home office. Country merchants
were bombarded with advertising matter, by what a writer in
Harper's Magazine has called 'postal torture methods.' A

thousand agents of the Selling Force, intensively trained in
every argument that had ever been raised for and against the
cash register, combed the countryside, itching for an opportunity to 'do Good,' that is, get a worried store owner to discuss his cash sales, his credit sales, his cash received on account, his cash paid out, what happened in making change as
an accommodation — any or all of these basic retail store activities. Once the country dealer had sashayed up to the
sample room of the local hotel about eight o'clock in the evening 'just for a look,' once he had seen the glories of the big
$600 number, it was almost dead certain that in no time at all,
to paraphrase the recollection of one of the disillusioned mes-
siahs from Dayton, the countryman would tumble right into
one of those big six-drawer 'white elephants.'

When he woke up he had a twenty-five cent cigar and a
contract. The register, he then observed, was shipped F.O.B.
factory. He could not change his mind because the contract
said he could not. There was no use in taking it down to the
local attorney to read, either. Even a tobacco lawyer could
not have upset it. The register was usually financed on a
time-payment plan, and the dealer who fell behind was likely
to see the Company 'pull the register.' When the 'show wagon'
backed up to the store and the 'elephant' got aboard it would
'take all that had been paid right back home with it.' Patterson's drummers were drilled at the factory in the merchant's
side of the cash register argument. The drummer never sold
a machine. He sold a 'system,' and hoped for an argument,
knowing that he would soon catch the dealer in a net of ad-
missions about losses which, the man from Dayton always
pointed out, would more than pay for the register. Thus Big
Business and high-pressure salesmanship came to the sleepy
little crossroads stores, sometime between the Centennial Year
of 1876 and the Louisiana Exposition of 1904.

A merchant could, of course, get a register from Butler Brothers, jobbers to the country trade, whose only drummer was a catalogue. The Butler Brothers machine would handle cash, record sales, and sound an alarm just as the National did. It also came in cherry, walnut, or oak finish, priced at $25 to $45. Either the National or Butler's 'Excelsior' would add some hurrah to any store, and show the folks that they had a live-wire dealer in their midst. Many country retailers, when they abandoned the old ways of keeping books, adopted a sales-book or ticket-register system, such as the old McCaskey Register, based on a duplicating book. The customers received a copy of an itemized statement on a duplicating book. The dealer snapped the original under a wire spring mounted on a board, all the sales to each customer grouped together, with room for up to 500 customers. The sales-book system did away with the waste books, journals, and ledgers, and provided a continuous record for both seller and buyer.

In the heyday of the old account books, when a busy store owner held a piece of paper in his hand which he wished to preserve, what did he do? He slipped it between the pages of his ledger until the old book was filled right up to bursting with notes about almost anything: out-of-stock goods, money due him on notes, comments on crops and money. There might also be a word about the lodge, the next election, a church affair, some legal struggle, as 'David Stickley personally appeared . . . made solemn affirmation that the within . . .' and so on. A loose slip floated out of David Hamlin's account book from Hammond, New York: 'Jennie: The Newspaper pattern is for the lining of the sleeves you will have to cut both larger and longer for you. in haste Libbie.' Elijah Miller used the back flyleaf of his book to say 'I have this day warned the legal voters in Hanover to meet at the time and place & for the purposes within mentioned by posting in Hanover a true and attested copy of the within warrant as the law directs. Attest, etc.'

A scrap tucked away in the old book of Jacob Sincendiver of West Virginia shows that he was a militia colonel when West Virginia and Virginia were one, and that he issued a call for an October muster day. Another notation says the state of Virginia is debtor to Jacob for four days' service at Harper's Ferry, 18–21 April 1861; and that Virginia owes him for a load of hay and 130 bushels of corn. We wonder whether he ever got paid, and suspect he did not. Personal affairs, local annals, the procession of the seasons all found their place among these informal files. 'Dea. Obediah Littefield Commence taking the Gazette 8th day of January, 1825, for 4/6 as per agreement,' wrote a clerk in a Kennebunk, Maine, store; George Scriba noted hastily in the back of his book that Perry Allen of Mexico, New York, wanted a bushel of seed corn; 'Potatoes dug by Francis Smith'; Sophia, a 'hired girl,' got two dollars a month.

'Caleb Todd died on the night of the 6th Jany,' wrote a recording angel in a Connecticut ledger, adding that he had loaned a yoke of oxen to Asaph Merriman 'to carry a load of hay to New Haven *some time since*.' He had almost forgotten! Among the treasures in the same 136-year-old book a modern investigator found to his great pleasure a collection of maple leaves in the fullness of their autumn glory — leaves so old that the form and color had been transferred to the paper by process of nature's own direct lithography.

James Kilham, of Lewis County, New York, wrote of larger affairs. On the flyleaf of his book it stands:

'Great National Money Panic
In the year of 1817 & in the year 1837 & in the year of 1857. A great money panic in the last month of 1860 & the Commencement of the year of 1861 on the acct. of the Rebellion in

the southern states. They seized all the United States forts.'
Meanwhile life went on. A 'set of gravestones' cost $14. Kil-
ham paid out $1 'for my share of singing.'

Amos Carpenter had a clerk named Anthony McGowan up
in Waterford, Vermont. Anthony was paid $22 per month,
and 'one dollar more conditional if he earns it.' But trouble
with labor is not solely the burden of modern enterprisers.
Pretty soon Anthony got docked; and again 'Anthony Mc-
Gowan lost one day and a half, and after four o'clock Saturday night.' Then one day, the old book says, Michael Kelly
started in, for the same wages plus the same incentive pay,
and Andy appears no more on the pages of history. Carpenter
turned out 79 sheep into the west pasture 8 April 1864 —
early, it seems — and Dolly got shod all around.

Horses were an important part of the life and times, for the
horse did all that we now expect of the farm truck, the jeep,
family sedan, and field power tools. Besides, a horse was good
company on a lonely farm. 'We Kild old Nell in 1891,' Dave
Hamlin wrote. We know what he meant. We can guess how he
felt.

Henry Fonda of Montgomery County, New York, mounted
a 'Table of Interest at 7 Per Cent in £- and Shillings' on the
back cover of his ledger, Timothy Morse sprinkled his ledger
with 'receipts' for homemade medicines, cakes, and sausages.
He made pills for man or horse, and best of all, 'Drops to
make an old horse young.' Timothy knew how to make hair oil
for neat grooming and advised frequent application and brisk
rubbing. He also had a formula for opodeldoc. Since this useful 'receipt' is not easy to come by, here it is in full:

Opodeldoc

Take one quart alcohol, one pound of castile soap, 2 oz. gum
camphor, 1 oz. oil of ambre. Place the alcohol in a pot of hot

water. Shave up the soap and keep it hot until all dissolves when it is done for use.

Sometimes a tired man might muse and nod at his desk, as did Caleb Morgan of Poughkeepsie, New York. He was idly doodling one day, a surprisingly aimless occupation for him, solid member of the Mill Street Methodist Church that he was, and he carelessly put himself in a fair way of being abused by a rascal. As he set it down in the back of his receipt book: 'Wrote my Name on a piece of Blank paper at desk this day — and Searched for it soon after and cannot find it. I fear some person may have made use of it in an unlawful way. C.M.' A store owner of the South, E. J. Lide, scribbled desperately on his account book, 'Suit of clothes for who!' Incidentally, a study of country store records in the South has demonstrated that most stores were honest, if not always accurate. When errors were spotted, they were just as often in favor of the customers as the store.

When old account books were filled up or discarded, either because the store or the storekeeper no longer existed, or because the accounts were being kept in a new, current book, the discarded folios often had a further history of unexpected service. When Chauncey M. Brewer, general merchant in the little village of Battle Creek, Michigan, a hundred years ago, had filled up his Day Book I on 14 November 1851, he cut a rectangular hole or well through the center pages; not all the pages, and not the covers. The result was a secret cache for his surplus cash. A modern historian recently tried the experiment of slipping a wildcat bank note of circa 1850 into the cutout area. The bill was an exact fit. Closed up and filed away, the scuffed old daybook looked innocently like what it was not — an old out-of-date record book.

Fitch Kelsey's ledger from Liberty, Illinois, became a family scrapbook after Fitch died. Temperance tracts were pasted over the old records of Dr. and Cr. — newspaper verse, too, showing a nice taste for sentimental poetry. Eliza, known to her father as Eliza Lane, but in her own secret dream world as Eliza Lanetta, started, but alas did not finish, an original composition which she entitled 'Evening Hymn of a Child.' It begins promisingly enough:

> *One evening i was wandering*
> *Beside a river fare . . . faire*
> *Wild roses and blue violets*
> *I'd pluck to deck my hair.*

Here the poetess falters. Of the second stanza we have only this fragment:

> *The birds were singing over me.*

A new feminine hand shows up at this point, with little jottings of tiny family expenses, and of the earnings of a seamstress: 'Cash for sewing in Alton, $1.20.' On a blue Sunday we get a little more of the family story in the handwriting of the seamstress:

> *How few the widow pity show*
> *When they perchance ere long may need.*
> *How few regard her bitterest woe*
> *Tho they have hearts that yet may bleed.*

Wit and humor found their way also into the old account-books-turned-scrapbook. Typical joke of 1855:

'Why did Joseph's brethren cast him into the pit?' asked a Sabbath School teacher.

'Because they doubtless thought it a *good opening* for a young man,' replied the pert scholar.

Somebody took Tobias Lord's 'Waist Book,' formerly used in his general store at Wells, Maine, and filled it with poetry clipped from the Boston *Transcript* and the *York County Herald*, as well as tedious moral essays by Samuel G. Goodrich, prolific old 'Peter Parley,' who graduated from a clerkship in a Danbury, Connecticut, general store to become fabulously successful as a literary hack and publisher, accumulating millions of readers and a comfortable fortune. An account book with a long and varied history and a charming end was that of Nathaniel Dike. Dike was a veteran of the Revolutionary War, who served in 'the Lexington alarm' from Killingly, Connecticut, and removed after the War to Allegheny County, New York, where he ran a country store. After his death a James Dike appears and disappears in the old book. There are lumbering records. One J. A. Major appears, and a slip still lies between the pages: 'Lent this book several years ago to a Party and — when it came back four pages had been removed — some *cussedness.*' Then another Major appears, a fisherman and loving artist of the native trout of New York waters.

To memorialize his triumphs, this Major had turned the big book around broadside so he could draw on its maximum width. For five successive pages he drew great trout just as they looked to him when he took them. They are described specifically: 'Trout caught April 24, 1877, by R. E. Major in the Canecadea Creek, over 1 lb.' He got a fine companion for the first, a one-pounder in the Limekiln that August. There was another from Whitney Creek in May 1893, another from Genesee in 1890. The best of all was a 1½-pound fish of 1891. Each is lovingly drawn in the artist's firm line, right after the lumbering records.

Stories and plots are suggested by the notes and scribbles, the successive ventures, which accumulated in old store books and were handed along for generations. They are fragments, never resolved, hanging in mid-air like unfinished music. Personalities enter and leave the scene. The imagination rises to the bait. What hand put the October leaves from a Connecticut maple away so carefully in a 136-year-old book? Did Mrs. Kelsey acquire another husband and protector to console her widowhood? Did a thief make off with Caleb Morgan's signature and put it to 'unlawful use'? Did Andy McGowan ever amount to anything?

We cannot tell. In regard to these matters, the accounts are still open.

A MAN OF MANY PARTS

MANY TRIBUTES have been paid to the contribution to American life made by the old country doctor, the lawyer, and the preacher, whose special places in the community may be understood from many appreciative and sympathetic accounts. The keeper of the general store, though he existed by the hundreds of thousands, has never received his due as a leader and as a civilizing influence. One might speculate about this. Being a merchant was not a learned occupation, and there were all kinds of merchants, some quite temporary. It was not hard to get into the business of running a store, as one Michigan wit used to remark; it was just hard to *stay* in.

Many men of low capacity or unstable temperament tried their hand at a store, as they did at farming, trapping, lumbering, or fighting. When a store failed to prosper, and creditors outnumbered debtors, the owner could take shelter under lenient bankruptcy laws, or skedaddle 'over the hill' as did Denton Offut, Lincoln's employer at New Salem, and many another.

Yet if we were to cut a profile of the really successful country merchant, we should find ourselves charactering a very flexible, a very versatile and durable man, with astonishing skills and accomplishments, and a considerable knowledge of the world. The whole complex of buying and selling presented many more difficulties than the merchandising of the twentieth century. His knowledge of his community was minute and intimate, his contact with it more continuous than that of the doctors, the lawyers, or the clergy. His store was the necessary core of crossroads life, the best hope that the spot might some day grow into a town.

The country merchant's opportunities to become a judge of men were exceptional. As salesman, middleman, issuer of credit, banker, supplier of necessities and some luxuries, as shipper of farm crops and local manufactures, the country trader had contacts with all his neighbors and with the larger commercial world. As a cash buyer he was in the market at all times, his policy, 'Cash given for anything he can make money by.' As a seller of store goods he was willing to take his pay in 'anything eatable, drinkable, wearable, or burnable, at fair prices.' In many instances the more prosperous merchants took on outside activities, not as a necessary supplement to their incomes, as did the petty storekeeper who cut hair or did cobbling as a side line, but as employment for capital or energies not needed in their store business. Some, when in funds, speculated in wheat or in western lands. Others underwrote a lumbering operation in the wintertime, made a turn in shingles, bought and shipped hemlock bark to the tanyards. William Battel, father and son, two generations of storekeepers in the town of Torrington, Connecticut, 'had also a manufactory of potash,' as did many others.

Stephen Thacher, as industrious a Maine man as ever came down the pike, not only kept at his dwelling 'a large stock of all goods usually found in a country store,' but also found time to be postmaster, judge of the probate court, raise Merino sheep, and keep an 'Academical school, with thirty scholars.' The local power-site, with its mill, frequently belonged to the owner of the general store. In a region of older, more mature communities, such as southern New England, with an easy access to distant markets and large centers of population, the country dealer took on some of the characteristics of the city merchant, shipping provisions himself in the coastwise trade, collecting goods of local manufacture, and trading them on his own account with New York, Virginia, the Carolinas, and even the West Indies. Following the opportunities of the changing times, the merchants along the seaboard often gave up retail trade for the newer industrial enterprises requiring larger aggregations of capital and the corporate structure — canals, railroads, banking, insurance, and manufacturing.

The store owner enjoyed a favored position because he had the opportunity of constantly enlarging his frame of reference. There was, perhaps, no other rural citizen, living within a radius of ten to twenty miles of the store, who touched life at as many different places as the retailer. Through the necessity of disposing of the country produce that he took in from his customers, the trader had connections with commission dealers in distant cities. He traveled regularly once or twice a year to one of the commercial capitals on the strenuous business of filling out his broken assortment of goods with new merchandise. He was in touch with stage lines, freight forwarders, knew steamboat or coasting captains, money brokers, and brushed up against men of large affairs among the importers and jobbing houses in the cities. He wrote and received letters when both were uncommon experiences.

Though not a man of professional education, the merchant somehow acquired as he went along a good knowledge of busi-

Waiting for the mail — a country store memory reaching far back to ancient days when the recipient of a letter paid the postage and could not peek until willing and able to put up the rhino for postage due.

ness law, especially the law of contracts, of mortgages and promissory notes, of partnerships and bankruptcy, of fraud, of agent and principal, and of those troublesome matters of consignment, common carrier, and insurance which are apt to arise when a boatload of flour sinks at the Falls of the Ohio. Farmers who 'forgot my specs' turned to the merchant on those momentous occasions when they had to write a business letter. He had the necessaries, a quire of writing paper, a well of ink, blotting sand, and his thoughts flowed as the farmers' could not from the tip of a goose quill. When death came to a customer of the old store and his will was read, the trader turned out like as not to be the executor. This was so true that a generation later the old safe was usually found to contain more old wills, letters of administration, and accountings of estates than anything else.

The merchant of the stagecoach era, wrote one of the few of the genus to try his hand at describing his own class, 'is a general *locum tenens*, the agent of everybody! And familiar with every transaction in his neighborhood. He is a counselor without license, and yet invariably consulted, not only in matters of business, but in domestic affairs. Parents ask his opinion before giving their consent to their daughters' marriages; and he is always invited to the weddings. He furnishes the nuptial garments for both bride and groom, and his taste is both consulted and adopted. Every item of news, not only local, but from a distance — as he is frequently the postmaster, and the only subscriber to the newspaper — has general dissemination from his establishment, as from a common center; and thither all resort, at least once a week, both for goods and for intelligence.'

During long winter days and evenings trade was slow. Many account books show as few as six or eight customers in a whole day. This was the country dealer's opportunity to improve his mind. He had the time and, since he did a small stationery business, he often had a few books around — Parson Weems' *Life of Washington*, *Pilgrim's Progress*, histories of Greece and Rome, some of the English poets. There was the Bible, too, and works devoted to its interpretation; tough octavo sermons, bound in calf, today's stickers on the shelves of antique shops and old bookstores, corners scuffed, the pages foxed, backstrap torn from much handling. They seem dull enough reading to us, but it was stimulating fare to our hardy ancestors, who enjoyed honing their minds on theological argument. Thus the country merchant acquired a local reputation as 'a great reader' and as a well-posted man.

If a man wished to give himself an extension course in some

vocational subject there were handbooks on the mercantile life, such as J. Montefiore's *The American Trader's Compendium*, books on agriculture, in case he had a farm, and ready-reckoners which would tell him how to find the capacity of bins and boxes, how to calculate interest for an odd number of days, and how many bushels of West India salt made a ton. There was an extensive literature on herb medicines, such as Wilkinson's *Family Medical Practise;* and the ambitious clerk poring over his law book is fixed in our minds as a symbol of the national faith that you cannot keep a good man down. The image is, of course, of the lanky frame of Abe Lincoln, extended along the rough counter of the Berry-Lincoln store in New Salem, the future President's nose deep in the *Illinois General Statutes* — which Berry owned, being the constable — or in Blackstone's *Commentaries*, which Lincoln found at the bottom of an 'empty' barrel, bought to accommodate a 'mover.'

The store often acted as a subscription depot for popular magazines, the newspapers of the nearest city or the little weekly sheet with 'patent insides' which was published in the nearest town. The store owner's contacts with the weekly *Argus* or *County Clarion* were close and frequent, as an occasional buyer of circulars and printing, as an advertiser announcing the arrival of seasonal goods, and sometimes as country correspondent sending in the news from his neck of the woods. 'Most of the mails have been carried on horseback, and it is quite uncertain about your getting the paper today,' an editor in Taunton, Massachusetts, wrote to a general store down the line, adding that money and news were scarce, but that there was 'snow in abundance.'

Equipped by his natural endowments, by experience with men, polished — somewhat — by reading and reflection, strategically situated with the local world revolving around him, the country storekeeper was pushed forward by all these circumstances as a leader in the affairs of the church, school, and town, the lodge or the militia. If there was a school teacher to be hired, the merchant was apt to shoulder the burden of the correspondence, satisfying himself about the prospective teacher's moral character, his ability to teach reading, writing, and arithmetic up to the rule of three. He had to be sure also that the new teacher could deal firmly with those twin problems of rural pedagogy, the big and the backward. He had to wade patiently through letters of application, such as this:

'The subscriber makes a tender of his services to the inhabitants of the second school district in Swansea as a teacher for the term of three months to commence on Monday the 3rd inst. And he assures those who may think proper to intrust their children to his care, that if the most strenuous exertions on his part can prevent it, their confidence shall not be misplaced. Hoping by assiduous application and unremitting attention to ensure the patronage and meet the approbation of his employers — Jos. D. Nichols.'

The storekeeper, who was often required to diagnose a consumption or prescribe a good medicine for all-around use by the whole family, was also expected to know how to extract beans from small boys' noses. If he was musically inclined, he might lead the Silver Cornet Band. The merchant was the natural custodian of the madstone, if the township was so fortunate as to possess one. What is a madstone? When a small, hard object lodged in a deer's stomach, it was sometimes surrounded by a calcium deposit to form a smooth, round 'stone,' the madstone, which made the deer twice as hard to kill, it was said, as the ordinary kind. The virtue of the stone was that when applied to the bite of a dog, it told whether or not the dog was mad. If the stone would not adhere, the dog did not have rabies. If the dog was infected, or in cases of snake bite, spider bite, or bee stings, the madstone was popularly believed to bring relief and drive out the poison.

At election time the candidates were thick as blackbirds around the store. Here, too, the tax collector set up for business, announcing, 'Taxes are now due and payable . . . bring last Year's receipts.' The electoral rolls were often deposited at the general store, along with the school trustee book. The back room was the polling place, where the voters gathered to select a supervisor, town clerk, justice of the peace, assessors and collectors, commissioners of highways, inspectors of election, overseers of the poor, hogreeves, and constables. The country merchant was often also the town clerk, or treasurer, his cubicle, safe, and store books suggesting his fitness, no doubt, for clerkly tasks. Often the merchant was deep in politics, holding various offices through the years, rising enough in the esteem of his constituency to go from some humble office such as hogreeve to sit for a term in the state legislature; and for years afterward there would be some people who would point him out and say, 'You wouldn't think that that man had been in the legislature, would you?'

In states having the grand jury system, the merchant, if his name was drawn, was almost certain to be appointed by the judge to act as foreman. He would swear with one hand upraised, the other upon the courtroom Bible, that he would diligently inquire and true presentment make, that he would keep his own counsel, that of his fellows, and of the people of his state, that he would present no person from envy, hatred, or malice; nor leave anyone unpresented through fear, favor, affection, or reward, or hope thereof, but that he would present all things truly as they came to his knowledge.

The rural trader was a hustler, often a lover of gossip and a sort of walking newspaper. Yet he sometimes sat silent at his books, lost in work or, like other men, in the vagaries of his imagination. A man with executive gifts, he managed his own affairs and those entrusted to him by others as well as any man could have done in his place. Looked upon as 'well-to-do,' his sympathies generally with the moneyed classes, he regularly disregarded his own interest in supplying the needs of those who could not pay. Often sharp in a trade, the merchant usually headed the list in supporting church, lodge, or any movement for a public improvement. He knew as well as the town physician or pastor the sins and secret griefs of his customers, their ills, aberrations, and follies. Like the doctor and pastor he discreetly kept his own counsel, and without the restraints of church discipline or the Hippocratic oath. He was spry as a cricket, tougher'n green elm, well-meaning on the whole — a man who in a less favored situation might hope to see hard service and die a sergeant. Plato, who in his ideal Republic assigned the role of shopkeeper to the weak and unfit, would have found the country traders a tough set if he had been able to visit the American republic.

In some of his incarnations, the country retailer could talk Choctaw and knew Mary Jemison, the 'White Woman.' Such a one was old 'Dote' Thompson, who started his general store in 1856 in the Genesee Valley at Moscow, now Liecester, in Livingston County, New York, and was still going strong in the 'eighties. Thompson was a dead shot with his long-barreled Kentucky rifle. Its gleaming barrel, polished stock, and ornate brass trimmings were always kept in scrupulous condition. A story of his prowess comes down through the years as seen through the eyes of his grandson when a small boy. About fifty yards from the store there was an elm tree, eighty or ninety feet high. One day the loafers at the front of the store noticed a squirrel sitting on the topmost branch of the elm, swaying with the breeze, just as grandfather Thompson came out of his house across the road and approached the store.

'Dote,' said one of the boys with a wink at the others, 'I suppose you've seen the day when you could pick that squirrel off'n that limb with that old rifle of yours?'

Thompson walked over and looked at the squirrel. 'Huh! I can do it now,' he said simply.

With the glance at the rest of the crowd, the interrogator replied: 'I'll bet you a pound of tobacco you can't.'

'All right,' said the merchant.

He walked back to his house, got his rifle, and returned. Without a word he carefully measured the distance with his eye, brought the gun to his shoulder, and crack! went the old gun. Down tumbled the squirrel. The grandson retrieved it, shot right through the head.

'Well, Hart, you'd better come in and buy that tobacco.'

That was all that was said. At the time, Thompson was past seventy-five years old.

Since Indians have been mentioned, perhaps the encounter of a storekeeper's wife with two red varmints looking for trouble may serve as a reminder that the wife of a country merchant had to adapt to her environment as resolutely as her husband. John Post kept a few articles for sale in his home at Utica, New York, around 1790. Two Indians came to the building on one occasion when they knew the trader was away. Mrs. Post was in the storeroom alone. Saucy Nick, the leader, demanded pipes, 'backer,' and rum. To enforce the point, he shut the door, drew his hunting knife, and drove it hard into the wooden counter-top. Mrs. Post faced the Indians across the counter, the knife still quivering between them from the violence of the blow. Pipes, 'backer,' rum — at once. The lady shouted for a hired man, while appearing to comply with the demand to draw rum from a cask. She stooped, apparently to fill a mug. Instead she came up from the floor with a heavy iron rod in her hands. As Post's man arrived on the run, Mrs. Post swung the bar at the knife, knocking it behind the counter, safely out of the reach of Saucy Nick. Calmly, she told the handy man to throw the rascals out!

The position of the rural merchant as community leader is reflected in his active part in the affairs of the militia. When the Wells and Arundel Artillery Company was organized in Kennebunk, Maine, on petition graciously granted by the governor and council of Massachusetts, Maine being at the time only a 'district' of the older state, it was composed of young men of Kennebunk and Arundel who could set off an 'artillery coat' to advantage. William W. Wise, son of Michael Wise and a partner in his store, was elected first lieutenant. Two small brass cannon, supplied by the government, helped to carry out the artillery motif. The patriotic ladies of Kennebunk presented the Company with a flag which became the subject of a spirited interchange between Miss Sarah Grant, for the ladies, who taught the maidens of Kennebunk, English and embroidery, and Barnabas Palmer, the captain, also a country merchant.

'Sir,' wrote Miss Grant, turning her attention from print and tambour work to military matters, 'In compliance with the request of the ladies of this town, I have executed and in their behalf, send you this standard. As a donation to you and the Company of artillery you have the honor to command, you will please to accept it. Let peace be your motto. But if the awful clangor of arms from a foreign and invading foe should summons you to unfurl it in the presence of the enemy, may it be sacred to liberty . . . Let that spirit which animated a Spartan band animate your breasts, and surrender it only with your lives. If . . . it should trium-

phantly wave . . . remember that it was given by females
who believe that humanity no less than valor, is an ornament
to the soldier.'

Storekeeper Palmer replied gallantly, asking Miss Grant
to 'present the grateful acknowledgment of the Company to
the respected ladies' and to 'assure them that we shall always
be ambitious to deserve their approbation.'

All able-bodied men between youth and middle age were by
statute members of the enrolled militia under the uniform
militia training law passed by Congress in 1792 and confirmed
and amplified by the various state legislatures as state law.
For as long as the recollection of the old French war and the
two British wars still lingered, one of the great occasions in
American rural life was the annual May gathering of the
farmer-soldiers for their evolutions and exercises, and company inspection. In September there was a general muster of
the whole regiment. Not every company was as well-turned-
out as the boys of the Wells and Arundel Artillery Company.
In most instances, however, the captain, at least, had what
passed for a uniform, and sometimes a French 'chapeau' with
a cockade or a red and white feather nearly a yard long, according to one old account. The soldiers came in what they
had, homespun in the border settlements, or a 'hammer-tail
coat and bell-crowned hat' at the New England trainings. As
the captain threw his colors to the breeze and the drums rolled,
the company formed its front, the tallest men at the ends, the
shortest in the middle. The company commander shouted his
orders, heavy on the last syllable:

'By file from line into column of sections on the right,
March.'

And so a day of patriotic fervor and delicious excitement
was well begun, not to end until late that night when the weary
patriots trudged home with a sheet of molasses gingerbread

and a headache. Spring muster day was a time for relaxing from the rigors of a hard winter, for a brief escape from solitude, a time for apples, nuts, buns—and rum all around. A man liked the feeling of resting his musket against the counter at the general store, reaching down into his jeans, fumbling in a pocket full of tackle for a few coins to lay out against some plunder — an ox muzzle, a piece of checked shirting, a razor, or 'bandanno' handkerchief.

The storekeeper was, like as not, an officer, a source of perplexity to European travelers who had never before seen a brevetted major draw a gallon of molasses from a barrel or weigh out two ounces of China tea. If not a major, the store owner was, then, a lieutenant, or at least a corporal, recalling the folk tale of the storekeeper's children who, on hearing that their father had been advanced to the grade of corporal, asked, 'Are we corporals, too?' To which the father replied: 'Only your mother and I are corporals.'

Since the general store was located at a spot most convenient for its trade, the 'training field' was usually right beside it, or at least no more than a whoop and a holler down the road. On muster day the parade ground was bordered by temporary booths set up for the sale of cakes, gingerbread, and hard cider. Before the ceremonies, the general store was full of men lying about on the counters or sitting around, their chairs reared back so the legs of the sitter could be thrown comfortably upon counter, box, or barrel — anything that brought them nearly on a level with his head. During the day there would be a turkey shoot, foot races, family picnics, wrestling, and an election of officers. After the election the successful candidates were expected to treat the company with cakes and a barrel of cider or rum. Ardent spirits were no less necessary at trainings than at such other important occasions as weddings, elections, funerals, births, and barn raisings.

One Maine man lost his election as captain of the militia at Morrill because his rival was able to produce one more gallon of rum than he did. Trade was brisk at the store as the citizenry assembled in 'tow frocks and shirt sleeves' with muskets, shotguns, rifles, butcher knives, sticks, pitchforks, a plow coulter, or sheet-iron sword belted on with a bull chain, the whole armament rather suggesting the pikes, scythes, and hayforks of the embattled peasants who followed Monmouth to disaster at Sedgemoor.

On one occasion, the militiamen who came improperly armed were dismissed. Resentful, they formed their own temporary company of irregulars, charged the main body, and chased them into the general store where the soldiers found sanctuary among the barrels and counters. At one muster, a John Boynton, wishing to salute his captain in an appropriate manner, charged his gun so heavily that it burst. Liquid patriotism continued to play a prominent part in the musters. At a general training at Otis, Massachusetts, one tavern alone (and there were three!) did a bar trade of $116, with whiskey at three cents and brandy at six cents a throw. Long before five o'clock in the afternoon, when they called it a day, the line of the company was usually badly sprung, and, as one annalist ruefully says, 'the Captain's feather got a dip of about forty-five degrees.'

Between the larger wars, the militia was called out occasionally in various local affairs, such as the Black Hawk War, or Iowa's comic opera 'Honey War,' a boundary dispute with Missouri over a strip of land, heavily timbered, and valuable chiefly because so many of its big trees were filled with wild honey. The 'Honey War' produced one deathless declaration of martial sentiment. When the troops asked about rations, they were told that they were expected to supply their own. A nameless Nathan Hale called from the ranks:

'We're willing to shed our blood for our beloved territory, and if necessary, to kill a few Missourians, but we're not going to do that and board ourselves too.'

Fortunately, hostilities were avoided by the appointment of a Congressional investigating committee, that sovereign remedy. Peace was celebrated with speeches and refreshments.

The years during which the training days flourished were also the years when leveling sentiments were supreme in the country districts, making the whole idea of the officer and the man repugnant to a staunch admirer of Old Hickory. Discipline was hard to enforce in such a democratic army of soldiers-for-a-day. We can sympathize with the militia officer, furiously brandishing his sword, bawling orders.

'Fellow sogers — dress! Dress.'

To which Barefoot replies from the ranks: 'We are dressed — most of us.'

And there was the predicament of the company captain, evidently of French descent, who in the excitement of parade, the piercing treble of the fife, the thumping of the big bass drum, and perhaps of his own heart, shouted in desperation, '*Garde d'honneur,* WHOA!'

In fact, the whole institution of trainings and musters could hardly have been sustained for as long as it was had it not been for the taste of the native American for military trappings and that love for titles which Mrs. Trollope noticed with such asperity in her observation of our domestic manners. Gradually the muster days fell into disrepute because of poor drilling, brawls, over-indulgence in New England rum, or hard cider, and the rising sentiment for temperance. As one observer of the musters said, with down-east understatement: 'The cause of temperance and morality was not materially advanced by them.' If muster day had its uses, they certainly were not of a military nature. It provided the fam-

ilies of the soldiery with more fun than a fair as they trundled
down from the clearings and hollows, to watch the wheelings
and facings, circulate among the booths, gossip with the
neighbors, and thrill to the field music.

In the midst of this amiable hubbub was the bustling storekeeper, his emporium crowded as at no other time with young
mothers, each with a baby on her arm and another at her feet;
the young fathers in homespun, muskets held in the crook of
the arm. Never was the stock so thoroughly fingered, never so
many requests for samples, and never the trader more alert to
petty pilfering as he weighed out a bar of lead or bent over
the row of jugs waiting to be filled at the molasses barrel. He
was treated with the deference due the man who brought the
necessities which made life possible, and the little extras which
made it bearable. When they looked at him they saw the man
who bought their wheat and pork, advanced them goods when
they had no money, hired their school teacher, drilled their
troops, marshaled their Independence Day parades, and could
if need be, fire an anvil, make the eagle scream, or propose a
toast in felicitous phrase to Stephen Decatur, 'brightest ornament of our infant navy,' or to the local militia: 'When in-
sulted, every citizen a soldier, and every soldier a citizen.'
Usually as much of a personality or 'character' as any other
in a day when 'characters' were more common than now, the
owner of the general store was the subject of endless quotation
and anecdote around country fireplaces and kitchen stoves.

Long current in the Middle West was the tale of the country storekeeper intent on a checker game in the back room.
When his attention was called to the fact that a lady customer
was waiting up front, he is said to have whispered: 'Sh-h-h-h,
keep still and she'll go away.'

The idea of a merchandiser who looked with distaste on
goods that were in brisk demand tickled the risibilities of gen-

Vendue.

WILL be offered at Public Sale, and positive- ly sold, on *SATURDAY* the 16th day of *November* inst. at the old building near David Mann's Store, in the borough of Bedford

A Variety of

StoreGoods,

and sundry other articles, among them are

Cloths, Casimer, Calico, Muslins, Shoes, Hats, Bonnets, Winter and Summer Roundabouts, Jackets, and Pantaloons, four STOVES, 2 Clocks, Patent Ploughs, *One Dearborn WAGON,* and *Harness,* one Water Wagon, an elegant riding HORSE, saddle and bridle.—*ALSO,*

Household & Kitchen

and a variety of other articles too tedious to mention.
☞ Sale to commence at **10** o'clock on said day, and continue until all is sold.—*Terms* made known on the day of sale. S. M. BARCLAY, *Assignee of*

T. R. GETTYS.

Bedford, Nov. 9, 1832.

Many a man took a try at storing, only to come down the pole faster than he had gone up. And so his assignee hung out the red flag and held a vendue in the interests of the store's creditors.

erations of customers and created a whole class of folk anec-dotes resting on what might be called the Fast Seller motif. Ezra Jones of Pemaquid, Maine, took a fall out of Uneeda Biscuit.

'Nope, I ain't got 'em,' he said, 'an' I ain't a-goin' to try to keep 'em any more. Jest as soon's I get in a new lot, why, every one comes along an' wants 'em. Fust thing you know, the whole blamed lot is gone, an' I'm as bad off as I was before.'

Frank Bailey, who ran the general store at Sanibel, Flor-

ida, also took a dislike to fast-moving items. When asked for
Noxzema, he explained: 'I don't bother with it — too hard
to keep in stock.'

A Vermonter of the same stripe, name of Stockwell, who
kept the store at Marlboro just west of Brattleboro, once
called out in alarm, 'Hey, don't take all those pencils. If you
do, I'll have to order some more.'

Country folks liked personalities, especially if they had a
little salt to them. The merchant was likely to be the chief figure or hero of local jests and stories which eventually mel-
lowed into the folksay of the region. Sometimes he was the
butt, especially in yarns where the stolen hams, combs, pelts,
or chickens were sold back to the rightful owner. The people
liked to repeat the jokes he got off, and recount marvelous
tales of the customers he skinned, and the ones who proved too
'cute' for him, the thieves he caught, and the debtors he
brought to book.

As must be the lot of all men, the proprietor of the crossroads store could not attend his own funeral, except in a
highly unsatisfactory way. He could not hear the eulogy, or
know the judgment that the community passed on his life.
The country trader might not appear an extraordinary figure in a bevy of congressmen or root doctors. Perhaps he was
no great figure as men were measured in the greater world of
state and nation. To those who traded at his store and knew
him in good times and bad, he was the real grit.

We get some sense of what a country merchant meant to his
township in the obituary columns of country newspapers. We
may read how Robert W. Carr died. That was 'Butch' Carr.
'Butch' conducted a general store and post office at Fayette,
Illinois. When 'Butch' died he was carried to the cemetery in
charge of his lodge brothers, the Modern Woodmen of America. It was February. The store thermometer stood at zero.

Long lines of farm wagons fell in with the procession, lighter spring wagons, buggies, and a few surreys, all filled with 'Butch's' neighbors and customers, wrapped in buffalo robes, their feet feeling gingerly for the soapstone which had been hot and toasty when they left home. Nobody said very much beyond the little phrases people use to conceal their thoughts.

But the procession which bounced and teetered over the frosty ruts was one of the longest ever seen in Greene County.

THE DRUMMERS OF PEARL STREET

A COUNTRY MERCHANT, seated in a New York omnibus, handed his fare up to the driver through a hole in the roof. The door flew open, and he stepped out into the Broadway of a hundred years ago. Glancing at the iron-fenced city Park with its pleasant fountain in the near corner, and at Barnum's Museum, its front covered with great gaudy paintings, noticing the signs of the wholesale houses across the way on Park Row, he turned and passed through the swing door of Coleman & Stetson's imposing Astor House at 221 Broadway, grateful to escape the slow crawl of New York traffic.

The medley of noise dropped off to an endurable murmur; yet component parts of the universal bedlam could be picked out. There was the rattle of hacks and great drays bumping over the new 'Russ' pavement, named after its inventor, Horace P. Russ, and laid along Broadway past the Astor House in 1848–9, the clop-clop of heavy horses, street cries of petty traders, shrill warnings from boys pushing handcarts and wheelbarrows. Newsboys raised piercing voices — 'Y'ere's the Tribune, Courier and Inquirer, Express'; or 'Evening Post, Sun, Mirror, Commercial Advertiser.' A scissors grinder

hammered his bell insistently. The oysterman blew on a rau-
cous fish horn. Public porters threaded in and out of traffic.
Hotel porters steered mountains of trunks, satchels, portman-
teaus, and boxes ahead of them with sharp cries of warning,
the names of their houses painted on each side of the little rig.
Charcoal men strolled the city streets, and wood splitters with
iron wedges that dangled and rang out as they walked, and
'Sam, Sam, the soft soap man,' announced in a loud voice to
the housemaids that he was coming for their kitchen grease.

Taking a firm grip on his carpetbag and satchel, the visitor
walked slowly up the steps which led to the lobby on the second floor. It was not easy to make his way through the piles of
luggage and swarms of people who clogged the way. His manner was diffident but his eye missed nothing. He saw the house
porters, leaning easily against the marble pillars, waiting for
orders. As he traveled toward the desk he caught a glimpse
down long corridors of the eating saloons, one for ladies and
families, the other for single male guests like himself, the
'long table' set for dinner at three o'clock in the afternoon.
Luxurious parlors gave off the vast hallways, awash with
velvet, lace, Turkey carpets, and gilded mirrors, satin
couches, rocking chairs, pianos, and ottomans. Where in
tunket could a man get rid of a chew of fine cut that had been
'used up considerable'? Nowhere in there, he noticed, was
there a suitable place to deposit a black quid except under the
sofa. Children rolled hoops and flew about the corridors, dart-
ing in and out among the boys who hawked newspapers, one
more trial to a travel-weary country merchant. It was a great
distance — in every sense of the word — from his back-
country store to these pile carpets and brilliantly lighted
girandoles.

The countryman passed a factotum at a wicket who tended
greatcoats and parcels. There was another niche where soiled

boots were cleaned and burnished. A clerk sat in a little sentry box beside the magnetic telegraph, which now connected New York with Boston, Buffalo, Washington, and intermediate cities. He sensed the existence of other recesses: a closet with basins of water, and furnished with towels; a desk for writing, with pens, ink, and paper. The merchant put his satchel and flowered carpetbag down on the marble floor. While he waited for the room clerk's attention, he observed among the novel conveniences, a wirepull by which a guest could signal for a waiter from the seclusion of his own room.

The arrival of a country merchant at the Astor House, say in the year 1852, or at any of the other New York hotels of the first chop, did not go unnoticed — at the Irving, the Prescott House, St. Nicholas, or the United States Hotel. Lounging in the lobbies at almost any hour were men who took a keen interest in arrivals, their eye trimmed for the western merchant who held a good bill of eastern exchange, or carried in his pocket a letter from the squire back home, endorsing him as a good risk. One of the great hazards among Pearl Street jobbers who were 'in the country trade,' was the lack of reliable credit information regarding the character, ability, and financial circumstances of the southern and western country traders who came to the city in an open-to-buy position. The West was filling up. Businesses of all kinds multiplied. As the frontier fell back, the lines of communication grew constantly longer and more attenuated, the need for credit information more urgent, the information harder to get.

In 1841 Lewis Tappan created a new kind of business in New York to meet the needs of an expanding economy — the commercial agency for impartial credit reporting. Tappan's new enterprise, styled *The Mercantile Agency*, met a pressing need successfully and was not alone for long in its field. Among the competitors was *Bradstreet's Improved Commer-*

cial Agency. Both have had a continuous existence down to
the present through a succession of proprietorships, coming
together finally in today's corporation of Dun & Bradstreet,
Inc.

Tappan described the purpose of his agency as 'procuring,
by resident and special agents, information respecting the
standing, responsibility, etc., of country merchants residing
in the States of New York, Ohio, Michigan, Illinois and the
New England States, New Jersey, parts of Missouri and
Pennsylvania and the territories of Iowa and Wisconsin, for
the benefit of such merchants in this city as approve the object
and become subscribers to The Agency . . . The information obtained is from attorneys, cashiers of banks, old merchants and other competent persons. It is not a system of
espionage, but the same as merchants usually employ — only
on an extended plan — to ascertain whether persons apply-
ing for credit are worthy of the same and to what extent.'

There were certain signs by which the New York commercial gentlemen sauntering through the lobbies of the hotels
could recognize a visitor who intended touring the wholesale
district. He would have a memorandum book of his needs
which he consulted frequently, making erasures, alterations,
and additions, and probably right in public; for a man who
had traveled hundreds of miles and had already spent upward
of a hundred dollars must be ready on the instant to give his
memory every possible assistance. He had to recall the state
of his inventory exactly. As he judged the market and demand, so would he prosper in the year to come.

Those who had made a study of the country merchant as a
type or 'character' would expect him to have his hair cut in
the old Brutus fashion, ragged and shaggy and brushed down
over his forehead. His pantaloons were about a decade behind
the mode in their cut, being made in the old comfortable fash-

ion of large seats and plaited fronts tapering entirely too much toward the bottom, with straps underneath his boots which should not be there at all. The cowhide boots were coarse and clumsy, the right one exactly like the left, and there was a huge blanket coat topped by a long beard and a fur cap. The neckcloth was too full and looked untidy. Although his clothes were all old in cut, perhaps the most remarkable fact about them was that they looked quite new, as though worn only on special occasions, as briefly as possible, and then laid aside quickly after each churchgoing or ceremonial. There was a pleasant suggestion about such a man that if he treated his clothing with such care he could probably pay his bills.

So there was a rush to the hotel register to inspect the name and residence of the stranger and verify his occupation from the clerk. The merchant, refreshed, could no sooner step into the lobby with the thought of a stroll down Broadway toward the Battery and Castle Garden, than he would be greeted by men with whom he was not acquainted, offering an oyster supper, theater tickets, a visit to Barnum's American Museum, just across the way, and as a starter, would he care to step into the Astor Bar for a dollop of brandy or a mug of flip?

If he accepted the last suggestion he would enter a large, finely decorated room, lighted from the roof, since it was the floor of a central court around which the hotel rose for several more stories. A fountain played in the middle. Newspapers from other cities were ranged on two long tables. A dozen readers lounged in chairs before two blazing fireplaces, smoking cigars which they obtained from a young man in a small enclosure. Others stood with tall glasses of brandy-and-water at the bar which stretched down one side of the room.

Thus the trader from western Pennsylvania or the valley of the Ohio, the ancestral butter-and-egg man, came up against a New York sharper, the drummer of Pearl Street. Narrow, crooked Pearl Street was the wholesale business center for importers and jobbing stores in all lines a hundred years ago, standing as Worth Street does today to the textile trades. For fifty years, approximately from 1800 to 1850, Pearl Street was the most important, as well as the most irregular, business street in the city, lined with warehouses, pennants fluttering over the retail shops, and the red flag hung out in front of auction rooms where the jobber and his retail customer might both find themselves bidding for a piece of Calcutta cotton goods or a lot of Birmingham hardware. 'Pearl Street contains all the large warehouses,' said Baron Axel Leonhard Klinckowstrom of Sweden after his visit of 1818. 'Here everything is sold wholesale. The shops are well supplied with goods and this street is considered the richest, though its appearance is less brilliant than Broadway.'

Ten years later, Charles P. Forbes, compiler of *The Merchants' Memorandum and Price Book*, lists the wholesale dealers who sold merchandise of interest to a country merchant, the hardware firms, dry goods, crockery, and West India goods, which included groceries. All were located in Pearl Street or near by. 'It is very narrow, and the houses are very high,' wrote Lady Emmeline Stuart Wortley in her account of her American travels in 1849–50. 'Waves and billows of merchandise of every description and denomination seem pouring over from the brimming stores and warehouses, into the inconveniently narrow street.'

Here the jobbers bought by the bale or the package from importers or manufacturers, broke the big bales and boxes to make up small lots, and sold by the piece to country traders. For this middleman function the reputable warehouses charged an advance of six to eight per cent on a fair valuation. Some followed the principle of 'One price, and no deviation,' like Nelson & Co., which dealt in men's clothing at 51 Cedar Street, permitting the customers to examine the goods at their leisure and providing them with a catalogue which gave printed figures for every item — the sack coats of Kentucky jean; blue blanket coats, sack and half sack; cottonade pants of French, English, or American make; the figured vests of Farmers' satin; the white cotton shirts with muslin or linen bosoms. Other houses followed the policy of letting the buyer look out for himself. There every price was negotiated.

Not every jobbing house drummed trade with a staff of high-pressure salesmen, but most of them did. A treatise on merchandising noted in 1856 that drumming was 'now almost universal.' The system continued to expand up to the time when commercial travelers took to the 'road' and the country merchant stayed at home. The corps of Pearl Street drummers was made up of young men, shrewd, genial, droll storytellers, adroit at flattery and quick at accommodation to the prospective buyer's mood. A man far from his own stamping ground, and a little bit lonesome, could not help liking them, with their free cigars, wine, and tickets. Each one wove all this hospitality in smoothly with the address of his own place of business. There he had prints of a splendid style on view, a very desirable article that sold like hot cakes in the country trade, priced at only two-and-six, undoubtedly the cheapest goods in Pearl Street.

When country merchants met on the cars, in stages, on the boiler deck of a river steamboat, to talk of trade and jobbing, some said there were more sharpers in New York than in Philadelphia, and that the New York market was more unstable. They cited the auction watch swindle, in which the rustic paid a bargain price for a good watch, which was then switched for a worthless one during the wrapping up of the parcel. They warned of tricks in the wholesale trade. The jobber left out part of the order, some important country staple such as blue cloth. When questioned he promptly credited the item, with profuse thanks for having the matter called to his attention. Correcting the 'mistake' built character and so made the country customer less suspicious of overcharges elsewhere, usually made on goods the actual value of which was hard to determine. The custom of drumming came in for heated discussion, with some defenders who pointed out that the drummers did show their lines, introduced new ideas, that the retailer did not have to buy unless he wanted to — and that anyway the custom was universal.

The country dealer, resting in his room at his hotel, was not without warning of importunities yet to come, for the business cards of the drummers were already streaming up to his room, with lithographed circulars, catalogues, and printed price lists. When he returned to the second-floor lobby he was ambushed. The drummer presented in his person a piquant contrast to the general store owner. He had about him the air of the town. In fact, in many instances, he lived at the hotel, his employers paying the difference between the cost of living at a good boarding house and the two dollars a day it cost to board and lodge American plan at the Astor. The drummer was also sometimes known as a borer, 'probably from some resemblance in qualities to a worm that infests fruit trees,' according to a Philadelphia newspaper. The drummer dressed in the height of style. His trousers had the full-cut leg, in checks or plaid, and were trimmed with braid down the side seams. He was shod not in boots but in the new lace-up shoes, his neck dressing smooth, not dowdy, topped with a green flat scarf; his hat of beaver. He wore a moustache and side whiskers and made a dashing figure with his walking stick, and shawl of a rich wool plaid gracefully draped over his shoulder;

an art in itself and one not to be mastered without hours of
practice.

The borer was expert in his knowledge not only of cotton-
ades and calicoes but he was also required by the exigencies
of his occupation to be something of an epicure in tasting the
town. He knew the city, from the Battery to the new Washington Square Park with its young trees and the look of the
country about it. He could guide a wondering visitor to
Fowler and Wells' Phrenological Cabinet containing busts
and casts 'from the heads of the most distinguished men that
ever lived . . . Mummies, Pirates, Robbers, Murderers, and
Thieves, living and dead' — where a country tourist could
also get his own head examined. The New Yorker who
drummed successfully in Pearl Street was also, if required, a
discreet guide to the temptations the city afforded. If a countryman desired to be separated elegantly from his cash at a
gambling dive, the drummer knew all the places where a man
could throw a card. He knew where the cozy saloons and 're-
treats' were, under the stoops of old brick or brownstone
dwellings, a proper setting for serious drinking. A part of the
borer's value to his employers was his acquaintance among
'waiter girls' and such of the city's ladies of light virtue as
had not yet been rounded up by the police or the Magdalen
Female Benevolent Asylum.

'The country merchant is booked on his arrival, is capti-
vated by courtesy, is attracted by appeals to each of his ap-
petites and passions,' wrote the author of a mercantile guide
of 1850, 'is coaxed, decoyed, and finally ensnared or cap-
tured.' Yet so skillful and ingratiating were the drummers in
their art that they could and would guide the trader as readily to a church as to an assignation, and praise him loudly,
too, for his preference, provided only that he be responsive
when told of the A-1 articles the drummer sold for cheap

prices. 'I keep at number so-and-so Pearl Street,' he would say, slipping his arm through that of the man in country dress.

The drummer was always most familiar and affable. He inquired with keen interest about 'the times' in the dealer's part of the country, probing carefully about the amount of hard cash he had with him, supposing that he did a dashing business in his store, fishing for the quality of his business references. Earnestly the nimble borer warned his new-found friend against rascality, and shook his head more than once over the business ethics of his competitors. 'I grieve to say it, in Pearl Street a great many persons, who while they sell goods and merchandise by wholesale, also cheat and deceive by wholesale.' An attentive young drummer in the jobbing line would warn most particularly against the iniquitous system of selling goods at auction.

It was a great temptation to any honest Johnny Raw, in the city from some little crossroads Paw-Paw or Stovepipe Corners, to sidle into Water Street as he heard the dulcet voice of the crier say, 'Once, twice, going — gone,' or cocked an ear to the neat tap of the auctioneer's hammer. Here were kerseys and flannels, Liverpool hardware, East India cottons, a chest of tea, a case of shrub, all presumed to be going for a song, at 15, 20, or even 50 per cent under what the regular jobber would charge him. The auction system had a solid reputation with the interior merchants of Indiana, Missouri, Tennessee — all the western and southern regions — for bargain prices, especially in regard to imported goods. The auctions did, in fact, turn over merchandise faster, at lower overhead cost. They gave the established wholesalers and the little United States mills a stiff run of competition, starting with the boom days after the second war with Britain. It was the fond hope of certain British politicians — Lord Brougham,

Robert, the second Earl Grosvenor, Lord Folkstone, and Sir
Robert Peel, heir to a great calico-printing works in Lanca-
sire — that they might make the United States such a vast
dumping ground for British goods that they could smother
American industry while it was still in its trundle bed, choking
off its breath with millions of yards of English alpacas and
balmorals. During the 1840's, a new set of conditions amelio-
rated the struggle, as changed conditions — steam naviga-
tion, establishment of the bonded warehouse, the stunning
success of American manufacturing — favored the native
middleman as against the 'foreign' agents.

The fight was a hot one while it lasted. As an early uprising
of the middleman issue, it recalls the acerbity of later contro-
versies over mail-order selling, and the independent retailer's
tussle, still going on, with the modern drug, grocery, and auto-
supply chain stores. American importers tagged the auction
system as 'foreign' because it represented foreign goods, for
the most part, and foreign interests. They organized mass
meetings, and fought the auction rooms with pen, pamphlet,
and the use of the boycott.

'Auction business is growing very unpopular in this town,'
wrote Jacob Peabody, veteran auctioneer of Salem, Massachusetts, to a British correspondent. 'The grocers have
formed a powerful combination, not to buy at auction for one
year.' The auction question even got into politics. Heavy
pressure was exerted by the 'respectable' American importers
and wholesalers on city and state governments, and on Congress.

The part taken by the country merchant under these circumstances comes out clearly in an auctioneer's letter to an
English friend which said that the hundred crates of 'ware'
had arrived safely by the *Lucilla*, but they had found the market so poor that 'we must endeavor to retail the residue by

single crates to country dealers as we find them come into the market. The Dealers in this city of your acquaintance are not pleased with your making consignments to us and will not do anything that will assist in making advantageous sales on your acct.'

A country trader must often have heard it said against the auctioneers that they were a menace because they had a monopoly. There were forty-five licensed auctioneers in New York in 1816, including vendue master Philip Hone, who made a fortune quickly and sensibly retired from the hammer to become Mayor of New York, and to keep a salon and a diary, too. It was said that the auctions simply drew a special class of inferior goods to the United States, expressly manufactured for the auction market; that the United States was becoming the dumping ground for all of Europe's seconds, damaged or 'tender' goods, contraband and distress merchandise. Less was said on the other side. Lower prices had their own kind of eloquence. The psychology of the city jobbers, interested in maintaining the *status quo*, was bad; for the protests of these indignant, righteous men, that goods were going for less than production cost, or that they might have been smuggled down from Canada or up from Bermuda, only added zest to the retailers' speculative spirit, as some two hundred men gathered to peer in the twilight of the auction rooms at the packages and pieces. What if it was true that each lot represented a loss to the seller, and to the United States Customs House? So much the bigger bargain for the successful bidder!

The greatest danger in buying at auction was Peter Funk, colloquial name for the fictitious bidder. Funk meant deception and humbug. A countryman, say from Connecticut, would step into an auction room off Broadway to see a piece of good linen which appeared to be going . . . going . . .

at six cents a yard; and there were fifty-five and a half yards of it.

'An awful sacrifice, Major,' says the master of the hunt, casting an encouraging glance in the direction of the new-comer.

'Seven,' shouts the excited visitor, and surges forward to claim his prize.

'Eight,' snaps Peter Funk, the professional underbidder.

'Nine,' says Connecticut, boldly, and *whack* goes the mallet.

'Sold! Fifty-five and one-half yards of Irish linen at fifty-nine cents,' touching lightly on the *fifty*. A clerk beckons, goes back behind a screen to a desk, and makes out a bill for $32.74.

Connecticut is outraged; a mock auction in so respectable a place as Broadway! He finds a policeman near the Tombs and the auctioneer is unceremoniously seized. As the culprit passes Chambers Street and sees that he is really headed for jail, he gives up his protests and hands the money back. The greenhorn trader has had a sufficient lesson in one kind of auction — sufficient, that is, unless he continues to turn a deaf ear to the admonitions of his drummer friends. In that case he is eligible to be gulled sooner or later on an auction watch.

If a country dealer was adept at evading the plots of the drummers to get him under some kind of an obligation, not wishing to be be-drammed, be-dinnered, and be-suppered, he might gaze upon various metropolitan wonders at little or no cost. Supposing that the time was early March 1852, he could step out on the street knowing that a full moon was due; but if it clouded over he could watch the lamplighters on their rounds of lighting New York's 8000 oil lamps and 6000 gas-lights. On Thirty-third Street there was a sight, the city's first iron bell and watchtower, where a policeman twirled in his chair, a hundred feet up in the air, keeping an eye out for

The allure of auction goods at distress prices drew many traders from the Corners onto the premises of 'Peter Funk,' colloquial name of the crooked auctioneer. Above, the 'auction watch' swindle is worked against customers, whose innocent rusticity is indicated by their having the heads of common farm animals.

chimney fires. The out-of-town visitor could ride uptown, by hackney coach for twenty-five cents a mile, to Reservoir Park to look at the Distributing Reservoir for the Croton water system at Fortieth Street or he could hire a carriage for two dollars, 'within the lamp and watch district.'

A trip to New York would hardly be complete without a visit to Matthew Brady's National Gallery of Daguerreotypes on the top floor, three flights up, at 205–207 Broadway, on the southwest corner of Fulton Street, and just a block south of

the Astor. There Presidents, senators, lawyers, judges, bish-
ops, great ladies, military heroes from generals down to ma-
jors, could be inspected ; and of course a ravishing picture of
Jenny Lind, to top off the heavy fare of Jacksons, Polks,
Clays, and Websters. The visitor could also pose for his own
likeness, though he would not be able to sit in front of the
ground glass of the master himself, since Brady was in London at the time, exhibiting and winning prizes for his pictures
at the Crystal Palace.

A country merchant from the back settlements did not en-
dure the long trip to eastern seaboard markets for goods alone,
but for the excitement, too, of seeing the world, and the nourishment of the imagination to be found in viewing Miss Fanny
Wallack's Rosalind at the Bowery Theatre or in showing up
at Metropolitan Hall at '7½ o'clock' to hear Professor Williams' astonishing lecture on mental alchemy. The physical
trials of a long journey were formidable, often involving a
start on horseback, then a river steamboat for another leg on
the way, with a finish in the steamcars or in unheated stages,
jouncing over frozen, rutted roads. For days on end the traveler got little or no sleep, risked catching pneumonia in the
wet and cold. It is not surprising that a merchant, before undertaking such a journey, consulted the almanac, made his
will, and recorded a preference about whether his casket
should be displayed open or closed.

Hotels were crowded at even the stiff price of two dollars a
day. The expense of travel was so considerable that even allowing for favorable prices in the eastern markets, a man
would have to maintain a brisk run of trade to offset the costs
incurred and the time lost while he was away from his stand.
Once launched on the way, it was agreeable to savor in advance the welcome he knew he would receive upon his return
home. A local citizen who had walked familiarly in the streets

of Boston, or Baltimore, or New York, who had sniffed salt
water, whose boxes of goods bore the marks of the country's
most respected wholesalers, could stand on an even footing
with any judge, colonel, or politico in his home county.

In a day when the greatest shortage of all was the lack
of news, the returned merchant would be endlessly cross-
examined on his experiences; and he would be expected to
deliver a lively account of the ways of travel, of how Philadelphia looked, of the crowds, the gaiety, the scandals, the
snow and rubbish in the streets, the very atmosphere of New
York. The men back home would want to know that it had
been a cold, late spring; that collections were slow, buyers
cautious; that the jobbers were heavily supplied and able to
move only small lots. Personal contact and experiences endowed the goods of the merchant who bought in the East with
intangible values that could not be matched by retailers who
were served by the jobbing trades of interior cities such as
Cincinnati, Louisville, or St. Louis.

The neighbors and customers would want to know, as a very
practical matter, the trend of trade for the products they had
to sell, and for store goods. Were goods going to be high or
low? The answer settled the home market for the season. The
storekeeper was expected, as a result of his six weeks of mingling with the great world outside, to bring back new ideas
which would benefit the whole township — about the new
patent cooking stoves; about new varieties of apples, pears,
and cherries. Was there a promising kind of flint or dent corn
well calculated for the manufacture of whiskey? What was
the trader's opinion of the latest fanning machines and cultivators? What about the new 'power' — meaning a treadmill
or capstan-like arrangement, operated by horses to convey
a flow of power through tumbling rods to a grain separator.

One authority on nineteenth-century commerce, Edwin T.

Freedley, advised the country keeper of a general store to sell reapers, mowers, separators, corn shellers, seeds, and fertilizers, letting them go at cost, if necessary ; because if he helped the farmers of his town to produce three to seven hundred dollars above what was needed for their taxes and subsistence, instead of one to two hundred dollars, the country dealer would be well on his way to wealth. And, said Freedley, he 'should never visit the city to replenish his stock, without endeavoring to bring back something that will afford suggestions to his neighbors and customers.'

Not all country retailers had to undertake the privations and expense of a six-weeks' journey. A New Englander could make his spring visit to Boston and return in about a week, usually in May. In 1853, Mark Cone started out from his Vermont store for Boston on May Day. How fortunate would it have been if a Hawthorne had been a witness to the departure and recorded the scene in an American notebook. We have only one clue from which to reconstruct the moment. 'Hubard Smith fell out of the wagon,' Mark's diary says. 'He was looking at some pretty girls.'

A man felt anxious until every box, bale, and package was under his own roof. Goods did not always come through safely. Israel Brayton, who kept a general store at Swansea, Massachusetts, was abused by a scoundrel on one of his freighting trips. He told about his misfortune in an advertisement in a Boston newspaper:

'Taken from behind the Baggage Waggon, between Boston and Milton Hills, on Monday afternoon, by cutting the rope with which it was fastened, a basket containing knives, forks, a few snuffers and trays, pocket knives, slates, Naples soap, brass lamps and candlesticks — reward ten dollars.'

The buying trip of a hundred years ago would perhaps be unique in this respect: there might be no necessity of taking it again. With the rapid extension of the railroad network across the country, the stay-at-home drummer was about to be superseded by the traveling salesman, and it was the merchant's turn to stay at home. The Scovil Manufacturing Company, of Waterbury, Connecticut, made a pioneering experiment in sending out a button salesman, Merit Welton, through the Middle West in 1832. Not a peddler, Welton had the distinguishing characteristics of a modern commercial traveler; he did promotion work, carried no stock, sold from sample cards, took orders according to sample, accepted no barter goods, and the Company made delivery later by freight. The results of this novel effort, as it happened, were disappointing. Nevertheless, Welton hung pictures of the Scovil factory in the public rooms of countless hotels, gave a set of firemen's buttons to the head of the Cincinnati Fire Department, collected useful information about credit ratings of customers, and learned more than had been known before about the kinds of buttons the public wanted.

Sometimes the chance to go drumming came to a likely country store clerk, who showed a knack for trade. Levi McCollum, who worked behind the counter of a general store in the village of Battle Creek, Michigan, a hundred years ago, found himself in the enviable spot of one who could pick and choose. He had a fine job that paid him $550 a year. Another merchant, at Jackson, was offering him $50 more per annum to come to him. A Mr. Kendall of Kalamazoo also made the offer of an eligible situation, and, to climax it all, Levi wrote to his father, 'I have been offered one thousand dollars for year to go to New York as an agent to travil through the west for a Dry goods House, but I think six Hundred here is as good as one thousand there.'

The practice of sending out commercial tourists had been well established by the eve of the Civil War by manufacturers in search of their markets and by the jobbing houses of all the wholesaling cities, with the addition of a husky newcomer, Chicago. The Chicago drummer became quickly the personification and byword for hustle and perseverance. He bobbed up beyond the reach of steamboats, beyond the railheads, his trunks loaded on lumber wagons. He found his way to the store, any store. One irrepressible Chicago wholesaler, John V. Farwell, even hired bill posters to precede his drummers as they worked their way through Chicagoland, and posters lettered in red were slapped up on the walls of stores and barns, announcing 'Our Travellers Will Soon Be Here!'

At the same time, business practices were changing. Freight rates were falling. The postal service was improving. Stocks of goods could be filled in at anytime, and so less capital was tied up in inventory. Turnover speeded up. Credit terms began to shorten. The discount for cash became general, with the result that the country dealer had to look more critically at the customer he was in the habit of carrying from one year's end to the next.

With the drummer appearing punctually at regular intervals, the storekeeper purchased smaller lots but stocked a wider variety. The country merchant put in perishable goods for the first time, and even gave a little bow to fashion. 'Shelf goods' in consumer packages were still few, confined to medicines, hard soap, tobacco, and the new novelty of canned foods. The cracker barrel was supreme as a fact and as a symbol of an age in which the clerk weighed, measured, and hand-wrapped every purchase. Yet change was in the air. Home manufacture was fast disappearing. The old wool wheel and the flax wheel had been sent to the attic. United States manufactures were gaining in volume and in repute against European imports. Connecticut, Massachusetts, and Rhode Island poured out a torrent of thread, cloth, nails, buttons, jewelry, clocks, and brass goods. A farmer could get hold of more tools and light hardware than he had ever seen before.

With the arrival of the 2 x 4 scantling, tied together by cheap factory-made nails, homes and stores did not have to be framed any longer with heavy timbers. Americans were adapting tools such as axes, spades, and hay forks from the traditional British forms to characteristically American designs, and making them in unprecedented quantities by the use of interchangeable parts, the subdivision of labor, the application of power, and the mechanical handling of materials in process. Each year saw more guns, reapers, threshers, mowers produced by what came to be called 'the American system of manufacture.'

New inventions were a matter of such general interest that the daily newspapers often devoted half a column — an important amount of space in the 1850's — to listing and describing the patents issued by the U.S. Patent Office for the current week: patents for an improved reverberatory furnace, a carbonic acid gas engine, a new safety valve, a water meter, new chucks for lathes, a new way to feed logs into a sawmill, better methods for panning ores, new seats and running gear for railroad cars. Slowly, but with gathering speed, the 'American system,' with its emissaries, the 'knights of the grip,' worked its changes on country life and the institution of the country store. Old Jed Barber, his gray hair, long-skirted coat, high beaver hat, and ivory-headed cane all tokens of the age that was passing, wrote indignantly to a friend, without pausing for punctuation: 'Travelling by cars the telegraph oil gold silver and iron are exciting people.'

The merchant on a buying trip had a serious piece of business before him, the laying out of about $5000 in wanted merchandise, mostly staples, but also including specialties suited to his particular community, such as military goods or

Masonic regalia. He had to investigate new categories of merchandise as they came on the market, such as the new vulcanized fabrics, sold by specialized jobbers, the 'India Rubber' warehouses. In New York, Molyneux Bell, at 58 Canal Street, was the sensation of the dry goods business, because he had the novel idea of manufacturing ladies' cloaks, talmas, and mantillas before a buyer had appeared. The rise of the ready-to-wear industry meant that the country storekeeper could stock ladies' garments made from the same stylish and *recherché* patterns as those worn by women of high position in the centers of fashion.

The visitor also needed a sharp eye for novelties that might 'go'; dollar clocks, for example. There was a rage for gold pens and the new self-sealing envelopes. A retailer from the back country who had been thinking of sprucing up his store might drop around at Fraser's Manufactory, corner of West Broadway and Reade Street, to see the latest style of showcase. If he needed a safe, the old reliable was Herring's Patented Salamander Safe. Fire in the country usually meant total destruction. Yet when A. M. Cable's general store at Deposit, New York, burned down, and all the heavy timbers and double floors fell in on his Herring safe, heating it up like a retort, Cable found his books and papers safe and still legible. Just such a Silas C. Herring Salamander safe, with heavy double doors, medallions, and date, 1843, may still be seen in daily use, after 109 years, in the little office back of Clarence F. Stotts's store at Colebrook, Connecticut.

Stationers printed and bound-up memorandum books for country dealers listing the articles that a general store handled, with room at the left margin for the owner to put down the quantity he wanted before he visited the markets, a wise protection against the blandishments of the Pearl Street drummer with his smooth tongue and tempting loss leaders.

At the right side of the page there was space for jotting down the prices paid. Being made of all-rag paper which would stand repeated erasures, the book could be kept and used for years.

One such memorandum book, bound in scuffed old leather and marbled boards, has the title *The Merchant's Memorandum and Price Book*. The preface brings to our eyes the country retailer at work in the wholesale trade, still feeling the fatigues of his long journey and the novelty of being in a great city. The hurry and confusion, the noise, all were upsetting — so much coming at a man all at once. In such a situation the book was his friend, 'A General Remembrancer for Mercantile Gentlemen . . . embracing the leading articles of merchandize in common use for the country trade.' The merchant could choose from among nine kinds of coffee. Thirteen teas were listed by type. Spermaceti oil, candles, and flasks of olive oil were listed, as well as five brandies and fifteen wines; rum from Jamaica, Santa Cruz (St. Croix), the Leeward Islands; also New Orleans and Yankee rum. Sugars included the refined loaf and lump, Havana white and brown, and Muscovado, the latter raw, coarse, and lumpy, requiring a portable mill and a boy to break up the lumps before it could be sold.

Braids, ribbons, and gimps are a reminder that much of the clothing of country families was always cut and sewed at home. All the tools that a shoemaker or cobbler used were in the book, showing clearly, as the mail-order catalogues did fifty years later, just what goods people actually bought and used. Shoemaking, or at least shoe mending, evidently went on in every household as a matter of course. Drugs and medicines were listed in English and Latin, classified in the pharmacology of the time as balsams, berries, barks, extracts, flowers, gums, oils, roots, seeds, salts, and elixirs.

For his own needs the merchant would find money scales and till locks, iron or brass and plain or fancy; also account books, books for cyphering, bills of exchange and bills of lading; blanks for leases, powers of attorney, and deeds. An interesting section, and a significantly long one, listed military goods, serving especially the ceremonial side of the military arts, a reminder again of the social importance of muster day. Plumes, lace, gilt, and spurs appear; eagles and tassels, swords and epaulets, as well as pistols, horse or pocket; and powder flasks, flints, shot pouches, and gun worms.

When a country merchant had thoroughly canvassed the buying opportunities of Pearl Street, stepped around his last sidewalk blockade of goods boxes, bumped into his last self-important clerk, peered into the dark interior of his last jobbing store, shaken off the last drummer, written the initials of the supplier beside his last purchase, it was said in the commercial lingo of the day that his memorandum book was 'ticked off.' Then he had no more to do except book his passage home and visit with other country retailers of his acquaintance, comparing invoices and discussing the prospects for trade. Perhaps an advertising display for the local *Palladium*, with lots of black type to announce its importance, began to take shape in his mind, something along this line: 'The Subscriber respectfully informs friends, customers, and the public generally, that he has just returned from the City of New-York, where he has personally selected an entirely *New Stock of Fall and Winter Goods*, suitable in every respect for this part of the country. Fall suits from 7 to 12 dollars.'

The merchant looked forward eagerly, we may suppose, to his welcome home — home, where a man could sit at his ease on his own nail keg and clean his fingernails with his Barlow knife, scratch his stomach without embarrassment as an honest American freeman should be able to do, and chew his fine-cut without concern for ankle-deep Turkey carpets or silken ottomans.

After the traveling salesman appeared, the owner of the general store was glad enough to stay at home and keep in touch with markets, prices, patterns, and new introductions through his genial friend, the drummer on The Road. The commercial tourist was a popular figure, with the trade, and with small boys and stove-side sitters. He brought with him the very taste, the acrid, exciting smell of the city, and seemed a shining figure, a modern, commercial incarnation of the knight-errant, scouring down the pike in a buggy, his lance a Westfield whip, his helmet a derby hat, his buckler a tin sample case.

But at first his life was not a happy one.

PART TWO

1 8 6 1 – 1 9 2 1

*'The world is changing. In
the direction of condensing.'*
—— GAIL BORDEN

THE MAN WHO BROUGHT THE NEWS
FROM UP AND DOWN THE LINE

HENRY DRESHLER, a drummer from Newark, New Jersey, was tossed into the clink in Baltimore on a raw January day on a charge of selling goods without a license. Since it took him several weeks to get out of jail, and the penalty was a fine of from four hundred to six hundred dollars, it is unlikely that Dreshler ever troubled the merchants and police of Baltimore again. It may well be that he bitterly regretted ever becoming a 'travelling agent' at all; for the same indignity might have been visited on him in Washington, D.C., Pittsburgh, Memphis, Cincinnati, St. Louis, Chicago, or Philadelphia.

'Philadelphia!' exclaimed an anguished Committee of the

Society of Commercial Travellers appointed to prepare a memorial upon the subject of the unjust drummer laws, 'Philadelphia! whose pattern-cards and specimens of manufactures, spread by commercial travellers, have poured millions into her coffers! Baltimore, whose commercial travellers swarm throughout the southern states. Pittsburgh, whose furnaces and mills, but for her commercial travellers, would long since have been silent!'

Still a novelty in the commercial life of the 'sixties, the first salesmen on the road represented manufacturers rather than the near-by distributors of staple goods, and they stopped only in cities and towns. Not until the 'seventies or 'eighties was the man with the heavy sample case commonly found touring the country districts in his hired livery rig. The licensing laws directed against 'foreign' salesmen, proceeded on the assumption that the traveling man was the rival of the local merchant, despite the fact that he sold no goods to the consumer. The laws were a belated expression of the old mercantilist theory of restriction and monopoly, which regarded the idea of a free-flowing commerce as quixotic. Against it the commercial travelers urged the benefits that would accrue from free intercourse between city and country, between states and geographical regions, such as frequent replenishment with fresh stocks, novelties of invention or fabric, style changes, and more accurate and up-to-the-minute news of price changes. Yet for years the travelers had a rocky road with the local authorities. E. P. Briggs, a hardware salesman, was arrested in Memphis 'on suspicion of offering to sell' and would have spent the night in jail if he had not had fifty dollars on him to guarantee his appearance in court. Briggs paid up when he got to Washington and St. Louis, and added the license fee to the cost of the goods he sold.

Gradually the local jobbers and retailers came to see that

they paid for the licensing system. As the West developed and Chicago and other cities loosed their own army of drummers on the smaller towns and villages, it finally became good civic policy to remove the restrictions.

It was generally supposed in the drumming fraternity that the local jobbers tipped off the police about strangers who were seen carrying packages around town, and therefore might be suspected of violating the law. Baltimore was the worst city of all from the drummer's point of view. A man with a bundle could scarcely cross a street or light out down an alleyway, without being scooped up for a ride in the paddy wagon. The Maryland law of 1868, in which the unfortunate Dreshler had become entangled, was typical of many in its provisions and intentions. It provided that no person who was not a permanent resident of the state 'shall sell, offer for sale, or expose for sale within the limits of the city of Baltimore, any goods, wares, or merchandise whatever, other than agricultural products and articles manufactured in the State of Maryland, either by card, sample, or other specimen, or by written or private trade lists or catalogue, whether such person be the maker or manufacturer thereof or not, without first obtaining a license so to do.' The fee for the license was three hundred dollars, a deliberately prohibitive figure.

The traveling men spoke up vigorously against artificial trade barriers between states. 'The hardship we protest is . . . that an honorable citizen . . . may, for showing a novel texture, or explaining a new process or recent invention in some matter equally concerning the well-being of every citizen of our great Republic, rich or poor — be thrown into a criminal's dungeon.' The ordinances designed to place obstacles in the way of the salesmen recall the statutes regarding peddlers. The distinction between the two classes was obviously slight in the minds of the lawmakers. Cincinnati permitted a New Yorker, Robinson Jones, representing a house of more than a million dollars in capital, to work his trade and 'peddle by sample, within the city limits of said City,' but it was specified that Jones was *not* privileged to occupy a stand in a public market, street, alley, or commons with table, bench, or otherwise.

Just when the stay-at-home drummer, who lounged elegantly around the Astor House, was succeeded by the hard-driving salesman on the road cannot be determined precisely. It did not happen all at once. The change was slow and halting. The two systems existed side by side for years; but certain outside margins can be indicated. In 1823 an English traveler observed: 'In the United States there are no commercial travellers; consequently, the shop or storekeepers are obliged to repair to the large towns, to procure the different articles they may want.' After the panic of 1837 in which many wholesale concerns broke because their customers failed to pay their bills, businessmen started checking country credit more carefully than ever before. They sent out clerks from the jobbing stores not primarily to sell goods but to investigate the responsibility of their retailers, collect overdue accounts, and make friends generally. It was a natural step to accept orders, and finally to seek them actively; and so the agents on collection trips became the first traveling sales force.

A veteran traveling man recalled in the 1870's how tentatively the new idea of the traveling agent was tried out in the Boston area during the late 1840's. 'What profound secrecy was enjoined by the Seniors . . . That mysterious trunk in one of the upper rooms, samples and pattern books privately collected together, privately packed, and the trunk as privately sent to the depot, the young "Traveller," and those remaining at home, having the words "say nothing" firmly impressed upon them.' The species must have multiplied, for the

term 'drummer' had come into vogue by 1854. Yet the change
was so gradual that a diarist of 1889 recalled that 'a generation ago,' which we can take to be just before the Civil War,
the traveling salesman 'was hardly known in this country.' It
has been estimated that there were a thousand of them in the
United States in 1861. The Committee of the Society of Commercial Travellers, whose pamphleteering against the 'drummer laws' has already been mentioned, estimated that there
were 50,000 of the railroad tourists in the north central
and northeastern regions in 1869. This either was an over-
enthusiastic figure or included part-time and transient workers who floated in and out of selling work, since in the next
year, 1870, the Bureau of the Census found only some 7000
commercials.

By 1874 the membership of the drummers' state association
in New York was 'over one thousand' and the President was
saying that the total number of men on the road in the state,
members or not, was 10,000. With trunk and carpetbag they
found the market for dry goods, groceries, clothing, men's
furnishings, hats and caps, woolens, fancy goods, small wares,
drugs, medicines, jewelry, glassware, hardware, boots, and
shoes. The manufacturer or jobber of every sort of line, from
crockery to carriages, was sending out men who 'by the aid of
the Photographer, by drawings, or by the newly-discovered
Heliotype process, may present designs from which to take
orders, all . . . to the mutual advantage of both buyer and
seller.' The *New York Herald* stated in 1877 that the figure
was up to 100,000 for 'professed' traveling agents, but
thought that half a million would be a more likely figure.
Again the government figures are more conservative; 28,000
for the 1880 census and approaching 93,000 in 1900.

In any event it is clear that the old trade custom of the
little merchant seeking out the supply for his store went out

with the stagecoach. The railroad trains, which gave one old lady the impression of 'bilin' and bustin' and steamin' on't along, not stopping to take up nobody — not stopping to set down nobody — and runnin' over horned creeters like all possessed,' brought the 'package express,' faster movement of goods and passengers — and the modern salesman. Postage rates were reduced in 1851, an indication of an expanding service to commerce. Distance limits on letters were removed in 1861. First-class letter postage dropped to three cents in 1863. In the same year free delivery was established in forty-nine cities. The decade saw the introduction of the registry system and the railway mail car. The penny post card came in 1893.

Faster, cheaper mail service, together with the telegraph, provided the means for a new kind of close contact between the country buyer and the city seller. Another stimulus to business was the provision in the postal law of 1875 under which newspapers and periodicals were handled at two cents per pound, and the country weekly newspapers delivered free of carrying charges in their home county. This change had a bracing effect on country journalism and on advertising. Advertising and the new kinds of neat consumer packages with pictures and brand names on them, went hand in hand. People were learning to ask for the patent medicines, stove polishes, soaps, oatmeals, and crackers they read about in the advertisements, all of which had profound effects on the mentality of the country store owner and his ways of doing business.

Now for the first time the country achieved unity in a commercial sense. The tight little economy of village and town, of city and state, based upon the apprentice, the master craftsman, the water wheel, and freight movement by team and wagon, gave place to a more spacious era. Farm crops and factory goods could find their place in a national market, tied together by shining steel rails. Under pressures that could not be resisted, the restrictive laws with their apparatus of licenses, informers, and penalties took their place beside the spinning wheel, the wigs, and small clothes which were relics of an older order.

Called variously railroad tourists, trade interviewers, solicitors, knights of the grip, drummers, agents, missionaries, commercial tourists, or just commercials, the salesmen were lineal descendants of the bagmen known to the English inns where the sample room, the anecdote of the road, and a certain occupational guild spirit had already developed. Many of the first commercials in the United States were, indeed, English veterans of the pattern card, whose boisterous behavior and distinctive dress did much to nourish a native American prejudice against salesmen and Englishmen.

The country trade was worked by drummers who represented wholesale houses specializing in one line or another, groceries, queen's ware, shoes, and other staple goods. Ready-made clothing was brought to the country trade by salesmen representing jobbers, and later directly by factory representatives. Among the specialists were the crockery man, the cracker man, and the irrepressible tobacco salesman with his magnetized tack hammer and lithographed tin signs, who boldly nailed his manifesto to the store door.

Quite distinct from the jobbers' men who called in regular rotation on the same territory, were the agents for new inventions and specialties, a high-flying crowd, who never expected to come that way again. The slicked-up drummer who sold a sewing machine, cash register, patented washing machine, or lamp was a persuasive critter, with a white vest and snappy suit, a freshly-shaved chin, and a cordial handshake. He had a suave way with country merchants which charmed them into

buying goods they did not always need, and in big-store quantities. He concentrated on one line, and did a rattling good job
of putting a 10 x 12 order into a 2 x 4 store. The tales he told
to his colleagues over a Sunday of sales made and goods
shipped were not all fairy tales. With his polish, his encyclo-
pedic stock of stories, and his high salary, he kept pretty close
to the electric-light towns where the people handled more cash
than out in the sticks. There, he felt, was his best chance of
swelling the merchant's bill to the limit. With sweeping gestures and rosy talk of five-gross orders here and ten-gross
there, the salesman promoting a new kind of dye or friction
match soon had the dealer feeling that he could hardly mention the pindling little quantity he could really handle. So to
keep the esteem of the specialty man — whom he would see a
year or so later, if ever — the store owner sometimes acquired a stock of stickers, goods that grew gray with age on
the shelves, a tribute to human gullibility when a fast talker
got on the subject of 'quantity at a price.'

The book agent was the prototype of the species. These
canvasers indeed made the study of human nature a science,
each having his own style of 'approach' in stalking the prospective buyer and his own method of pouncing to close the
sale. If there had been a Linnaeus to provide a Systematic
Classification of Drummers, he probably would have put the
religious book salesman of the post-Civil War period into the
same genus as the early Yankee peddler who, a couple of generations before, had sold Polyglot Bibles, all in English.
There were subscription book salesmen beating the bushes
with Civil War histories under their arms. For each county
there was at least one mass-produced tome filled with slapdash
accounts of local Indian artifacts dug up, and the first fulling
mill, with a section of woodcut portraits of the county's
worthies, published at so much per 'cut,' and flattering biog-

raphies of the 'prominent farmer' or 'leading merchant' —
that is, the subscribers.

The men who were out bucking 'the road' thought of their
occupation as a profession, and their function as a high one.
They kept the mills going and the wheels turning. They were
the governors of trade. Business could not hum without the
helping hand of the hustler with the satchel and sample case.
The traveler saw himself as 'the ambassador of supply and
demand, the advance courier of the "latest out." ' He was 'to
trade what the statesman is to politics and government.' As he
produced an 'interchange of ideas and intelligence between
two different sections of the same country' he carried the flag
for civilization itself.

The author of *The Commercial Traveller's Guide Book*, of
1871, gave an imaginative quick study of the twentieth century when merchandise would move from coast to coast.
'Though goods may not reach the Pacific coast in twenty-four
hours after leaving New York,' as one enthusiast prophesied,
'the time will not exceed forty-eight hours.' He predicted that
the want ads of our time would offer jobs in some such terms as
' "Wanted, a commercial traveller for North China. He must
be able to speak Chinese fluently, and be master of the white
goods trade"; or, "A Russian, familiar with the Tartar lan-
guages, desires a commission from some manufacturer of
woolen goods as commercial traveller in eastern Russia and
Siberia." '

The drummer was not, on the whole, a speculative man, but
in one of the few books of reflections on the calling, Charles S.
Plummer adds a few touches to the self-portrait. He saw the
drummer as a natural orator, a skilled diplomat, a walking
market letter, an expert on sports and the arts. Drummers
liked to dwell upon stories of aggressive salesmen, anecdotes
of their quick wit, the ingenious stratagems by which the vic-

torious commercial confounded his competitor and, as they
said at the time, 'brought home the Beechnut,' bringing an
ancient expression up to date by switching the key word —
'bacon' — to the name of a famous branded grocery item.
Wherever a hamlet sprang up, or a town, and an improvised
clapboard structure appeared with 'General Store' scrawled
on a crude sign, the drummers would appear almost as fast as
the flies. Salesmen quoted approvingly the couplet:

> *Commercial travellers will find their way*
> *Where wolves won't dare to stray.*

The older traveling men, when in a reminiscent mood, liked to
recall with satisfaction the names of men who had graduated
from the ranks of the railway tourists to high position and
great fortune. Marshall Field was a salesman on the road. So
was Aaron Montgomery Ward. John W. Gates once sold
barbed wire. King C. Gillette was a drummer who tried to
think of some article the buyer would use once, throw away,
and come back for more. He got his idea while shaving — the
Gillette Safety Razor. George W. Cole got tired of selling
varnish and invented '3-in-1 Oil.' A little later the drummers
might have claimed, had they wished to, Huey P. Long, who,
as a drummer for Cottolene, a cotton seed-oil shortening, and
for flour and patent medicines, rode the parishes of Louisiana
and learned all too well how to manipulate his fellow citizens.

'Of course you all know him,' says the author of a friendly
sketch of the commercial traveler, 'that jolly, joking, tender-
hearted, generous and hailfellow who is "well-met" on every
trip . . . Bouncing about on "limiteds" and way-freights, a
twenty-mile drive — or a five-mile walk — he covers his territory and keeps the remote and isolated section in touch with
city ways. The boys gather at the grocery to hear him talk.
The country merchant advises with him . . . the duel of

banter is passed when the confidence is reached that "that man and his house are square." '

The drummers were certainly great hands for a practical joke. A new traveler would be introduced to a strange salesman whom he supposed to be a customer, for the fun of watching him 'sell' a colleague. In the days of the licensing laws, another gambit was to make elaborate arrangements for a strange drummer, masquerading as a detective, to crash his way into the hotel room of the appointed victim. The hoped-for denouement was that the green tourist would attempt to bribe a fellow salesman: 'Can't we just settle this thing right here?'

The Daughters of the American Revolution decided to put a plaque on the Pavilion Hotel in Montpelier, Vermont, the plate bearing some deathless prose about how Lafayette had been entertained there. The celebration was set for a June afternoon. The spandy-new historical tablet was carefully veiled by a flag until the great moment came. A whiskey salesman, staying at the hotel, looked the situation over and got an idea which he quietly put into effect. That afternoon the people assembled, the band played, the orator of the day pointed to the flag and, rising to his climax, exclaimed, 'When the American flag is lifted, you will see words to be read by generations unborn.'

The flag was whisked upward. A large card appeared, and on it the words:

'Wilson's Whiskey — That's All.'

Every shipping clerk or stock boy in a jobber's warehouse hoped that he might some day put aside the broom, the brush, and blacking pot, say good-by to marking cases, and go on the road, telling yarns that were escapes from Joe Miller's joke book, or cribbed from John R. Walsh's *Chicago Jokes and Anecdotes for Railroad Travellers and Fun Lovers*, and blowing up his samples to the trade. His chances were good if he was young, energetic, and had a winning personality. When the head of a firm decided that a lad might hatch out as a drummer, he gave him a few weeks' training in prices, the line of merchandise, and mentioned a few maxims. Never let the prospect sense that you are in a hurry to make the next train. Never 'sass' a customer. Smile when the dealer says 'I've already bought your line.' The salesman who drops a crippled wing weakens his chances, so put on a good front — and smile. Always have your samples in good order. Expenses? Keep them down; 'there is too much money spent by young men on cigars.' Don't sell merchandise you can't deliver. Don't 'throw dirt' at the competition. Never admit trade is dull. Watch your credits. Keep in touch with the home office.

What a glorious prospect, to drop one's own post cards and circulars into the mail — 'Will be calling on you with a full fall line on such-and-such date.' He would see the country, make new friends, be practically his own boss, with control of a large personal trade, and command a handsome salary. To a country boy hanging around the little store at a four-corners, the drummer was a gay bird of passage, his home where his hat hung, a hero to be compared favorably with the engineer on the fast freight. His confident bearing and city ways made the counter-sitters, man and boy, seem like wild creatures who had ventured briefly out of the brush. There was an ineffable, worldly grace about his gesture as he proffered his pasteboard on a first call: 'My name and connection, sir.' Under the fixed stare of many pairs of eyes, it was notable that the commercial's suits were on the dashing side, his shirts dressy, his collars stiff; but his manners were as comfortable as an old shoe. He smoked good cigars — no drumheads or stogies for him — and certainly knew his way around.

Legend, with some assistance from the travelers themselves,

The penny post card heralded the day and hour of the railroad tourist's arrival at the crossroads to unveil his 'line' for the spring, or fall, trade.

had it that the drummer was a gay one with the ladies. He was at home among the mysteries and niceties of the polite world. He knew how to undress in a Pullman berth, and called the porter 'George.' He ate dollar dinners, knew how to order a

meal from the bill of fare, and could handle a complicated lay-
out of knives and forks without turning a hair. When he sat
down in the dining room of the West Side Hotel even the ca-
naries seemed to chirk up as he casually examined his knife
and fork, and ran his napkin over them, at the same time
carrying on a running fire of persiflage with the delighted
waitress. He called her 'Sister' because, as he said, his father
had been a traveling man too.

The drummer usually dropped off the afternoon accommodation from Kansas City, for example, said 'Howdy, Sonny,'
if there was a small admirer at the 'dee-po' to greet him, and
lugged his samples over to the country store, where he sat
down on the counter, mopped his brow and expressed a desire
for a chew of tobacco. The male population gathered around
while the visitor told the 'one' about the Swede and the Irish-
man, the Latest One that was going the rounds in the big city.
When the time came that there were more automobiles than
teams standing at the store's hitching rack, the salesman
added to his repertoire the latest Ford joke of the day, a bit of
whimsy on the lizzie's diminutive size, its extraordinary light-
ness, its tinniness, its high-strung nervous temperament,
cribbed from a paper-covered pamphlet sold by the train
butchers, 'Ford Smiles — Jokes About a Rattling Good Car.'

'Say, Pop,' he would say, 'I heard a new one when I was in
Saint Looey last week. Seems that this lighthouse keeper had
a beautiful daughter, but being out there on a pile of rocks,
as you might say, she hadn't had much experience. Well, one
day . . .'

In fact, the commercial traveler became the central figure
himself in a kind of *sub rosa* folklore. There was a whole class
of anecdotes: 'Have you heard the one about the traveling
salesman and the farmer's daughter?' They combined fact
and reputation. The fact was that the drummer often did drive

long distances, jogging along through the back country in a
'livery rig,' and he often did have to 'put up' at a farmhouse.
The reputation was that no female could resist his invitation
to amorous dalliance.

To a country store clerk earning ten to fifteen dollars a
week, whose personal knowledge of the earth's geography extended some twenty or thirty miles from the store, the drummer cut a shining figure. He was in touch. Didn't he know Cap
Anson personally? And John L. Sullivan? Well, he said he
did. He spoke casually of distant cities: 'As I was coming
down Fourth Street in Philly last week, I saw . . .' Such
easy knowledge of the world was enough to strike dumb a
youth who had seen Chicago once and would not dare hazard
such a familiarity as 'Chi.' The traveler would whisper hor-
rific tales of graft in high places and knew who was going to
win the election. Sometimes he possessed astonishing skills in
entertainment, and could lend a rich bass voice to the singing
of Pentecostal hymns at a prairie prayer meeting, or 'render'
a light, secular number at a country social.

If he could play the fiddle, a fiddle was found, and he would
saw off old-time favorites such as 'The Devil's Dream,' or
'The Mocking Bird.' Sometimes he did a few card tricks, accompanied by a delightful patter, and bit by bit the circle
around the stranger got all the news from up and down the
line.

There were occasions when the jolly soap or cracker agent
found his match, as an entertainer, in the old merchant himself. Charles Nuffer, who ran a general store near Watertown,
New York, was known to be a remarkable athlete. Among his
exploits it was recounted that he put up the cross on St.
Stephen's church spire in Croghan, and then did a handstand
on the cross. Nuffer would be talking with apparent seriousness to the dry goods man from Syracuse lounging in front

Pranks and yarns around the hotel lobby created the folklore of the American traveling salesman — which still awaits the touch of an inspired collector and storyteller.

of his counter. Suddenly, without effort or preparation, he would jump backward, high into the air, and end up standing on top of the counter. He could also, on request, jump into and out of an empty barrel or escape from a strait jacket. The drummers were entranced.

The skillful drummer started to work his trade by not mentioning trade at all. That came later, when a mood had been established. A few observations on the money market and the latest quotations on produce provided a discreet link between sheer entertainment and the state of the country dealer's stock. Meanwhile the salesman meditated on the store's current credit standing back at the home office, and decided whether to sell hard or to hold back.

After supper at the hotel, a drummer found it pleasant to let out his belt a notch and tilt back on the hotel piazza, if the weather was mild, jingling the loose coins in his pocket, the seals and emblems of his fraternal orders dangling prominently from his heavy watch chain. He lifted a quill toothpick from its chaste little gold case. Taking his ease in the twilight, he greeted local acquaintances as they passed by, chatted with other drummers, watched the flashy girls who in every town put on their finery in the evening and paraded arm in arm down to the depot to see the last train come in.

Travelers in all lines felt the tie of common interests. They exchanged data on hotels, news of railroad rates and wrecks, compared notes on business booked. As the postman feels a special interest in biting dogs, the commercial who must have his trunks and samples with him — on time and intact — was particularly alert to the whole evil race of baggagemen. Over Sunday, before the automobile and the week end had been invented, the drummer tried to button up at a good hotel in a good-sized town. One Sunday in 1874, for instance, there were thirty-two salesmen at the hotel in Keene, New Hampshire. The winter before that there was one occasion when fifty young salesmen spent Sunday in Bangor, Maine. The men chatted about the new salesmen who were coming up, the old timers who had dropped out, and strong sentiment developed for the need for an association, such as the railroad conductors had, which would provide sickness and death benefits. Pictures of wives and children were shown and discussed, though one

hotel stenographer has left us the tart observation: 'The majority of travelling men are single — that's their story.'

Often the drummer, after making a sizeable town, also
worked out from it into the country. He hired a rig, a dinner
of oats for the horse, and if necessary 'coat livery,' which
meant that if he did not have a heavy coat with him suitable
for wintry days, the livery stable would rent him one. Down
to the beginning of World War I, it was as much the business
of a traveling man to know horses as to know his own line of
goods. It was worth a lot in time and personal comfort to have
a sharp eye for a spavined old skate, a kicker, or a parrot-
mouth.

One of the country tours of Foster Haviland, the Arm and
Hammer Baking Soda man in upper New York state, was a
charming, pastoral idyl — at least it started out that way.
Haviland must have thought that the life of a salesman fell
in pleasant places, as he headed north from Glens Falls with a
two-horse wagon, a companionable driver, a dog, and a small
arsenal, just at the beginning of the open season on upland
birds. It is a melancholy duty to report on the two weeks that
followed. The first time Haviland shot at a pa'tridge, the gun
kicked him over a log and the second barrel went off, catching
the dog broadside with the full load. A few days later, and
dogless, the amiable driver loaned their rifle to a needy stranger who immediately made off with it. The next night their
gamebag was stolen from the wagon when it was left in the
hotel barn. The remaining gun fell out on a piece of particularly rough road, denting the barrel so as to make the gun
useless.

Otherwise, everything was fine. During a leisurely progress
through Essex County, Haviland would see a tree beside the
road with a good-sized trunk and tell the driver, Alex Russell,
to *whoa*. Then he would open up his grip and take out a
poster. Climbing up on the rail fence, he adjusted the oblong

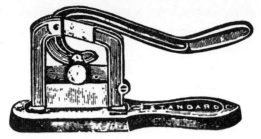

When almost every rural male 'chewed,' the tobacco plug cutter was a necessary item of store equipment for slicing off a fruity nickel or dime's worth of eatin' tobacco.

card, heavily waxed to stand off the weather, until its position and visibility just suited him. Tap, tap went the neat little hammer, and the palette of the New York state autumn landscape was enriched with new color, a deep orange, flaming behind the words 'Arm and Hammer Soda' in bold letters as black as a stack of black cats.

The grocery jobber's man covered his trade about once a month. Dry goods: two to four times a year. The shoe man: about twice a year. Drugs: every two months. Books and stationery, annually. The hardware salesmen with their heavy steel trunks made their rounds two or three times a year. The traveler for the men's clothing companies had to handle two big trunks, one for the patterns, another for the models. He often drove a wagon and team owned by his firm. He called seasonally, with the summer line in the early spring, and the winter line in the early autumn. The canners' men booked their orders before the pack was put up.

After the salesman had left, the country merchant frequently sent fill-in orders to his connections in the jobbing cities. The jobber was expected to exercise discretion in serving the rural customer's interests. For example, Mrs. J. Q. Rapp, of Jeffersonville, Illinois — a village whose population has shrunk and whose name has kept pace, being now shortened to Geff — sent seven orders to Bishop Brothers, Cincinnati wholesale grocers, over a period of three months in 1872. One for forty dollars' worth of crackers, cigars, nuts, candies, and oranges brought back this scribble on the invoice: 'Yours to hand, goods shipped today . . . did not ship oranges, thinking that they would be too high for you; are worth today from $9 to $10 a box. If want them at that price please let us know and we will ship.' A dry goods jobber wrote: 'The style of shawl you order is closed. We send one which we think will suit in its place.' From Sprague, Warner & Company in Chicago came the word, across a bill, 'Too cold to ship cheese or ink.'

Country dealers expected wholesalers in different lines to co-operate in exchanging mail and in combining shipments. Mrs. Rapp often enclosed orders for other lines of merchandise in her grocery order. 'Yours to hand,' replied Bishop Brothers, 'and order executed to the best of our ability. We handed West Brothers & Company (China and glassware) your order.' One autumn Bishop Brothers picked up a $836 dry goods order from McAlpin, Polk & Co., packed it in combination with their own. Relations were informal. Sometimes a small order for one dealer was shipped to a near-by merchant who was receiving a larger shipment. The dealer got word with his invoice where to pick up the merchandise: 'Shipped with J. M. Tracy's goods.' Sometimes the bill showed that the market had changed: 'Coal oil has advanced since Mr. Eaton was at your place.'

On their trips drummers sent ahead advance notices of their arrival, or an explanation, if they departed from custom. 'I'll be at your place 4 days after mailing this circular, Samuel Ward, salesman.' 'I have been North for my health. Will be along as soon as the Weather gets a Little Cooler. Thanking you for favors,' and so forth. In the old days when a drummer had the confidence of a country dealer it was his until he abused it, retired, or died. Others 'made the town' simply to be in line should any of those contingencies arise.

Critical portraits of the drummer usually delineate the high-powered specialty man who was making, literally, a 'tour.' For him it was now or never. This was the man with the 'heavy' manner, who gave the porter orders in a loud voice and affected a Byronic manner with the local girls. He was the bumptious individual who condescended to observe, 'I see you sell fancy wares,' at an unpropitious moment, drawing the crisp rejoinder, 'No — we just *keep* them.' The *New York World* thought of the drummer as having 'unbounded cheek,' a passion for euchre and smoking cars. *The Daily Freeman* of Kingston, New York, was even more detailed in specifying what it found objectionable in the drummer type. He was 'a being oiled and curled, redolent of musk and plated with brass, full of well-studied lies and subterfuges, the idol of silly school girls and female waitresses at country hotels, the envy of beardless boys who tried hard to acquire his mannerisms and learn his style of profanity.'

If some traveling men were bold and brassy, they merely possessed to an excess the qualities necessary for survival in a lonely and trying occupation. It took courage, unquenchable optimism, and a sound stomach to stand the life of the road in the wooden coach days. The 'early bird' call in the hotels came between four and six in the morning. All day the drummer hustled sample cases. He met each situation as it came up: the man who always tried to get an extra discount, the merchant who thought that when he sent in an order, the house should get out the hand organ and declare a champagne celebration. He had his own nominee for Meanest Man in the World; the retailer who liked to abuse a commercial traveler in his own store.

At noon the salesman grabbed a hasty sandwich and before

he ate again he made a long evening's ride to the next town large enough to have a water tank and a hotel. There he got his meal and his mail. The mail might be a complaint from his boss, the sad story of how a stock clerk had scrambled up the order of a valued customer, or a crisp letter from the credit man, frankly skeptical of the drummer's judgment in a matter of extending credit, and explaining that he had not shipped the order. If neither the mail nor his afternoon snack of peanuts and train bananas had given him indigestion, the traveler might sup on cold leftovers under the gelid eye of the hotel parrot. When the winter nights were so cold that the trees gave off crackling reports like the fire of a Gatling gun, and blankets and mattresses were worn and thin, the tired drummer climbed into his iron bed with a lamp chimney wrapped in a towel to keep his feet warm. In an electric-light town, a single bulb cast a yellow glow as it hung in the center of the bedroom, not enough light to read by but strong enough to reveal the cracks in the plaster and the coil of rope provided in lieu of a fire escape.

The end of the week did not always see the commercial traveler 'Sundaying' agreeably with Messrs. Knit Goods, Cutlery, Crackers and Guns at Keene or Bangor. Sometimes he had to bunk up with a complete stranger. Sunday night meant paper work, writing up orders and his weekly expense account. And Sunday nights he often sat in an unheated depot, listening for the sad, lonesome whistle of the slow accommodation that would move him and his traps on to his early Monday morning customer.

> *The hotel bus from the midnight train*
> *Brought only one passenger through the rain;*
> *A commercial tourist weary and sad,*
> *For trade had been poor and collections bad.*

In the days when men wore shawls, it was of first importance that the drummer have 'a good, heavy, full-size, warm,
traveling shawl,' and wear flannel underwear at all seasons;
that or the best knit goods, or 'perforated buckskin under-
clothing.' It was recommended that outer clothing be of wool,
winter and summer, with cotton half hose, a soft hat or cap,
and stout, easy shoes, a sack overcoat for winter, or a cloak
and overcoat combination. The shawl was a fixture. 'In winter
or summer the traveller should always have his shawl with
him.'

'I know of no exposure so great, so trying to the young
man, as that to which the travelling salesman is subject,' declared William H. Baldwin, President of the Boston Young
Men's Christian Union; and he did not mean exposure to
pneumonia or cigar smoke. He gave a vivid sketch of the critical moment. The drummer's customer suggests the 'social
glass.' 'Shall we indulge?' he inquires, courteously. It was not
an uncommon contretemps. Even the pettiest retailer knew
the adage to the general point that — spend a dollar when
you come, and you shall have a glass of rum.

The shoe traveler or the flour man is keenly aware of the
nice bill he has just made. The customer is thirsty. In that
fatal instant he has 'broken that sacred promise which he may
have made to the dear anxious mother as he left the old homestead in the country for his new city life.' Here is a scene. One
has a sense that he has seen a lithographic print which caught
the pathos and drama of the moment, the mother's anxious
face and ample figure on the porch, the waving hand of the
departing son, haycocks around a stackpole, and oxen in the
background, and father in high boots, flat-crowned hat, and
spade beard, a goad in his hand, guiding the oxen at drawing
firewood for the winter fireplace. Perhaps Currier and Ives

did record the scene and Mr. Peters simply never found the stone.

The Reverend T. De Witt Talmadge, the Norman Vincent Peale of the 'seventies, a popular preacher of great note and influence, who added regularly to the liveliness of New York's Monday morning newspapers, and whose devotional works occupied half a page in the Montgomery Ward catalogues, preached to an assemblage of drummers in 1877 at his great tabernacle in Brooklyn. He recommended to the railroad tourists that they take along with them on their tours a serious secular book and a Bible printed in large type, the valise in the right hand, as they set forth, and 'your blanket and shawl strapped in your left.' He admonished them in the most vigorous language, with startling gestures, not to pack their playing cards or brandy flask, a reference which recalls the anecdote of the excited gentleman who burst into a railroad car and called out:

'Is there a drummer in this car?'

'Yes, sir. I'm a commercial traveller,' came the reply.

'Ah, just loan me your whiskey flask, if you please. A lady has fainted in the next sleeper.'

Gambling was also enumerated by the Young Men's Christian Union speaker as a dangerous outlet for bored salesmen. A man could, after all, become weary of coal smoke and cinders, rough roadbeds, cold-hearted customers who said 'I've bought your line,' the endless routine of pack, unpack, pack, unpack, and pack. He could stare at the smudged wallpaper in a stuffy little room or the coiled rope which *might* get him to the ground safely if the dreaded cry of 'Fire' was raised in the small hours of the morning. He could easily stray into sin out of a simple need for the warmth of human companionship.

President Baldwin came next to the 'Social Evil.' Turn

away, he exclaimed, from 'the low and degraded of the female sex . . . let the No be promptly uttered.' Study to avoid the company of the opposite sex 'where you would not gladly welcome the unexpected presence of your dear mother or sister.' And he spoke gravely of one other temptation. Letting a customer take a peek at his samples on a Sunday might mean that he would have to book an order on the Sabbath Day.

In his Brooklyn sermon, the Reverend Talmadge went over the same ground, rising to a solemn climax of pulpit metaphor. As in a vision, he saw the last day of the drummer's life upon this earth, probably spent in a railroad coach or a strange hotel. 'The train of your earthly existence is nearing the depot of the grave,' he shouted in sepulchral tones. 'The brakes are falling, the bell rings at the terminus, the train stops. ALL OUT FOR ETERNITY!'

Some years later, two traveling men, knowing the pitfalls and hazards of the traveler's life, met by accident in a crowded hotel in Boscobel, Wisconsin, read together chapters six and seven of Judges, and were inspired to organize The Gideons, their slogan 'A Bible in every hotel guest room.' Special texts relevant to the life of a traveling man were prominently emphasized in the front of the Gideon Bible. There, in boldface type, was the offer of consolation to the commercial who was sick, who had tired of sin, who was in trouble or discouraged, who felt himself yielding to temptation. The Twenty-third Psalm was suggested to the lonesome and restless. The charity of the thirteenth chapter of First Corinthians was prescribed for the salesman who was losing confidence in men. The drummer who was fighting against unscrupulous competition, say some fast-moving crowd who offered the country retailer an alluring premium, a mission rocking chair or a wall thermometer, could find comfort and the courage to go on in the words of the Psalmist:

'Fret not thyself of evil doers, neither be thou envious against the workers of iniquity.

'For they shall soon be cut down like the grass, and wither as the green herb.'

It was inevitable that a group of Americans with strong social instincts should sooner or later band together. There were flourishing traveling men's associations in Minnesota, in Canada and Michigan, in the 'seventies. St. Louis had its Western Commercial Travellers' Association. In Boston it was the We Help One Another Association. The Detroit group offered insurance benefits to travelers between the ages of twenty-one and forty-five, subject to a doctor's findings after auscultation and percussion of the chest. It was necessary to determine whether there was a clear and distinct respiratory murmur over both lungs; and whether the pulse intermitted. In another field of service, the Association had been able to persuade the railroads to issue the drummers special Saturday-to-Monday tickets, good for round trips at a one-way fare.

New York state was not the first, but not the last either, to organize for the improvement of traveling conditions, burial and sickness benefits, annual banquets with speeches and dancing, and to taste the solemn joys of parliamentary ritual. In the state it was distinctly a Syracuse idea. James H. Eaton was invited to take the chair at the organizational meeting held at the Globe Hotel. A Committee was appointed. A constitution and bylaws were adopted, and officers elected. By 1877 the New York group had well over a thousand members, a magazine of their own, and a new lay-over ticket on the Erie.

The social functions of the drummers threw the Syracuse newspapers into an ecstasy of journalistic excitement. The banquet was 'sumptuous.' The table 'groaned' with soup, fish, oysters from raw to smoked, boiled meat, cold dishes, entrees, vegetables, relishes, ornamental pieces, roasts, game (prairie chicken, antelope saddle, wild turkey, quail, venison), pastry, and desserts. There were elaborate confection pieces such as 'The President's Baggage,' 'Pyramid de Fleurs,' 'Temple de Fantasie.' It was of course a 'festive board,' and 'mine hosts' were 'au fait.' There was no strong drink, because, as the President pointed out, 'the presence of our wives, sisters and perhaps sweethearts, is one of the most gratifying features of the evening.' The guests 'discussed the viands.' The incoming President made an address and the retiring President read a poem about how the drummer came down like a wolf on the fold, and boasted the goods and the buyers he'd sold. The 'feast of reason and flow of soul' continued through the toasts and was followed by 'the mazy dance,' with music by the Professor; first the stately Grand March, then the quadrille, the Lancers, the waltz, Caledonian, and Polka. As 'trade's merry messengers' warmed to their work, the music shifted to Monnie Musk, the Virginia Reel, and a mad Gallop with 'the *élite* and beauty of Syracuse — and even other towns.' After the ball was over the newspaper editor looked back wistfully, and forward expectantly: 'The "drummers" have departed. They are a jolly lot . . . Great preparations are on the *tapis* for the third annual dinner and reception [of the] vagabonds of trade.'

As the commercial travelers caused a new profusion of goods to appear in the country stores, other items lost their importance or disappeared altogether, such as whale oil, hoops and shoe pegs, cone sugar and hemp seed. The additions always exceeded the casualties. The judgment of the time upon itself was that it was an extraordinary era. Every year brought new wonders — illuminating gas in the cities, the magnetic telegraph, Hoe's printing press that rolled off

10,000 newspapers in an hour, Daguerre's beautiful invention, gun cotton, chloroform, and John Wesley Hyatt's dainty 'Celluloid' — what would they think of next?

A look at the stock of a good, lively country store at the time of the Philadelphia Centennial in 1876 would have been enough to convert any citizen to a belief in progress. Lamps and lamp chimneys, and the whole class of merchandise known as 'kerosene goods' would seem to be a marvel to eyes that had strained to see at night by means of a lighted rag, soaked in beef tallow and draped over the edge of a dish. Equally startling would be ready-made 'overhalls,' and shirts all ready to put on, from Troy, New York. The three-dollar shoe would be as exciting as the dollar watch, the oil stove, or the Langtry bustle. As the century wore on to its end, it seemed that the world was filled up with jardinieres, fifty-cent corsets, stereoscopes, cuckoo clocks, watch fobs, gramophones, and chewing gum. What a bonanza of goods to choose from, and still more coming all the time — granite kitchen ware, barbed-wire fencing, screens to keep the flies out, toothbrushes to produce the modern dental smile.

The day had passed when store goods meant stern necessities such as powder and shot, salt and tea. Clever little gimcracks, notions, and novelties blossomed all over the place. Butler Brothers, jobbers to the country trade, and then located in Boston, were the great five-and-ten-cent counter men. Though they sold a general line of merchandise to the country trade, cheap, mixed counter goods were their hobby. Every little crossroads store stepped out with a five-and-ten counter, as a result of Butler Brothers' enthusiasm, piled high with a medley of inexpensive articles usually sold in different specialized trades. The dealer kept his prices up on goods that he regarded as his regular lines, and used his

counter business to bring in the bargain hunters and put some
ginger into the day's trading.

As the assortments grew larger, the customers began to feel
the stirrings of a sort of civic pride concerning the variety of
goods which could be found at their local store. A good, live
store presented, after all, an agreeable contrast to the bitter
scarcities of earlier, harsher days. Thus the folklore of the
Complete Stock motif came into being.

It was told of Henry Hull, who kept store at Hinesburg,
Vermont, that a customer tried to stump him by asking for a
goose-poke. The goose-poke was a device placed around the
neck of a goose to keep it from going through a fence. Hull
said y-e-s slowly, hesitantly; then triumphantly produced one
from the clutter at the back of his store.

The loafers around the livery stable at Hardwick, Vermont,
offered five dollars to any drummer who could ask for an article that Mr. Way at the Hardwick general store could not
supply. One commercial tried to cop the five dollars by asking
for a coffin. That was too easy. Undertaking was often combined with running a general store. Mr. Way had the only
stock of coffins for miles around.

Another joker came into the store and said: 'I want to buy
a pulpit. Do you have one in stock?'

Mr. Way had to think hard. Then a smile broke over his
face.

'We-ell, I guess I have. I had forgotten about it. I bought
all the furniture from the old Methodist church when they
remodelled. I put the pulpit up over the carriage house thinking there wouldn't be much call for it. Glad I can accommodate you.'

Another rural inquirer for strange merchandise asked a
New York state man whether he could furnish a live toad.

'Yes, you go down in the cellar,' directed the store owner. 'In the southwest corner is a board about four feet long. You raise up that board and you'll find a toad.' The man followed instructions, and there was the toad. It was in the winter-time, too.

The period from 1870 to 1900 was the great age for the drummers. After 1900 the traveling men were more numerous than ever, but their imaginative appeal faded. The drummers themselves seemed to have changed, or perhaps it was the world that had changed. At any rate, they did not seem to make the impression they used to. Their contacts with the public were less intimate. That may have had something to do with it. When the salesman took to the road in his open run-about he disappeared from the smoking car. The depot saw him no more. It was easier to drive into a 'Tourists Taken' out in the country than to stop at the 'Star House' in town. He no longer Sundayed with the hardware man or the shirt man. Friday night he stepped on the gas and got home for the week end, being, as it finally turned out, a married man after all, happy in his choice of a wholesome country girl who could bake Sally Lunn and play 'Red Wing' on the Pianola ('Now *you* can play the piano as well as anyone.'). The drummer's great day had been earlier; when he was a near-by figure, when the young country was feeling its oats, prosperity could be assured by voting for McKinley, and a robber baron might steal a railroad with reasonable assurance that he could keep it.

Those were the days when a popular drummer could lounge on the counter of a country store, wave his Havana with the bright band still on it, and feel himself the leading character in a satisfying drama. As he joined the group around the stove, the boys were delighted to be both audience and supporting cast to an accomplished actor.

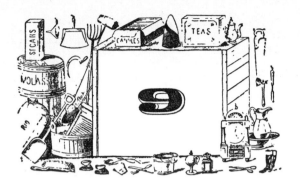

FROM CRADLE TO COFFIN

THE COUNTRY EMPORIUM of general merchandise seemed by the 1870's to have reached a triumphant climax in its long effort to bring the city to the country and to link the country with the city. Old men who reached the fullness of their years after the age of the internal combustion engine liked to recall the atmosphere of the store of their youth as one of austere simplicity, though their own fathers would have been perplexed at such an opinion.

Usually the gable end of the store faced the street or roadway, the ridge running at right angles. One style of building, often put up about this time in a village large enough to support a business block or row of several different businesses, had a permanent awning along its front, made of corrugated, galvanized iron — called a 'tin roof' — supported by iron pipes for columns. There was a new fashion for the store building to have an iron front, which was distinctly a false front, with engaged columns and vaguely Corinthian curlicues worked out in cast iron. The store in open country or at a crossroads location had its gable end squared off by a façade, or false front of wood, which ran up to an imposing height, though everybody knew it pretended to be something it was not. Sometimes an unroofed porch or platform ran across the front of the store, with steps at each end which a walker mounted to get to the front door, but its functional use was that the height was just right for loading heavy goods directly into a farmer's wagon box. Somewhere handy to the front door were hitching racks, and off to one side, a long, low, open-faced horse shed sheltered the customers' rigs in bad weather — such as may still be seen occasionally behind a country church.

Yet it was, after all, the interior of the store and what it contained that made a well-run country store seem in the Centennial year of '76 no less than a World's Fair exhibition itself, with the products of all nations, the fruits of all science and industry on parade. 'An Omnibus Store,' the *Philadelphia Merchant* called it, especially characteristic of the newly settled country districts of the West, yet also to be found easily within forty miles of Philadelphia itself.

'It is a grocery store,' continues this contemporary account of the little store that seemed to have *everything*, 'with tea, sugar, coffee, spices, molasses, dried fruits, etc.

'It is a hardware store, with cutlery in variety, axes, rifles, divers mechanics' tools, kitchen utensils, agricultural implements, bar-iron, nails, etc.

'It is a shoe store, and men, women, and children can alike be accommodated with foot gear.

'It is a confectionary store, and there's a goodly row of glass jars of candies for the sweet tooth.

'It is a drug store, and medicines, dyestuffs, paints, varnish, putty, tar, etc. are at your service.

'It is a trimming store, and pins, needles, thread, tapes, ribbons, etc. await your call.

'It is a jewelry store, with the adjuncts of clocks, watches, violins and jews harps.

'It is a hat store, and you must not be positive that bonnets are not on hand.

'It is a brush store, and bristles and broom-corn are in readiness for a customer.

'It is a crockery store, and you may buy queensware, earthenware, glassware and stoneware.

'It is a book and stationery store, equal to the ordinary requirements of the vicinity.

'It is a tobacco store, and smokers, chewers and snuffers can be supplied.

'It is also the post-office, and the merchant is the postmaster.' He will have almost any article you can call for, the trade paper said, and will most agreeably make a note to get what he is 'just out of.'

In the interior arrangement, the dry-goods counter usually ran along the right side, as you faced the store from the front entrance, and was heaped with drills, sheetings, calicoes, button molds, and trimmings. Little touches might be seen which showed how new refinements were reaching the country trade. Napkins and towels came already hemmed. Work shirts were sold already made up. There were satchels for traveling, now that people could move around more. Cotton thread came on spools, 'run off' by pretty girls called 'spoolers,' Wilbur Cross recalled, 'who easily found husbands.' The thread was displayed in a dispenser cabinet which sat on the counter. One type whirled around, shaped like a great cylinder, to show all the gauges and colors of 'Merrick's Six Cord Soft Finish Spool Cotton.' Another cabinet was made with drawers, one line of lettering on each drawer:

Sole Agent   O.N.T. Spool Cotton On white spools
George A. Clark

Large bins or 'boot boxes,' five or six of them, arranged according to size, from boys' up, stood along the floor, the lids loose for easy access. They overflowed with congress gaiters, factory-made shoes for men, high-button shoes for women. No individual packaging for each pair; that came later, after the introduction of the 'shoe box.' Some of the new styles were even shaped to the foot, right and left, an exquisite new comfort. A wire contraption hung from the ceiling, among the baskets and lanterns, a lady's bustle, serving no purpose other than to provide the silhouette and rear elevation currently prescribed; it was the fashion, and was advertised as having lots of 'shelf.'

Even the smells and redolences of the store were different as the nineteenth century entered its third quarter. The wet spot under the kerosene barrel contributed a new characteristic, raw and dominant. Among the good things to be seen and sniffed was a row of aromatic pails filled with fine-cut tobacco — one kind of consolation. Gleaming jars behind the counter offered another. They held a bewildering variety of corn kisses, hearts, Gibraltars, cinnamon red hots, lemon gumdrops, Zanzibars, and conversation candy — little lozenges called 'cockles,' a small crisp candy made of sugar and flour. Tucked inside each shell-shaped piece were little slips of tinted paper delicately printed with rhymes and sentiments. Often the mottoes were printed right on the candy. Some were the very pink of wit: 'Why is love like a canal boat?' 'Because it's an internal transport.' Some were daring: 'Did you wink?' and 'O you Kid.'

Smoking tobacco was just beginning to come in small bags. There was a device for snipping off the ends of cigars, over it the warning: 'Don't put your finger in the cigar cutter.' Cubebs were frowned on, but tolerated. Cigarettes were not sold at the country store, at least not at W. E. Parker's store at Harbor Springs, Michigan. Though his stock of goods was large, a subject of considerable local pride, and said to be

worth ten thousand dollars, Mr. Parker drew the line at selling packaged 'coffin nails.' He reflected the sentiments of his
community, that cigarette-smoking was a vice. The wicked
'tailor mades' were available, however, at saloons: ten for ten
cents. Community opinion on the supposed worth of the
Parker store inventory was probably close to the mark. Actual
inventory figures for a prosperous general store, located at
Canaan, Connecticut, for the year the Civil War ended and
the following five years are:

1865:	$12,184.99
1866:	11,723.87
1867:	9,726.25
1868:	9,599.28
1869:	10,596.20
1870:	10,478.31

Elegancies in the stock, such as palm-leaf fans and para-
sols, suggest that the hardest part of pioneering was over,
that countrywomen could occasionally promenade or just sit.
With the new cooking stoves went enameled kettles and cooking ware; and stove polish to keep the stove tops black and
shining clean. New shoes got blacked with the new convenient
paste form of blacking. Everyday boots were still softened
with a home concoction made of mutton fat or the same neat's-
foot oil that was used out at the barn to grease the harness.

For the shoes that had to be ready on Sunday morning to
go to Sunday school, there was Mason's Shoe Blacking (pro-
nounced 'blackin' '), put up in tin boxes with a yellow top.
'You didn't have to see the shoes to know that someone nearby
had been using Mason's — you could *smell* it,' wrote one who
'was there' in the 'seventies. 'I am sure I could recognize the
smell yet today.' A cuspidor was a necessary furnishing which
helped to make a farm kitchen cozy. Cuspidors, therefore,

were a standard store item — in tin, brass, or earthenware, hand-painted with flowers in natural colors — and sold for around a quarter. Chamber pots were for the bedroom; a welcome supplement on frosty nights to the little house out back with the stars and crescents cut in its door, and the interior decoration of chromos left over from the Grant and Colfax campaign.

Some stores sold fresh meats from an iced meat box. Canned fruits and vegetables were moved by the case to the farmers' wagons, though many did not have the money to buy them. Others were suspicious of them, and the legend that foods left in their cans became 'poisoned' probably dated from this time. Farm wives used 'glass cans' to put up hundreds of jars of meats and home produce in their own kitchens. At any rate, the meat people, the ice people, and the canners were hard at work on the food question and would in time banish the dull monotony of winter 'cellar' vegetables and salt rations.

For the baby and the trapper back in the hills, there was Gail Borden's new invention, condensed milk. For the dying there were coffins or simply coffin fixtures, if a man figured to nail up the box himself. Formerly a stark affair, death had new ornaments and appurtenances — heavy screws, the heads marked with weeping cypress and garlands, long steel tacks, nails in the shape of crosses, a set of four handles and a plate. The plates were inscribed 'Mother,' 'Our Babe,' or bore the square and compass of the Masons, the open Bible and I.O.O.F. of the Odd Fellows. There was, too, a simple, noncommittal 'At Rest.' The store had also a supply of 'mourning goods,' crinkled gray, black, and white lining materials, unbleached domestic for shrouds, usually kept decently out of sight until called for.

The remarkable number of barrels to be seen everywhere

around a country store, out back and down in the cellar, suggested the expanding productive power of the United States and the ability of the people to absorb the goods which the mills turned out. Empty barrels never stood around the premises for long. A farmer could use them in too many ways; for making cider, putting down sauerkraut, and at butchering time. There were always empty goods boxes, too, all made of soft pine wood in those days. The smaller ones were usually given to country youngsters, hungry for something of their own to take home. The lids were tacked back on the larger empties and they were stacked up back of the store. They sold for ten cents to a quarter each to farmers who converted them into feed storage bins.

Refined white sugar, once out of the reach of the average family, now came through in big quantities. It was quite a trick to blow the dust away, peck at the head of a three-hundred pound barrel with a hammer, and get the head off without spilling or getting dirt into the sugar.

Opposite the dry goods counter, with its row of upholstered cast-iron stools for the comfort of the ladies, there was another counter which ran parallel to it for the entire length of the main store. Showcases rested on it for candy, cigars, cutlery, and here the store cheese was kept under glass. Behind the counter were shelves for light groceries, tobacco, chewing gum, and patent medicines. The sugar and cracker barrels stood at the end of the counter. Nail kegs with their tops knocked in were arranged along the front. In some stores the grocery counter had an iron railing about eight inches high along the front, good for keeping the drummers and loafers from lolling there and getting in the way of the customers. There was always a back room behind the main store where 'a great hogshead of Porto Rican molasses lay on a stout frame near a large cask of beef in brine, a small cask of pickled mackerel, and a pile of dried codfish, at a safe distance from a barrel of kerosene oil.'

The cubbyhole where the merchant did his paper work also showed the spirit of change. The old stand-up desk, the quill pen, and black blotting sand were gone, and in their place the store had an up-to-the-minute roll top which gave an unbroken view of the store, equipped with steel pens, blotting paper, and wire penholders. The big store lamps overhead, with their dangling smoke bells, which were guaranteed not to explode, made the store seem a 'white way' compared with the candle and Betty lamp era.

The country store was now able to keep in stock all the goods thought necessary to getting the generations born, reared, and buried. People wanted more goods and could satisfy more of their wants than ever before. That supposes a changed farm economy. Crevecoeur's farmer, who kept a goose for its feathers, sheep for their wool, an orchard for cider, bees to fertilize the apple blossoms, and a little patch of flax or hemp for their fibers, had been obliterated by the cash crop specialist who produced commercially for the new national market, and bought what he needed at the nearest store.

This radical change created a demand for bigger, better, and more farm machinery and put the owner of the general store into the farm implement business. To the rear of the store, sometimes attached to it, was an implement shed. Here the men of the township gathered to inspect the newest developments in reapers, separators, rakes, horse mowers, plows, and cultivators. Here, too, were kept the inflammables, turpentine, linseed oil, tar, brimstone, and heavy merchandise such as household furniture, caskets, hay, grain, and patented feeds.

It would be a mistake to suppose that every trace of older days and ways was swallowed up all at once. Change is a kind

of great turning movement, with the past marching along beside the present, and keeping pace with it for a time. The
women still churned butter by hand in stone or wooden churns,
and 'put down' their surplus in big brown crocks. The chickens and eggs or garden truck and cheese, still flowed steadily
to the general store; but the difference was that they now represented side lines to the main business of the dairy, stock, or
grain farm.

Cities were growing like weeds, and the number of factories
doubling and tripling, yet the old village way of meeting local
needs had a stubborn vitality about it. The tin peddler with
his faded green wagon and flea-bitten white horse still made
his rounds, selling against the country store, and also sometimes *to* it. He still displayed his line of notions and pie pans,
stenciled canisters and coffee pots; but his planished ware no
longer came from an artisan's tin shop. It was formed by dies,
presses, and lathes under factory techniques. After the 1870's
the tinman, for the most part, had only to solder the parts together. He did it not as a self-employed mechanic but as a
factory worker.

The cobbler continued to work in his small shop down the
way from the general store, as did Grover Walter, who made
boots and shoes at Summerville, Illinois, played the flute dis-
mally, and enthralled the children of the neighborhood by a
greater accomplishment. He could crack a scaly-bark hickory
nut on his knee with his shoemaker's hammer. The cobbler
found that business was changing. He made fewer boots and
shoes to order and did more repair work. And there came a
time when he stocked a few factory-made shoes himself. As a
specialized retailer he hung out the bright new sign of a 'Boot
and Shoe' store and there it stayed — long after men ceased
to wear boots at all.

The tie-barn was still filled with horses, buggies, smells of a horsey and ammoniated variety. It was a vital spot, a kind of alternate headquarters for the loafers and tellers of droll stories. Wagons were made locally. The dripping wheel of the old mill still provided the power that ground the flour or sawed out rough boards. The local harnessmaker, with his trade sign of a wooden or plaster white horse out in front of his establishment, continued to be the man to see for a set of harness. The blacksmith was even more of a key figure, if that were possible, than he had been before, as farmers leaned on him for the repair of heavier, more complex machinery.

So the distant mill and the little near-by shop each seemed to supplement the other for a generation or so. Most of the mechanics and craftsmen who continued to flourish in the country districts were devoted to the service of the horse, and they followed their trades successfully until the automobile gave country life a new, faster rhythm. Old general store inventories show the importance of the horse, if any proof is needed, in such items as whips and collars, carriage bolts and axle grease, curry combs, brushes, horseshoe nails, and a stock of some fifteen hundred horseshoes. There were copper rivets for home repairs on the harness, cultivator points and mower teeth, lap robes and soapstone foot warmers. Just as a farmer bought fixtures for his grindstone and expected to make the mounting himself, he also expected to find whiffletree and felloe plates at the store. The wood parts, made of good seasoned hickory, he could provide himself. The automobile made over our lives; but the auto never gave us the warmth of the living animal — a friend, or sometimes an enemy, but never impersonal. Folklore gathered around the horse. It produced a race of traders. Does humor or legend gather around the used-car dealer? It was hard to feel about the car, for all its marvelous fifteen hundred parts, as our grandfathers did about horse-flesh: 'J. M. Irwin of Kane has a fast new horse,' the country correspondent would say in his weekly jottings for the *Patriot*. 'Those with ordinary three-minute nags are warned to keep out of the way or take the dust.'

The merchandise in a well-stocked country store of the later nineteenth century was a visual demonstration in commercial geography and tended to send the imagination winging on long journeys. Tea chests stood on the floor in their original straw matting, covered with Chinese characters. There was allspice from Jamaica and the East Indies; bags of almonds from Malaga and Valencia; just possibly some rare bananas from the West Indies, and indigo from Madras. There were cottons from Calcutta, and cassia bark might bear the markings of China or of Saigon or Batavia. Ginger came from Africa, peppercorns from the Dutch Guianas; green coffee in burlap bags from Mocha, Java, and Brazil.

Ships that touched at the Azores brought oranges and lemons. Figs, raisins, and citron were a reminder that Americans had long coasted around the shores of the Mediterranean. Salt came from Liverpool and the Tortugas; spice from Ceylon, fancy goods from Germany. All brought the flavor of strange place names — Campeachy, Turks Island, Madagascar — to the tight little life of town or county. Thus country store goods were linked, for those who might think of it that way, with the Spanish Main, the South Sea Islands, the doldrums, trade winds, and the Roaring Forties. The prairie farmer, who had never heard the heavy *clump* of a big roller hitting the beach, or had never licked sea salt from his lips was, whether he thought of it or not, a sharer in the schooner or packet voyages, which ended at the counter of the old familiar store at the four-corners.

With larger stocks a necessity, the country merchant began to give some thought to display. Showcases came in during this period. They had glass fronts, shaped like a mansard roof,

or curving back from the customer, the glass set in shining
German silver frames. The cases stimulated a limited amount
of departmentalization. At least they reduced the confusion.
Spectacles and inexpensive jewelry could be grouped together; knives and razors; braids, gimps, and trimmings
placed together; shaving soap, brushes, and toilet articles.
The age was getting more polite. A man shaved regularly
every Saturday or Sunday, according to whether he considered going to the store or to church more important. Manufacturers began to supply brightly lithographed posters to
be mounted in the store for advertising display. They developed special devices for showing off their goods. Thread
manufacturers had their cabinets. Dye companies and makers
of horse medicines provided the store with a variety of dis-
pensers designed to keep a comprehensive stock of their goods
in the store, and to make sure that it would be spotted in a
prominent position.

Since most of the merchandise that came into the store was
in bulk form, each sale was a slow and tedious affair. If a customer asked for plug tobacco, the clerk had to know whether
he meant cake or twist; if cake, he stepped up to the long
brown fruity-smelling slab, rested his hand on the heavy blade
of the cutter, and asked: 'Wanta five cent slice or a ten cent
slice?'

When the buyer had stated her wants in some article of dry
groceries, the merchant plunged a scoop into the bin or barrel
and out it came full of loose rice, beans, or coffee. He laid a
piece of flat wrapping paper on the scales, checked the weight,
folded and crimped the paper, tied it up with twine. There
was a nice, handy cotton twine called 'Tea Twine' for tea and
other light packages, sometimes plain white, sometimes a twist
of red and white together. The string came out of a holder
that looked like a beehive, or from the other kind, which

swung overhead and held the ball of twine in a sort of cage. Each parcel was wrapped once with a single string and tied in a bow knot. Loose pieces were carefully wrapped on a per- petual ball which was kept in the twine box. Time wasn't money, but string was.

Hardware items, like most groceries, were packaged in bulk; but carpet tacks were an exception. Here a start had been made toward consumer packaging as later generations came to know it. Early in the nineteenth century tack manu- facturers began using paper packages for ¼ lb., ½ lb., and 1 lb. quantities. These containers were shaped by the clerk on a wooden form and tied with string. Older people still remem- ber the wrapping paper used in the country stores; straw paper, it was called, brown and strong. The country retailer also needed a lighter-weight white 'tea' paper for making little cornucopias or cones into which he poured the customer's tea, spices, or other light goods and then crimped the top over to hold the goods in place.

Before the coming of the paper bag the merchant took a square sheet of wrapping paper, laid it on the counter, and poured or placed the merchandise in the center. The corners were then pulled together, crimped to prevent leakage, and tied. The resulting package looked like a modern bag and was just as substantial. It sounds easy; but just try to do up five pounds of beans or sugar that way and make a neat, present- able job of it. But the old-time clerk was just as adept at the tasks of his day as the modern check-out girl is at hers. Butter by the pound was spaded out of a crock or tub into a boat-like box of thin wood, beechwood sewed together and shaped rather like a tiny Conestoga wagon box.

Journals and ledgers of old general stores, early trade papers, catalogues, and item sheets of prices-current, fre- quently referred to 'papered coffees,' a 'paper of shoe polish,' a 'paper of corn starch,' a 'paper of farina in the one-pound size.' The 'paper' was the ancestor of the modern package or carton. A companion development to the neat carton was the paper sack or bag. The first paper bags were made right in the store by the clerks when they were not waiting on trade, dusting, or sweating over assembling a hay loader. No one knows today who invented the paper bag, or precisely when bags were manufactured in quantity by machine. This much is certain. Before the Civil War there were not any bags; and then after the war they were suddenly everywhere.

The first name in bag history that is recorded is that of Francis Wolle of Bethlehem, Pennsylvania, who was granted a patent application in 1852 for a machine that would cut roll paper, fold and paste it with flour paste, lumps and all, to make a bag. Wolle marketed his novelty in the Philadelphia area but found it tough going and made little progress during his first ten years. Production methods were primitive. Sometimes the flour paste ran out over the surface of the paper. 'Bags received,' a Beloit, Wisconsin, firm wrote to a bag plant in Chicago, 'Can't report on quality of bags until spring. Every package frozen solid.' Manufacturers soon seized upon the paper bag as a promotional device to advertise their products and supplied them, imprinted, to the trade at nominal prices, or gave them away as a premium with the purchase of goods. Many retailers, of course, had bags printed with their own chatter, embellished with a cut of an eagle, the American flag, a boot or shoe — whatever the job printer could dig out of his cut file.

A young man outfitting himself in order to keep a live country store would need a considerable variety of fixtures and equipment. He would need tin measures from a gill to a gallon; caddies and canisters for tea, coffees and spices, baking powder and saleratus. Every store had a cheese safe to keep the flies and mice away from the store cheese. One kind was made of wire, another of wood; or there was an elaborate arrangement of a cheese board, with a glass bell that could be raised or lowered by chain and counterweight. Every store had a cutter for roll paper, a feather duster or turkey wing for dusting, and a coffee mill with two big red or blue wheels. A fruit and sugar auger was needed for loosening dried fruit in the barrel and breaking up lumpy sugar. A store required a number of different kinds of scales, delicate tea scales with a little brass beam and tiny scoop, spring balances with a tin pan, butcher's scales with a marble slab, counter scales with a capacious scoop. If the storekeeper had a feed business out back, he also needed a heavy platform and hay and stock scales that would handle up to five tons, bought perhaps from Jones of Binghamton, New York — 'Jones he pays the Freight.' If he was the postmaster, there were also United States post-office scales for weighing letters and packages at the post-office window.

A good many legends have gathered around the country store scales. There was often an impression among the customers that the scales tipped in favor of the store. Yet some storekeepers were known for their 'down weight,' while others were scrupulously exact, like George Clark, who was Grand Trunk station agent, postmaster, and owner of the general store at Pennfield, Michigan, near Battle Creek. Clark was a just man. He would break a cracker, people said, to make the weight exact.

In connection with adulteration it is only fair to the country merchant to say that more often than not he was the victim, rather than the initiator, of roguery. It was a seller's market. Distant suppliers were tempted to 'shave' their goods in a day when trade was a trick and standards of identity did not exist. An estimate of the average man's mercantile morals appeared in a trade paper column called 'Brother Gardner's Philosophy': 'Remember dat while de average man will return you de k'rect change in a business transackshun, he'll water his milk an' mix beans wid his coffee.'

The manufacturer, the grower, the importer, and jobber all had a hand in adulteration, and even the articles used for adulterating purposes were themselves adulterated under the pressure of demand for 'cheap' goods. The cream was taken out of the milk, and it was fortunate if nothing worse happened to it. The mustard was sophisticated with farina. The coffee was mixed with tailings and leavings of the old crop. The middlemen then polished it, colored it with chemicals, changed the marks and packages. After arriving at a United States port, the beans were dumped out again, shoveled over, more coloring matter added to repair traces of damage in transit. Turmeric gave the beans a nice golden color; soapstone a stylish slate color. Spurious and exhausted leaves were added to the tea crop, alum and chalk to the bread, starch to the lard. Gypsum went into the pepper; pickles and preserves looked fresh and appetizingly green, thanks to salts of copper. Starch was good for stretching out baking powder. Chocolate was doctored with flour. Flour was the most common and generally useful of the adulterants; but it too was cut with plaster and potato starch.

The question naturally arises about how widespread such practices were. It is probable that price was the determining factor. Goods that were sold at the median or above for their class were, at least, pure; that is, they were what the bill of lading said, all tea or all coffee or all lard. Under that level the buyer was in a shadowland where he might very well get articles that had been damaged by sea water, temperature, or some other accident of transportation; or stretched out with substitute ingredients. If the language used in the advertisements of wholesalers addressed to the retail trade was a reflection of business realities — references were frequent to 'short weight cocoanut,' 'second class' goods, 'no chemicals,' 'sour coffee' — dishonest practices must certainly have been common among first hands. But it was the last man in line, the country merchant, who got the blame, the loss of character and good will.

The American Grocer advised retail dealers to 'Count, measure, weigh and gauge everything you buy.' One general store owner who bought his dry goods in Baltimore in the 'eighties found that on groceries he could do better in New York than in other markets. He spoke up strongly for New York, in interesting contrast to the reputation of the city around the middle of the century. 'I weigh all my sugar and coffee and other goods,' said the merchant, a little man, doing an annual gross volume of about $10,000; and he went on to say that he had 'found short weight in some of our nearer markets, but in New York the goods always hold out.'

In addition to built-in fixtures such as counters and shelving, the country store needed a coffee roaster for those customers who did not wish to roast the beans at home. The fumes of roasting coffee were one of the more agreeable additions to the composite store smell, and served as a deodorant, or at least cover-all, for the heavy odor of kerosene, the rankness of the onions, or the effects of mildew after a spell of cool wet weather. A handy tool was a fish fork, for spearing fish packed in brine. A collection of measuring faucets was a necessity, for drawing molasses and other liquids from their barrels. The latest thing was a refrigerated 'sliding cover Grocer's chest.'

Wire fly traps and fly fans were in the advance guard of new conveniences. We have to get our minds far back in time and circumstance to imagine the scale of the fly problem in the summertime before the woven wire screen appeared at doors

Buy Your

MOLASSES

OF

F. C. HUYCK.

4 Qts. to the Gallon and no sticking to the Measure.

We are using
MEASURING-FAUCETS. ✦
One of the Greatest Inventions of
the Age. We use no Funnel nor **stuck**
up Measure, but run the Molasses directly in the Jug.

IT'S A BIG CURIOSITY.

Call and see it!. Satisfy yourselves
that it will give better measure than
can be had by the old fashioned system

☞ **The Best P. R. Molasses selling for
70cts, per Gallon.**

A link between the mercantile and the industrial ages, the progressive little store of Francis Conkling Huyck, at Rensselaerville, New York, is recalled by its lineal descendant, the modern firm of F. C. Huyck & Sons, manufacturers of wool felt for countless industrial purposes. To the housewife, the company is best known for its Kenwood blankets.

and windows. On the farm the flies sailed directly from the
barn to the table butter. The sleeping baby was covered with
them, while mother sang sentimentally :

There he goes, on his toes,
Tickling baby's nose.

Certainly the country store swarmed with flies. Some goods
were covered with mosquito bar to prevent the flies from blowing. Flytraps and sticky curls of arsenic paper helped. The
clerk swung a fly switch of branches and leaves or his duster
to keep them moving. The store did what it could to 'mind the
flies'; but it was distinctly the day of chase the fly, not kill the
fly. There was an audible hum as the swarm settled on the
dried fruit. Flies gorged themselves on spilled molasses or
scatterings of sugar and smears of lard. The people shrugged
and lived with what had to be endured, since there were no
means of effectively shutting the flies out or cutting down
their numbers inside. One could not be finicky and manage to
eat at all, though like the saucy boarder, he might prefer his
flies on a separate plate.

Screens for doors and windows do not appear to have existed in 1864. There were four firms making wire products for
industrial uses in Philadelphia in 1857 — for paper making,
sieves, riddles, screens for cleaning coal, flour, rice, for making railings and trellis-work, but no mention of door screening. The U.S. Patent Office lists forty-four patents for window screening and window-screen parts before 1873; and a
patent was issued in 1868 for a wire-screen-making machine.
Allowing for the lapse of time between the issuance of a patent
and the assembly of machinery and capital for manufacturing in quantity; then allowing some more time for distribution
and public acceptance — without advertising, except in a
small way, percolating slowly from city to town, and reaching

the country neighborhoods last of all — it seems safe to suppose that the doors of general stores were not screened until the 'eighties.

A progressive merchant, Mrs. J. Q. Rapp of Geff, Illinois, known as 'the best business man in town,' had wire screening in stock in 1880. It must have been somewhat later, then, that a further attachment was invented. Some ingenious merchant took an old flour sack and cut it into one-inch strips halfway across, then doubled the uncut remainder, tacked it to the top of the screen door, and had himself an automatic fly brush. A customer entered. The strips of bagging fluttered violently. For the flies it was 23 skiddoo.

A store had to be prepared to handle goods of 'a coarse and drossy nature,' of great weight and awkward shape. F. H. Dean, at Monkton, Vermont, placed a heavy wheel or windlass in the second story, with pulleys and grapple hooks for hauling the flour and sugar up and down, while a man stood ready at the top to 'kick it out' or 'kick it in.' The same kind of tackle was used by William Lord to hoist hogsheads through the trap door to the upper story of his Brick Store at Kennebunk, Maine. Cellars were used for warehousing too. D. Thompson's store in the Genesee Valley was fixed up that way. 'Under the wide cornice at the peak of the store roof hung a huge wooden pulley from which two large ropes were fastened below' — his grandson, James Budrow, speaking. 'When I asked grandfather one day what it was for, he said, "You come down next week, when I am expecting some molasses, and you will see." '

The nearest railroad was six miles away. Freight had to be hauled in heavy wagons by four horses if the roads were dry, by oxen if wet. On this particular day the roads must have been wet, because when the wagon appeared it was drawn by oxen. There were two immense hogsheads on the wagon, and five or six men ready for the job of unloading. Great trap doors in front of the store opened up. The wagon was backed up to the opening with much hawing and geeing and liberal use of the ox goad. Heavy chains with iron hooks were attached to the casks and then to the pulley rope. A horse was hitched to the rope by a whiffletree. After two hours' time and many heavings, the molasses was finally lowered to the basement, resting on skids 'ready for the insertion of a big wooden faucet at the bottom. Quart, half gallon and gallon tin measures were on a convenient shelf ready to fill everybody's jug.' And every family had one, too, with a stout stick tied to the jug. You slipped the stick through the hole in the handle when carrying home the sweetenin'.

A new store would need a money drawer. Such drawers came with five tills, six hardwood coin hoppers, and a steel gong that sounded when the drawer was opened. The small retailer did not need a cash register; or if he did, he did not know it. The cash register salesman had not yet made his appearance with his non-cancellable contracts for the machine with ornamented cabinets, money drawers, porcelain-tipped keys, numerous bells, levers, wheels, and its important 'detail strip.' One thing he did need, the times being still plagued with counterfeiters, was the ability to keep out of his till any of the 5400 different imitations of good bank notes which were at one time known to be in circulation.

Cash or credit was the burning issue of the day among rural dealers. Mottoes and cartoons decorated the stores, pointing up the overwhelming preference of most storekeepers for cash. 'Credit is dead,' said one sloganner, 'Slow Pay Killed it.' 'Poor Trust is Dead' was lettered over the picture of a dead dog, with his name 'Trust' on his collar; 'Bad Pay Killed Him.' 'I

SMALL PROFITS & QUICK SALES.

THE GO-AHEAD PRINCIPLE.

A store proprietor was among the select few if he could tack up on his wall a sign stating that he sold goods on the cash basis — and stick to it.

gave credit,' says a dejected bankrupt. In contrast, the successful merchant, shown with a jaunty cigar and a paunch, says 'I sell for Cash.'

The old tradition of lenient credit made the cash system, however attractive on a theoretical basis, a daring move. Yet some dealers took the plunge. William T. Fulton, of Portland, Indiana, advertised: 'We will change no goods, make no tickets, nor keep any accounts in our minds against anybody.' Most merchants followed the 'trust' policy because they felt they had to. And those whose stores served a prosperous section, who knew when to grant and when to withhold credit, who relentlessly pursued the delinquent into the courts when necessary, usually died owning a farm, stock in the nearest bank, and a box of sound mortgages.

If there were more goods available than formerly, there were also more people with more wants. The central problem before the country, in an economic sense, was to build an in-

WONDERFUL DEATH BY CON=SUMPTION.

AFTER consuming thousands, Mr. **Credit** has laid down and died, at the "Rough & Ready store," in Winslow. Call on Abel Smith and he will preach his funeral sermon o=ver a lot of choice

Yankee Notions,

and a fine lot of Groceries, and a smart sprink=ling of **DRY GOODS**, togeth=er with White fish, paints, tin-ware, boots and shoes, thoroughly made, to order. Bring on your produce, and I will do your work cheap or sell you a pile of goods cheap.

Winslow, Jan 1. ABEL SMITH.

This is how a pioneer Illinois storekeeper and cobbler announced that he would grant no more credit. Another way to say the same thing: 'In God We Trust. All others cash.'

dustrial plant on a national scale which could produce the goods for a vigorous people who wanted better roads, better clothing, better homes, better nourishment for the body and the spirit: a forty-five-dollar reed organ in the parlor, a daughter who could play 'Why Should Sorrow O'er That Brow a Shadow Fling,' an ingrain carpet, and a bisque figurine of The Gleaners. Far from the country store setting, the new millionaires of industry and railroading and stock jobbing were building French chateaux on Fifth Avenue and the Gold Coast. The middling well-to-do kept a horse-and-buggy and added a piazza or gazebo. Expansion and a sense of destiny were in the air. 'Everyone talked about railroads, steamboats, mills, stores, town lots,' said a Michigan man, speaking of the world he knew in the 'seventies and 'eighties.

Through crisis and panic, through those occasional happy times when farm prices were high and goods were cheap, the country merchant kept in touch with the daily necessities and hearts' desires of his locality. If there is a time that can be fixed as the Augustan age of the general store, it was these years, the first twenty years after the Civil War. Life had eased up a bit from the labors of making pot ashes and stump fences. Flail and grain cradle, winnowing basket and dough-trough were gathering dust with the spinning wheel. The store did not seem as far away as it used to. A countryman could go down to the crossroads once in a while when he did not really need anything, just for the warmth of human society. It was good to settle into a chair beside the stove and ask a neighbor whether it was hot enough for him, or cold enough, or pleasant enough, as the state of the day and season might suggest. Sometimes it was more fun to get off some standing guy and hear an appreciative chuckle from around the stove than it was to see Beach and Bowers' Minstrel Show at the Opera House. For the cakewalking 'genuine burnt cork entertainment' came only once a year, while a customer in good standing could get in on the jollities and arguments down at the general store any time he wanted to.

It was easy to find an excuse on a snowy winter day to hitch up the team to the bobsled and dig out for the store. On a warm spring evening, come Saturday, there was no ritual more gracious than jogging along peacefully, hearing the music of a frog-and-cricket orchestra, seeing the farm families in their homes gathered around under the yellow lamplight, while anticipating a bit of 'visitin' ' at the store.

SITTIN' ROUND THE OLD STORE STOVE

THE MAN in the blue shirt hitched his poultry crate a little closer to the stove, reached around behind him for a cracker from the hospitable barrel, and wished it were not such a long way to the Herkimer cheese on the far counter. He was a personage, with a vast fund of anecdote, and reputed to be the first local citizen to see the Great Comet in 1882, and therefore best able to compare its brightness with the visitation of 1910; but on this day his topic was a Methodist camp meeting.

'Fellow over Lyndonville way says the Methodists had a camp meeting to the home of one of the elders and one of the brethren brought a stranger, a relative I guess it was, from out the state somewheres. The folks all sat in rows on the porch and sang a hymn or two. Then the presiding elder got up and asked each member for his testimony, beginning at one side — and no skipping either. Skinner responded. Brother Twombly told about how he was converted. Sister Bartlett got a bit worked up like she always did. Several hearty Methodist voices were raised saying "Amen, sister." So it went, one after the other. When the elder came to the stranger he said simply:

' "Next gentleman."

'The man looked surprised, stiffened up and said solemnly:
' "I am an Episcopal rector."
'The elder's eyes shifted to the next chair.
' "Better than nothing. Next." '

There was a nod of acknowledgment and a pause. A man on the other side of the stove craned around for a better aim at the old raisin box filled with sawdust.

'The bluejays are hollering. Guess we'll have some snow and cold by night.'

And then he resumed.

'Bill Freeland, who runs the American House livery stable over to Torrington, has thirty-eight stalls. Keeps 'em filled, too, and is willing to swap at any time. One day Bill told Fred Barnes, a young Danbury drummer with quite a hand at horses, to take care of a farmer who was itchin' to make a hoss trade.

'Fred went out and looked over the farmer's horse — eyes, teeth, legs, and so on; it was an old skate for sure.

'The farmer found a horse that he liked in the livery barn and asked:
' "What do you want to trade?"
'Fred said: "Your horse and one hundred dollars."
' "And fifty dollars," corrected the farmer.

'They finally called it a trade. The farmer gave his horse and seventy-five dollars. When the dicker was made, Freeland came out and watched while the harness was exchanged. As the farmer lifted the lines he looked at Freeland.
' "I know you're as crooked as a cork screw, but is that horse all right?"
' "As far as I can see he's all right," said Bill. But Fred noticed that he closed his eyes just before he spoke. Later Freeland told young Barnes "That horse's got the lightest rear of any horse in that barn. When that man touches him with a

whip his old buggy will be scattered from here to Goshen." '

There is an easy pause. Somebody says 'Nope, you can't judge a horse by its harness.'

'My muscles are all corded up with rheumatiz,' confided another member of the circle. He received a number of prompt suggestions for a cure.

'Carry a potato.'

'Tie a piece of cat fur around the place where it hurts.'

'Cut your fingernails on Friday.'

'Put on your left sock first.'

'Wear a ring made out of a horseshoe nail.'

'Chaw some Canady thistle root, like I do. Knocks the creaks an' aches right outa ye,' advised an old codger respected for his 'root n' yarb l'arnin'.'

The talk shifted to a couple who were known to be quarreling. The considered opinion was: 'They'll never comb gray hair together.'

The assemblage of loungers who graced the front stoop of the general store in summer, and ranged themselves around the stove in the winter, usually drifted in during the morning, to get their mail and read the announcements which had been tacked up since yesterday. There would be a G.A.R. installation and supper. A box social was to be held at the Swamp College district school. Mlle Carlotta would make a balloon ascension at the County Fair, and the thought came instantly that a fellow who got there early might be selected to hold one of the trailing lines.

Sometimes the regulars would make some small purchase, and then sit until somebody said it was time to go home. As one man said, he waited all morning for the morning mail. When it came, he started waiting for the afternoon mail. Another member of the junto would sit and talk until finally he would pull his watch out, take a look, and exclaim:

'Gosh, half-past ten, and I promised my wife I'd be home by ten.' Then he settled back with the remark: 'Wall, she's mad as she can be now. Might's well stay another hour.'

Before there were stoves, the rural philosophers gathered around the fireplace. Only the tavern and the barber shop have ever offered serious competition to the old general store as a place of male refuge, where a man could spit, scratch, and make up stories which everyone enjoyed and nobody believed, in an atmosphere of *gemütlichkeit*. The tavern's chief attraction was its stock of liquor. The country store was also plentifully supplied, down to the time when the local 'Cold Water Army' got busy. The barber shop offered free reading matter, but so did the store. Since the storekeeper kept the post office too, the newspapers were generally well read in the store before they reached the hands of the subscribers. Anyway, a visit to the barber shop cost money and was a sometime thing, while the trip to the store was a daily necessity. The store had the edge in another way. It maintained a checker game. The board rested on a nail keg — old, battered, greasy with use. When a checker got lost, a new one was improvised from sections of corn cob, with one set charred to make the blacks.

The loafers were hardly profitable to the proprietor; but they were accepted and their habits endured. In a day when almost every adult male raised in the country chewed tobacco, the store owner was forced in self-defense to provide a facility known as the spit box. Sometimes it was large, square, with the stove set right in its middle. Again it was a bucket or coal hod filled with sawdust. The spryer club members often preferred to open the door of the stove and drench the fire. There is a legend that some general store stoves had doors on all sides so the marksman could shoot from all quarters without moving.

The habitués were generally loyal to their club; that is, if

This chair is typical of those upon which the sitters sat, telling their wonder tales, noting the comicalities of human character, advising Pa what to do when he had 'a misery in his stommick,' or planning some plain devilment.

there was more than one general store in the vicinity, each one had its own clientele. This attachment to his premises was not always appreciated by the dealer, who would often have gladly parted with his uninvited guests if he could have done so.

'I am a storekeeper,' said one exasperated merchant in a newspaper advertisement, 'and am excessively annoyed by a set of troublesome animals, called Loungers, who are in the daily habit of calling at my store, and there sitting hour after hour, poking their noses in my business, looking into my books whenever they happen to lie exposed to their view, making impertinent inquiries about business, which does not concern them, and ever and anon giving me a polite hint that a little grog would be acceptable.'

However, the occupants of whatever there was to sit on — tavern chairs, the long wooden bench or settle, a scattering of kegs and dry goods boxes — were firmly established as a fixture in country society. While the merchant moved from bin to scales with a scoop or ruler in his hand, the town worthies whittled, discussed, and at times just sat, in a comfortable silence.

There was the 'Judge,' with a firmly-established reputation for wisdom; beside him, the local oracle, a man of too many words, a gossip, and something of a nuisance. The Great Objector never failed to introduce the doubt, the defect, the dark side of the argument. Younger men sat silent among the patriarchs, growing restless and drifting in and out of the circle unless some fun was up. The selectman or a busy doctor might stop by the store to warm his hands. A dog sprawled at full length under the chairs, a lesson in relaxation. There was often more silence than sound. Inside the store, the tick of the old wall clock, the rise and fall of voices, sudden gusts of laughter, the snapping of the fire, all muted sounds until a customer blew in, huffing and stamping and edging up to the warmth. Outside, a gust of wind threw snow against the doors with a raking noise. The pawing of a horse could be heard, the creak of leather as the horse nudged at the hitching rack or strained to reach a scattering of oats from yesterday's dinner.

This was the place and these the characters for local history. Here the 'masculine in-group,' as an anthropologist might say, handed down an oral tradition of bold rascals and colorful outlaws, departed captains and local kings; the memory of lost causes; of crackpots, frauds, fanatics, of hunting prowess, medical potions, and weather lore; of prodigies, heroes, ghosts, and odd personages generally. The group around the stove also acted as a sort of informal press association which gathered, processed, and distributed the news of the community and provided it with drama and incident, while entertaining themselves and the clerks with pranks and whoppers.

Sometimes the sitters seemed to be just a social club; again a forum for democratic debate. The topics discussed ranged over many fields of interest — the new preacher, who was in a state of grace, the idea of immaculate conception as well as some modern instances of the ordinary kind, crop prospects, aches and pains, and the proper way to train a bird dog. They talked of birth and death, of government and elections, and always of the weather. Here the old soldier 'shouldered his crutch and showed how fields were won.' And here the story of the awkward swain was passed around, how he took his girl to the county fair in a buggy. As they drove past the popcorn stand the belle remarked, 'My, that popcorn smells good.' And his reply, 'Tell you what, I'll drive up close's I can so you can smell it real good.'

Vivacious incidents from the lives of the neighbors were shaped into anecdotes around the store stove with rare mimicry and a superb sense of pause and timing. When Uncle Homer Mullinix tramped into Fayetteville, Arkansas, from the Ozark hills to make his will, his wife went shopping at the general store, which had just been hooked up to an early cow pasture telephone line. All finished up with the lawyer, Uncle Homer attempted to make his first telephone call to his wife at the store, just as a violent electric storm broke. As he cranked up the box and leaned into the long-necked transmitter the lightning struck the wire. 'It's her, all right!' he shouted, happily.

And they told, in Michigan, of Miz' Lou Esty, an itinerant seamstress who went from house to house to sew and mend. One evening at a neighbor's supper table it was mentioned that someone had broken a mirror.

'I've broke mirrors,' said Miz' Esty.

'And you didn't have any bad luck?' inquired Mrs. Thompson, her employer at the moment.

'Nothin' I can remember. Of course,' she added negligently, 'Esty died that fall, but I wouldn't count that.'

'Neither would I,' agreed Mr. Thompson.

Various jocular names were applied to the little coterie of relaxed countrymen whose quick humor, quirky personalities, and shrewd sense of values were synthesized into something that came to be called 'cracker box' philosophy. Sometimes they were called the Liars' Club. The justice of the peace at Gurleyville, Connecticut, named the ringside sitters at the Cross store there 'the House of Commons.' 'Everyone spoke the language to which he was accustomed,' Wilbur Cross recalled of the Gurleyville parliamentarians, 'however profane or indecent it might be. Never before nor since have I heard so many double negatives for emphasis; never before so many allusions to sexual and other functions of the human body or to the hencoop or barnyard. It was the raciest speech God or Satan ever put into the mouth of man.'

The stories about horse-trades were endless, pointing up a code of deceit under which the seller made statements of fact about the horse which would be sure to mislead the buyer, who also hoped to skin his adversary if he could. The real issue at stake, as both participants and interested spectators knew, was to establish the fact that the winner was the better man.

'Feller in Mechanic Falls used to be smoother n' a pussy-willow. Sold a team guaranteed to be willin'. The man that bought 'em couldn't get any work out of the horses, and went back to the seller about the deal.

' "I thought you said these horses were willing."

' "So I did," said the seller — trader name of Perkins — "They sure are. One's willing to stop. The other's willing to let him." '

Henry Hartwell was reluctant about selling a particular cow to Joe Fields, who had heard Mrs. Hartwell call out to her husband, 'Don't you sell the pail-filler, Henry.' Joe pricked up his ears at that. He just had to have that particular cow. It took one hundred dollars to get her. After he drove her home he soon found out what kind of a pail-filler she was—a two-quart one.

The box-stove democrats paid particular attention to the doings of those whose pretensions were somewhat in advance of the general run. Deacons and elders were a special target. From time to time a deacon, even as other men, was known to try his hand at a horse trade. One considered to be a 'leetle nigh' on a trade, volunteered to an eager buyer, 'Wall, I'll allow that you'll be real pleased to see that horse go up hill.'

The man bought the horse, but was soon back. 'The pesky critter balked at the first rise; tho't you sed she was a prime goer!' 'Not jest so,' answered the elder. 'I said you'd be pleased to see her go up a hill; naow wouldn't you?'

Another deacon was accused of putting water in his milk. He denied the charge vigorously. Then his hired man got mad and quit. Of course he talked. The deacon told the literal truth. He put the water into his milk pail first and then milked into it.

'Deaconing' the apples meant topping off the barrel with the best, but by no means typical, specimens. Prudent sellers have been known to 'deacon' *both* ends. A similar operation was known as 'stove-piping the potatoes.' A section of stove-pipe was inserted into a bag of potatoes. The big ones were dropped in outside the stovepipe. Then the pipe was filled with culls and little fellows, the pipe gently withdrawn.

The parson was seldom the butt of the joke. Usually he was credited with shrewdness, an apt wit, and the last word. For fifty years the Reverend Timothy Alden had preached to his little flock at Old Yarmouth, Massachusetts, and they had faithfully supplied the parsonage with firewood as a part of the salary agreement. Then there came a day one cold winter when the woodpile was exhausted and the congregation forgot their obligation. No wood was delivered on the day it was expected. The following Sunday the Reverend Timothy preached from Proverbs xxvi, 20: 'Where there is no wood, there the fire goeth out.'

Braman Ayers, a real old-time shouting Methodist, who preached in Berkshire County in the western part of Massachusetts, was driving past his brother's home when he sniffed the fragrance of his sister-in-law's own special version of johnnycake. It was just at noontime, too. So he reined in his horse and turned into the yard, to the dismay of his sister-in-law who knew his capacity. Quickly she pushed the fragrant yellow cake out of sight, and put ordinary bread on the tablecloth, reminding the minister, somewhat breathlessly, that it was time to say grace.

'Oh Lord,' said the Reverend, 'bless this food prepared for our use, and bless the johnnycake — *under the stove.* A-h-men!'

The pranks the 'House of Commons' boys enjoyed were crude and earthy by polite standards. Many were common and 'meaner than pusley.' Some of the boys would slip out and loosen the nuts on the buggy wheels of a customer who might be unpopular with the coterie. After he got well started homeward, loaded down with his purchases, the buggy would shed its wheels, one by one. A small circus had its main and only tent pitched beside the railroad tracks at Fairbury, Illinois, when the McDowell brothers, Elmer, Tom, and Johnny, had some kind of a ruckus with the circus roustabouts that left the McDowells feeling a mite aggrieved. So they thoughtfully tied a rope from the circus tent to the caboose of a P.T.& W. freight train which was standing near by. When the train pulled out, so did the tent.

It was great fun to turpentine a dog just to see Jowler jump and tear off howling down the road. Years ago one store had an enormous tomcat who had the full use of the premises and took his ease with a full sense of his hereditary rights. One day a clerk was painting an address on some shipping cases with a brush dipped in a mixture of lampblack and turpentine. Just at that moment the cat strolled by, his tail arched over his back, with an air of owning the establishment. The clerk reached down and daubed the cat from the rear with the brush. For a second the cat wore an expression of bewilderment and acute disbelief. Then the turpentine really took hold. He dug his claws in the floor and took off with a screech, charging right through the women customers, knocking down displays, and creating, it was agreed, a memorable scene.

When business was slow it was also good fun to get geese drunk on whiskey-soaked corn. That was easy to do since both ingredients were always handy.

'Uncle Jim' Rupert, who had a good run of trade in Rockport, Illinois, owned a dog called Jim Pug. Jim Pug was allowed to range around freely and do some scrounging at the store. Jim Pug was fond of eggs. When he was hungry he would roll an egg out of the tub in which it was stored, to the great pleasure of the crowd. This was before the invention of the modern egg case, with its flats and fillers. Eggs went to market in tubs packed around with straw, oats, or sawdust. Jim Pug was very neat about his trick, but he was choosey too. Unless the egg was fairly fresh he would break it and then let it lie broken on the floor.

Carson Rupert was always teasing the dog. One of his favorite tricks was to tie a string to a chunk of meat and give it to Jim. The dog would gulp it down, and then Carson would pull on the string. Jim would squat back, grunt, growl, scratch with his feet, and create a general disturbance each time the string was pulled. The boys were delighted. Jim Pug was quite an attraction and advertising medium for the store.

Evenings and wet days, the clerks tried to look busy when the boss raised his eyes from his books, and yet give their full attention to the high jinks around the stove.

'In nearly every New England village, at the time of which I write,' said Barnum, 'there could be found from six to twenty social, jolly, story-telling, joke-playing wags and wits, regular originals, who would get together at the tavern or store, and spend their evenings and stormy afternoons in relating anecdotes, describing their various adventures, playing off practical jokes upon each other, and engaging in every project out of which a little fun could be extracted by village wits whose ideas were usually sharpened at brief intervals by a "treat," otherwise known as a glass of Santa Cruz rum, old Holland gin, or Jamaica spirits . . . Our store was the resort of all these wits, and many is the day and evening that I have hung with delight upon their stories, and many the night that I have kept the store open until eleven oclock, in order to listen to the last anecdotes of the two jokers who had remained long after their companions had gone to rest.'

Impromptu comments made by a stove-side sitter would sometimes strike his auditors as having a special felicity, in which case they would be passed around and remembered. Someone saw old Creed Taylor roll a cigarette using a page torn from Hostetter's Almanac for his cigarette paper. The result was a fearsome thing, about six inches long; round, firm, and fully packed with fine-cut tobacco. One of the boys ventured to make an observation upon it.

'That's not good for your health, Mr. Taylor,' he said.

The old man snorted. 'I don't smoke for my health.'

It is a pleasure to report that Mr. Taylor escaped the consequences of indulgence in his king-size cigarettes. Local tradition says that whiskey, not tobacco, killed him; at the age of 113.

Again, the club members sided with law and order when a member had had a brush with the law, because of its appreciation of the artistic form in which the judge cast his verdict:

Little drops of whiskey, little bits of fun
Go to make the fine and cost, nine fifty-one.

The country store provided a receptive audience for the teller of tall tales. Two natives were boasting of their fishing prowess. Said Sam: 'I was usin' a bass plug I made myself out on Seymour Lake and I caught a small mouth bass. Believe it or not, but that bass weighed five and a quarter pounds.'

There was a polite silence. Then Ezry spoke up: 'That's nothin'. I was fishin' for bullhead last night down here at the mouth of the crick when I felt somethin' yankin' on my line. I pulled it up and found I'd hooked onto a lantern, and what's more the durn thing was lit.'

There was an incredulous silence. Then Sam said: 'Ezry, if you'll put that lantern out, I'll take two pounds off my bass.'

Uncle John asked Abe when they met down at the general store if he got his hay wet in the last shower.

'Nope,' was the reply. 'Just had a few scatterings to pick up. 'Bout half a load, I'd say. Had old Kit and Joe. They just can't be beat. I saw the shower comin' and started back on the run. It rained on the back of the hay frame all the way, but never wet my load at all.'

'Once when my father was going up to the lakes,' Frank Greenfield would say, referring to old Bill Greenfield who flourished in Saratoga County, New York, 'he saw a flock of pigeons on a limb and decided to catch them. He didn't have any bullets; so he put his jack-knife in the muzzle of his gun.

The knife split the limb open and then it snapped back, catching ninety-nine pigeons by their toes. Someone asked him why he didn't make it a hundred and be done with it. He just grinned and said he wouldn't lie for one pigeon.'

Bill came naturally by his fertile imagination, for his father before him, Abner, was known on occasion to 'get off some remarks.' Abner took Bill hunting one bitterly cold winter day. They set a stump on fire to get warm, 'but the cold was still so intense that the blaze, forty feet high, froze in a column. Abner went into a cave to get warm. He tried to talk, but no words came; so, after a pull at a bottle, he and Bill went home. On the next Fourth of July, Bill happened to go into that same cave, when he was startled to hear Abner's words, just thawing out of the air, saying, "Here, Bill, have a drink." '

City men seldom think about the weather while country folk seldom forget it. Weather was an intimate reality to a farmer, the phases of the moon, the slow turning of the seasons, or any striking portent in the night sky. Each out-of-the-ordinary occurrence was likely to be set down in the country merchant's chronicle; such as the Lewis County, New York, account book with a note on a year of drought: 'The hay crop in the summer of 1862 was about half a crop.'

Certain days or years were marked by extraordinary natural phenomena, such as a great storm, an eclipse, or a comet and so were remembered long afterward. The early pioneers in Illinois, for example, told and retold the story of the winter of the big snow. It was three feet on the level, they said, only some said four. Came in November and stayed 'til April. Hog and hominy got mighty scarce. And there was actual suffering when whiskey went up to a dollar and a quarter a gallon.

Just how the sun disappeared, just how the darkness came, and how the people felt was passed along from one tongue to another for generations. Such was the Yellow Day of 6 September 1881, which excited wonder and dread among the ignorant and superstitious; and similarly the Dark Day of 2 November 1819; or its great predecessor of 19 May 1780, when birds ceased to sing and chickens flew up to their roosts as though it were night. Cows bellowed fretfully at the pasture bars, and there was such terror abroad that 'men prayed, and women wept.'

In the Berkshire hills a local memory was the last summer of the Civil War when it got so hot that the thermometer hovered around 90 degrees for seven weeks, with no rain. It was told for years afterward how the smoke from the burning forests of Canada drifted over southern Berkshire, making the sun a red globe at midday; and August potatoes were no larger than marbles.

Maine men told of the great September gale of 1869, and in the vicinity of Belfast it was said that an extraordinary display of the northern lights in the autumn of 1811 foretold the second war with Britain. At Morrill, the aurora borealis appeared as armies marching and counter-marching. Formations that appeared to be platoons and regiments were seen to advance, then wheel and turn and retreat; and all the while the eerie lights performed the most complicated and endless evolutions of a military character.

At least one revered and stoutly rational almanac-maker, Robert B. Thomas, proprietor of *The Farmer's Almanack*, threw the full weight of his great authority against all fears and apprehensions, advising that instead of looking for signs about human destiny in the natural world, the husbandman and goodwife would be better employed at grafting their fruit trees, cutting wood, making sugar, 'and other matters.'

Probably the experience with weather which bit in most deeply on our racial memory was the season that our forebears called 'The Lean Year,' 'The Year of the Corn Famine,' or 'The Year Without a Summer.' In 1816, from New England to Pennsylvania, a cold, backward spring was followed by a summer of frigid disaster. Ice formed an inch thick in May. On 3 June there were three inches of snow in New York state, ten in Vermont. On 5 July the ice was as thick as window glass on the ponds. That month the corn and garden sass gave up and died. August was worse — a half an inch of ice. The unripened corn was cut down, the blades and stalks dried for fodder. Rations were short for man and beast in the northeastern part of the country that winter, with the 1815 corn saved for the 1817 seed. A summer's work gone for nothing, and empty stomachs, served as sharp aids to memory. Many men just quit, got fired up with the 'Ohio fever,' and emigrated to the western country.

A man could learn a lot about weather signs around a country store if he was of a mind to listen :

Frost comes six weeks after you hear the first katydid.

Plant root crops in the dark of the moon ; if you don't they will go all to tops.

When you blow out a candle, if the wick smoulders a long time, bad weather is in prospect. If it goes out quickly the weather will be fair.

When the camphor bottle is 'riley' a storm is brewing.

Frost is out of the ground when you hear the first frogs.

Plant corn when the oak leaves are the size of a squirrel's ear.

Tomato plants set out when the sign is in the Twins will bear smooth tomatoes.

The countryman needed the most reliable information he could get about rain. 'Rain before seven,' they said, 'Clear before 'leven.' When chimney smoke falls to the ground, that means rain. Sundogs predict rain. A ring around the moon means stormy weather. Rub a cat's fur the wrong way, and sparks will mean cold weather. The last Friday in each month sets the weather for the next month. Other signs of rain were frisky animals, the cry of tree toads, a mackerel sky, mare's tails streaked across the sky. A buzzing in telegraph wires meant a change in the weather.

A hard winter was coming when the squirrels put away a big store of nuts. This evidence could be validated by examining the husks on the corn. If they were thicker than usual and the apple skins were tougher, the squirrels were right! Not precisely weather data, but a useful saying around a farm was the rhyme:

> *On Candlemas Day*
> *Half the wood*
> *And half the hay.*

That is, on 2 February, the prudent farmer had better check up. If he had used more than half of his woodpile or half of the hay in the mow, he would surely run short before spring and he had better set about finding some way to replenish his supply.

A good deal of practical information about farming, before the days of agricultural colleges and government experiment stations, was passed around at the country store. A pig with a curly tail fatted easily. Eggs should be set so they will hatch in the sign of Cancer. Put a setting of thirteen or fifteen under the hen; always an odd number. Never set a hen on Sunday. When there was a death in the family it was important to 'tell the bees,' for they would die or go away if not included in the family circle in time of mourning. 'Cradle your rye,' the folks said, 'on the Fourth of July.'

A good listener could pick up numerous pithy sayings expressing general truths about human frailty along old store counters. 'If three persons of the same first name come together you may be pretty sure one of them is a fool.' This item of gnomic wisdom was obviously based upon sound actuarial probability. Another folk saying with more humility in it: 'If all fools wore white caps, we should all look like geese.'

This narrative has dwelt on traditional sayings, bodacious tales, jokes and capers, because the evidence is so abundant that the country store provided the perfect environment for the cultivation of these lively arts. And yet, to deal adequately with rural Americans as they were, it must be recognized that there was another side to the life of a farming people who lived upon the bosom of nature. They had a vein of sentiment and sadness, this breed of earlier Americans who were so close to the earth and the great galaxies of the night sky, who sensed the unity of the living world in field and wood lot, in the animals of the farm, and in the march of the human generations. Men and women who heard the cry of birth regularly in their own homes, who had hacked out a hillside grave in a February thaw, who had stood helplessly while a hail storm shattered their wheat or the cholera took their hogs — these people extracted a hard living from the soil and still found some sweetness in their days. Poetry lurked in their hyperbole and sudden laughter sustained them in their pains.

We have an impression of the droll stories told around the general store by a man with an original vein in him. We should not suppose that his perceptions were insensitive as he listened to the secret sound of snow water, trickling under ice at 'sugaring off' time. For men do not speak of such matters. A man could not in all decency say that he had lifted up his eyes unto the hills, unless he made it clear and plain that he was simply quoting from the Bible. He could not tell of a time when his heart leaped as he watched his mare and her colt at play in the upper meadow; but it was entirely fit and proper to discuss an interesting case of heartburn. And if he did, a good deal of lore about medicine and health would be made available to him at once, some having to do with the 'patents,' the proprietary medicines which stood in rows on the store shelves, some having to do with old medications made up from traditional family recipes and compounded in the home kitchen. None were without effect if they contained enough alcohol.

They generally did, as we shall see in the next chapter.

ONE FOR A MAN, TWO FOR A HORSE

'WHAT KIND OF WHISKEY are you drinking nowadays,
George?' the boys around the store would ask in the 'eighties
when George pointed his cane at invisible piles of rebel dead,
and recalled once more how the general had ridden up to him
on his white horse at Antietam, shouting: 'George! Stop the
slaughter. You've killed enough!'

'Never touch it,' George would say. 'Nothing for me but
Plantation Bitters,' indicating the shelf. 'I'll take a bottle
now.'

Nearly every country store had a patent medicine shelf beside the cattle powders and poultry remedies, which was not as
incongruous as it might seem. Many of the concoctions were,
like Dr. Bennett's Golden Liniment, 'for horses . . . equally
as efficacious as upon the human family.' The *curative powers*
of the Golden Liniment, its *emollient properties* and its

234

healthy stimulant effect, worked just as well on such equine disorders as poll-evil, spavin, ringbone, foundered feet, mange, and windgalls, as upon rheumatism, chilblains, erysipelas, bunions, and ingrown toenails.

Country people liked their pills and draughts. The solitude of life on hundreds of thousands of nineteenth-century farms, its introspective quality, the struggle to turn forest or prairie sod into a farm stimulated men to seek rum and whiskey as an anodyne, or the solace of the 'medicine habit.' A dose from a 'patent' bottle was reasonably certain to give the sufferer a boost, since the formula included either a narcotic or a good slug of whiskey. 'Had taken only one bottle when I felt the effect,' said Densmore Z. Smith of South Lincoln, Maine. Once the despair of eight doctors, Smith became one of the best friends the Dana Sarsaparilla Company ever had. He knocked off five bottles and felt like a new man.

Hostetter's Celebrated Stomach Bitters contained varying amounts of alcohol at different times, pleasantly flavored with oil of anise, coriander, and gentian. At one time the alcoholic content was twenty-five per cent and the recommended daily dose was six tablespoonfuls, or about one-and-a-half ounces of straight whiskey. No wonder some dealers sold it either by the bottle or the drink. Many a good church member of sound temperance principles accumulated an impressive collection of bitters bottles out in the barn, taking his daily dram as a preventive, a tonic, a builder-upper, a diuretic, and as an alterative, without dreaming that the blessed gift of the Vegetable Kingdom, straight from Nature's Own Laboratory, made him feel frisky because it was spiked. If he did, he never mentioned it.

Bitters were a large and popular classification. Quaker Bitters was for dyspepsia and the blood. The Quaker Bitters folks gave away trade cards showing chromolithographs of angelic little girls in pink and blue sashes. The tots presumably suggested the innocence and purity of the tipple. Drake's Plantation Bitters, a favorite of the 1860's and '70s, had a cryptogram on the bottle, 'S.T. 1860X,' which was the subject of endless argument and ingenious theorizing along the country store benches. The talk and the guessing helped to advertise the bitters. Alliterative names were in great favor, like Sands Sarsaparilla, Radway's Ready Relief, or Burdock Bitters. The 'S.T. 1860X' business was finally resolved as meaning 'Started Trade in 1860 with ten dollars capital,' but Mr. Drake, the bitters man, was reported as saying that it did not mean anything. It was 'our scheme to make people ask questions.' The idea was similar to that later devised by C. W. Post for his Postum, the celebrated coffee substitute: 'There's a Reason.' This slogan became famous but Post never disclosed what the reason was. At any rate, the basic ingredient of many proprietaries was Santa Cruz rum, and the 'misery' in the farmer's stomach was alleviated as the medicine 'took holt.'

Another bitters name of great note was 'Dr. Stoughton's Elixir,' a household remedy compounded of wormwood, germander, rhubarb, orange peel, cascarilla, and aloes. It came in a bottle with a special shape; it must have been short and fat, not tall and long. It sat stolidly and was hard to tip over. Stoughton's was so popular and the bottle so familiar that it became a figure of speech. 'There he sat, like a Stoughton bottle,' people would say to indicate one who was dull, heavy, or unresponsive. Today we can only conjecture what the Stoughton bottle looked like, unless the antiquarians who collect old bottles can tell us. Yet it remains as a measure of fame that a patent medicine bottle got into the language and the dictionaries.

There were fashions in medications. At one time pills were popular; again it was lozenges. Pastes and elixirs had their day. Sarsaparilla had a big run. The medicines were sold by agents on commission, and through them finally reached the retailers in the country trade. The dividing line between a drugstore and a general store was often not distinct. Drugstores sold dye-woods, turpentine, alcohol, liquor, paints and varnishes, glassware, often a line of notions and some groceries, non-proprietary drugs such as calomel and quinine — and of course the patent medicines. So did the general store. The agency for a 'patent' that was in popular demand amounted to a monopoly. Profit margins were enormous even in a day when long profits were the usual thing. The medicine shelf in the country store was regarded as a busy little moneymaker.

W. M. McNeil, of Lafayette, Indiana, who had sold a country store six dozen of Pain Exterminator at three dollars per dozen, which retailed at a dollar a bottle, paid the transportation on the order, as well he might, considering the few cents the stuff cost him. Of course, the Scot did not pay out *cash*. As he told his customer, 'I put in four extra bottles to pay part or all of express charges. I always pay one dollar in medicine on orders of six dozen or upwards.' The McNeil deal, with a spread of 400 per cent between the merchant's cost and the selling price, appears quite conservative compared with the easy money that was made out of the electric belt. This device, a drugless form of quackery, a thing of gimcracks and spangles which the patient wrapped around his middle, was alleged to work on the 'galvanic' principle, and at one time had a great vogue. Hustlers could buy it for less than ten cents and retail the belt, in the good old days, for two dollars and fifty cents to 'weak men' and to women with female complications. But the manufacturers of the bottled goods did all right too. 'Nature's Creation,' a consumption cure, which sold at five dollars retail, cost its maker twenty-four cents a bottle.

Contrary to popular belief, the medicines were not 'patented.' They were the secret formula of an owner who used the word 'patent' to suggest that the U.S. Patent Office had found in his formula qualities of uniqueness, new principles, or some new sort of use. In case a patent actually had been granted, the remedy then would not be secret, since its composition would have to appear in the patent specifications. This was the last thing in the world the 'doctor' desired. The fact was, the names were simply trade names that had been registered in Washington as the name of a commercial property. The formula was a mystery and the curative powers whatever the owner's conscience and imagination might be able to agree upon. A legal patent had another serious disadvantage. It would become public property in seventeen years. The registered trade name was good for all eternity.

The owners of a medicine business were either self-styled 'Doctors,' 'Professors,' Indians, or corporations which carefully personalized their products in their dealings with the public. The brand name was Dr. So-and-So's vermifuge or anodyne. On the label was the picture of a man, presumably the brilliant doctor himself, bearded and benign; a figure as reassuring as the white-coated Man of Science who adorns today's national advertising, fiddling with his test tubes and announcing astonishing triumphs and discoveries about vitamins and chlorophyl.

Strychnine was used in tonics, to give a good belt to the appetite. Morphine or some opium derivative was also a base ingredient in the pain killers which were advertised on billboards, barns, and the walls of country stores. There was a craze at one time for petroleum, under the name of Seneca or rock oil, and again for the tomato. The tomato came into favorable medical notice in the 1830's. It was discovered to be a 'powerful deobstruent,' whatever that sesquipedalian word may mean. Tomato extracts had their season in the sun under such names as Phelps' Compound Tomato Pills or Dr. Miles' Compound Extract of Tomato. Little was said about the formulas, which must have borne a strong family resemblance to each other, and to chili sauce, but great enthusiasm went into depicting their wonderful effects upon bilious attacks.

Dr. J. C. Ayer's Sarsaparilla was recommended for a harrowing list of disorders, including a very deep-seated one, 'debility peculiar to spring.' It contained 'the Sarsaparilla-root of the tropics, Stillingia, Yellow Dock, Mandrake, and other roots held in high repute.' No quantitative detail, of course; and no mention of *spiritus frumenti*, which was what did the business.

Robert P. Letcher, an influential Kentuckian in Congress, whom John Quincy Adams called a man of 'moderate talents, good temper, playful wit, and shrewd sagacity,' demonstrated his qualities in giving an account of the entrepreneurs of the cure-all:

'Any idle mechanic, not caring longer to drudge at day labor, by chance gets a dispensatory, or some old recipe book, and poring over it, or having it read to him (for many of these present doctors cannot read), finds that mercury is good for the itch, and old ulcers; that opium will give ease; and that a glass of antimony will vomit.

'Down goes the hammer, or the saw, razor, awl, or shutter — and away to work to make electuaries, tinctures, elixirs, pills, plasters and poultices' for expelling 'these supposed worms, which never existed but in their brains.' A man who might stand as the exemplar of the type was Thomas W. Dyott, an individual of vast energy and effrontery, who polished boots by day in a Philadelphia cellar and made shoe-blacking by night. Prospering, he conferred the degree of Doctor of Medicine upon himself, successfully spread a line of pills, drops, cordials, and ointments to the farthest western settlements, lived in high style, with an English coach and four horses, in the most elegant establishment of its sort in Philadelphia County. A colleague, 'Doctor' Swaim, was a former harnessmaker. An enterprising constable of Conners-ville, Indiana, barely able to write his own name, became trans-formed into 'Doctor' Chism, who advertised as a 'Root Doc-tor and No Calomel.' Gail Borden, eccentric inventor and homeopathic 'Doctor,' got his degree of medicine in his own cellar-laboratory. 'It is no use to be a doctor unless you put on the airs of one,' he said.

Although the patent medicine business was an ancient one, it rose to new heights of prosperity with the alliance between the medicine-makers, the newspapers, and the popular farm, family, and religious magazines. Advertising was what was needed for the promotion of the lotions, drops, ointments, bal-sams, berries, barks, and extracts. Once it was applied, they poured out of the 'medical warehouses' in a vast volume onto the store shelves. A popular journal characterized the 1840's as the age of 'rail-roads, Ericsson propellers, miracle-working pills, and medicated candy.' The publisher of the country newspaper got the advertising revenue and often sold the medicine too, along with his 'squares' of white space, his job printing, subscriptions, and stationery.

Philadelphia was the chief port of entry for bringing in English drugs and chemicals, as well as a seat of medical learn-ing; so that the city became known as 'the American medical center.' A 'Philadelphia doctor' was the object of hostile in-nuendoes from the irregulars who described the regular physi-cian as a monopolist and conservative, so wedded to his lancet and calomel that medical progress, as represented by yarb and root learning, had simply passed him by. The new school was aggressive. A Dr. S. D. Merriam, who set up at Ashley Falls, Massachusetts, and practiced Indian herb medicine, advertised that as a result of years spent among the western Indians, he could diagnose an illness without a word being spoken by the patient. This was formidable competition indeed for the doctor of the classical school who relied upon the stethoscope and often had to ask the patient to stick out his tongue.

An economist, writing in the middle years of the nineteenth century of Philadelphia's eminence in distributing medicines to the farthest clearings of the South and West, wrote: 'Wherever a few backwoodsmen have reared their lonely cabins, an agency for these preparations is established; and so remote and isolated are some of the frontier posts, that a box shipped hence cannot reach its destination in a year.' The total annual sales out of Philadelphia in 1858 of bitters, syrups, and cattle powders was estimated at a million dollars wholesale. Whatever effect these medicines had on public health, they contributed heavily to the prosperity of paper mills, glass works, printing and engraving shops, lithographers, box factories, magazines and newspapers. One medicine factory had a printing shop that turned out 2,600,000 almanacs for free distribution. All were enlisted in selling the great pyramids of pills which were drying in the pill room, the pills being made by passing the prepared material, which was in long strips, through grooved rollers, with much the same hand motion as a woman would use in rolling out dough for pies. 'The motion, we presume, is precisely the same when Bread Pills are made,' says the writer, slyly, after recovering from the experience of seeing enough pills to physic all creation 'with some to spare for the inhabitants of the planetary systems.'

The folkways of nineteenth-century America seem perplexing and inconsistent to us today. It was a time of prudery and sticky sentiment, mixed with a coarse realism worthy of a Restoration wit. A leg was a limb, or did not exist at all. Edward Everett of Boston draped his replica of the Apollo Belvidere, which was one way to harmonize the good and the beautiful. Canons of taste were precious and finicky. Yet widely circulated patent medicine advertisements dealt with frightening lists of symptoms; nor were they dainty when it came to a discussion of piles or tubercles.

There were doctors in Philadelphia, surely a city with as nice a sense of propriety as any other, who openly advertised their infallible cures of 'secret disease.' Dr. Hunter, 38 North Seventh Street, invited either sex to his 'private rooms,' 'without fear of interruption by other patients . . . those who have injured themselves by a solitary vice are also invited.' A hundred years ago, the *Public Ledger* was publishing half a column of this kind of advertising every day. It must have met a need. Newspapers accepted the advertising of Dr. Robertson's Vegetable Nervous Cordial that claimed to cure 'all nervous complaints, attended with inward weakness, depression of the spirits, head-ache, tremor, faintness, hysteric fits, debility, seminal weakness, gleets, and various complaints resulting from secret impropriety of youth and dissipated habits, residence in warm climates, the immoderate use of tea, the unskillful or excessive use of mercury, so often destructive of the human frame, diseases peculiar to females at a certain period of life'; and so on.

The nature of the pills for females becomes clear in the warning that The Portuguese Female Pills are not to be taken during pregnancy 'as they are certain to produce miscarriage during that period.' Madame Restell's Preventive Powders were advertised 'for married ladies whose health forbids a too rapid increase of family.' In this instance the price was not the usual dollar, but five dollars, a charge in proportion to the value of the service rendered. Madame Restell was known as New York's most expensive abortionist, not to mention her other curious activities.

The wounds, diseases, and impaired health of the soldiers who returned from the Civil War introduced the mental patterns of ill-health and self-medication. The printed word, in its new abundance, spread the news to the remotest hamlets of cures and recoveries no less startling than the miracles performed by the saints in ancient days, such as that of St. Placidus, who could ease a splitting headache by a laying on of hands, or St. Clare, who cured a colic with holy oil. Mr. Lewis J. Allen, of Battle Creek, Michigan, who fought with the Twenty-eighth Pennsylvania Volunteers, affords a case in point. One day he was greatly struck by something he read in a Detroit newspaper — possibly a paid advertisement? — about Dr. Williams' Pink Pills for Pale People. Feeling pale, he took one box. From that day onward he was completely free of his terrible rheumatism, without the aid of holy oil or the touch of hands.

An instance of the versatility of the country storekeeper in medical matters occurred when an emergency arose one day at the general merchandise emporium of Charles Nuffer, known as 'the Flying Dutchman.' Nuffer flourished at Beaver Falls, in Lewis County, New York, and was known to have the ability to 'lay on hands.' If a farmer got cut, or there was a nasty accident in the woods, Nuffer could stop the bleeding. Some said he possessed the lost Seventh Book of Moses and had second sight, a statement Nuffer never contradicted.

There was one particular day, long remembered locally, when Hannah Lefevre had the misfortune to back into the store stove — and it was *hot*. A great uproar followed. Nuffer, a sly man, solicitously reminded the singed lady — 'I'm a great one at laying on hands, you know.' But Martin, Hannah's husband, decreed otherwise.

A curiosity of the times were the bitters ads in the religious press. The temperance advocates read in their journals not only of missions and ministry and the testimony of those in grace, but reams of copy about bitters. The printed word had an august authority to the mind of a rural reader, appearing in publications whose views he revered on the great issues such as church dogma and party doctrine. There were often reports of the positive cure of desperate cases of 'consumption,' detailed and circumstantial, and vouched for by a minister of the gospel. It took an alert mind to distinguish between the editorial matter and the advertising, the account one pastor gave of his ministry and the tale of another about his 'breast complaint.' The reader needed mental equipment more subtle and more critical than most people possessed, if he was to resist successfully the advertisements illustrated with woodcuts of the saved, and filled with dark threats of the hearse, the worm, and the shroud.

The testimonialist often believed with the deepest sincerity in his own cure. He took the medicine. He got well. Responding warmly to humanitarian impulses, he shared his good news with others. Various devices were used to strengthen the evidence. The grateful patient often swore to the fact that he felt better before a notary public. The pastor of the Baptist Church in Brunswick, Maine, validated a cure in Morrill. A Mr. Hodgkins, a general merchant at Rockport, Massachusetts, said of Mrs. Pickering's torture, 'Her case is not overdrawn . . . My own mother is taking the Sarsaparilla with good results.'

What the medicine makers thought of these fortunate *post hoc* recoveries is not recorded. Even the regular doctors were shooting, so to speak, with a shotgun. They hoped that some one of many pellets would hit the mark. Whatever the men who concocted the patents may have lacked in regard to science, they were past masters at the *art* of medicine. Their profitable business was soundly based on the fact that the living cell tends to recover ; on the deep need of a hard-working populace, living in separateness, for a bit of theatre, a miracle they could believe in.

Joe Nontell, of Newberry, Michigan, helps to explain the patent medicine fortunes. Joe was a cook in a lumber camp. He coated dried peas with sugar and put them into a medicine bottle. Gravely he doled out his peas during the winter season to any jack who needed doctoring — 'with varying success,' reports a student of the folkways of the Upper Peninsula. Could more be said for the practice of a Park Avenue specialist? The medical advertisers stressed the importance of faith. The will to believe can play a powerful part in any program of treatment. Often an escape from a serious pathology simply cannot be explained upon rational grounds.

The patent-medicine makers, sizzling with enterprise, found another way of getting in touch with the country people to supplement their advertising in the newspapers and religious weeklies — the almanac. It was ready-made for them, already an old American institution, handed down from colonial times with the affection and authority of generations, laden with cultural and patriotic associations — Doctor Franklin, General Washington, and all that. They printed poems about Braddock's defeat, the correct history of the glorious revolution, recipes, proverbs, and parables.

Here the oncoming generation met up at a tender age with exhortations to frugality, temperance, industry, and piety. If the almanac formed the character of the young, it was equally an enormous influence on those in middle life. The

Read, Reason & REFLECT!

DR. PARMENTER'S
MAGNETIC OIL!
Will Cure Rheumatism!

TO THOSE AFFLICTED !

This Oil is warranted to ease more pain in less time, than any other medicine now in use. Call and test its Virtue; it removes the worst Rheumatic pain in 30 minutes; pains in the side, breast and back, in 20 minutes; Nervous Headache in 10 minutes; Croup in 20 minutes; Chilblains in one night, and is a sure cure for chapped hands.   The Oil acts on the System on the principle of Electricity, regulates the whole system, and is perfectly safe in all cases.   **PRICE 25 CENTS PER BOTTLE.**

PRINCIPAL DEPOT,
No. 9 Cooper's Buildings, cor. State & Green Sts.,
ALBANY, N. Y., and for sale by Druggists generally, throughout the United States and the Canadas.   Druggists, Merchants and Peddlers supplied at the lowest prices,

By Dr. WM. O. PARMENTER.

BAKER TAYLOR, PRINTER, 66 STATE STREET, ALBANY

The science involved in the patent medicine business was not that of medicine or of chemistry but of popular psychology.

farmer and the farmer's wife found in it practical information that they relied upon. The almanac told when to plant and when to reap, gave letter postage rates and stage routes, lists of the eclipses and the moveable feasts. Do not wean any farm animals, the almanac warned, under the Scorpion sign. Sow clover and alfalfa in Libra. The almanac provided long-range weather forecasting when there was no other convenient source for such information, and noted the places of the fixed stars at a convenient hour for every day and month — useful data for countrymen who could read the night sky like a heavenly clock.

Near the front of the pamphlet the reader always found the zodiac, with the picture of the Man of the Signs in the center of the page, surrounded by the twelve divisions or constellations with their beast-symbols. Each was connected by lines to a part of the human body. To many readers, and all children, this page was a mystery. To a minority it was a reminder that each sign 'governed' an organ or part of the body, thus keeping alive the belief, or at least its recollection, that the movements of the heavenly bodies have an influence upon human affairs.

To moral precepts and 'sayings,' bits of poetry and history, flights of sentiment and oddments of practical information, the almanac also added the spice of wit and fun. At one time, in serious vein, a page might be filled out with a household hint: 'To keep a stove bright, weak alum water mixed with "British lustre." ' At another time, and in another mood: 'To keep eggs from spoiling — eat them while they are fresh.'

By producing millions of almanacs and distributing them free, the patent-medicine companies gradually took over this valuable transmission belt for ideas, so that in time the declination of the planets got well mixed up with cures for neuralgia or torpid liver. As each year wore on to its end, about

November, an interesting bundle arrived at the country store, the heralds of the Christmas season — the new supply of medicine almanacs. They lay on the counters in great piles, so that Advent, to a wondering child, might seem the solemn season that marked the anniversary of Hostetter's or Ayer's. The rule was: Help yourself. Along with it went the honor system: One to a family.

As time went on, the editor's whimsical sayings, the moral earnestness, the personal touch were more and more diluted with advertising and medical hocus-pocus. The printing was bad, the format miserably small; but the habit was strong. There was still the loop of string for hanging the booklet on a nail behind the kitchen stove, where the green or yellow cover would be a daily or hourly sight, bringing 'glad tidings to the afflicted' for a whole year, as well as its own peculiar kind of literature of misery, with its own plot and story-line — of hollow-cheeked people who became plump and hearty, of little children, the light of their mothers' eyes, snatched from the grave by Mrs. Winslow's Soothing Syrup.

Even the margins of these tattered ephemera were pressed into service. There the man of the house did his figuring about taxes, income and outgo, his reckoning of how he stood in the ledger down at the general store. A man started in to make a daily jotting about the weather, and ended up by keeping a diary. No wonder the little books became grimy and thumbed before the sun once more entered Capricorn and it was again time to go to the store for another almanac showing the man with his insides spilling out, and those perplexing signs called Taurus, Gemini — a misprint, perhaps, for Jiminy? — and Cancer, which governed the health of the breast.

Here, at least, a close reader of the medical almanacs felt himself on solid ground. He had read deeply about cancer of the breast in his almanac. Or perhaps he had picked up off the

general store counter the booklet put out by Dr. J. B. Haines
& Co., of Cincinnati, Ohio, whose Piso's Cure was said to cure
cancer 'At Home.' Striking the note of public service, the
'doctors' published grave warnings against extravagant
claims and humbuggery, which shows that they understood
thoroughly the axiom that one way to acquire a character is to
deplore the existence of scoundrels.

It is not surprising that the 'doctors,' who had learned so
well how to live close to the folks through clever advertising
and publicity, became as real as a neighbor down the road.
'Doctor' Munyan, with his stern expression, high pompadour,
and up-lifted index finger — 'If the Sign of the Cross Were
to be Destroyed,' said Munyan millions of times in the newspapers, 'the Next Best Sign Would Be "The Index Finger
Pointing Heavenward" ' — was like a solicitous father to the
family, warning of perils yet to come. For years after *The
Ladies' Home Journal* had published pictures of the tomb-
stone of Lydia E. Pinkham, hystericky women kept right on
unburdening their hearts to their good, gray friend, whom
they supposed to be slaving away for womankind in her laboratory at Lynn, Massachusetts.

'Write to Mrs. Pinkham,' urged the Pinkham Medicine
Company, cordially. Believe it or not, they *had* a Mrs. Pinkham, too, ready to be put on exhibition, if necessary. But she
was not Lydia E., the inveterate letter writer and originator
of the Vegetable Compound; 18 per cent alcohol, as the label
said it was, after the Food and Drug Act became law. For
Lydia E. was dead, dead ere her prime, and hath not left her
peer. Since 1883 she had been moldering in her grave; but
with the help of form letters, a corps of industrious clerks continued to entertain and console Lydia's large coterie of Tired,
Nervous Mothers.

Dr. H. T. Helmhold, promoter of Buchu, became such a

noted figure that the story is told of an old lady in upstate New York who heard about the unveiling of a statue to Von Humboldt and asked, 'Was the doctor present?'

Susy Weiser, of Chambersburg, Pennsylvania, was taught to say 'A blessing on Mrs. Winslow' for helping her through her gripping, colicking, and teething siege. The Mrs. Winslow to whom Susy referred was that kindly nurse and female physician of thirty years' experience, she of the Soothing Syrup, and more adequately enshrined in the phrase 'the Florence Nightingale of the Nursery.'

'God speed her on her humble but happy mission!' exclaimed Mr. Weiser, father of the grateful little Susy, in the *German Reformed Messenger*. 'Away with your "Cordial," ' he said, ' "Paregoric," "Drops," "Laudanum," and every other "Narcotic" by which the babe is drugged into stupidity.' It would have given poor Mr. Weiser a nasty turn had he known that the soothing agent used by the Florence Nightingale of the Nursery was one-tenth grain of morphine sulphate to each fluid ounce.

The susceptible needed only a deft suggestion to feel the symptoms described so graphically on the bottle, and the pseudo-scientific lingo which worked upon them seems fantastic only until it is compared with typical folk beliefs that were widely held. Passed along from generation to generation by word of mouth, these cures, charms, empirical beliefs are of such remote origin in many cases that only the trained folklorist can follow the line of descent. Many sound like acts of propitiation offered up to some malign force or deity, a reminder that popular medicine had a long European ancestry behind it, and that a number of our own forebears saw apparitions and wonders, made pacts with the Devil, and knew a witch when they saw one. Folk medicine, believed in devoutly by some, scorned by others, yet kept alive by half-believers, dealt in such imperatives as:

Snake oil cures rheumatism.

Starve a cold and stuff a fever.

Wash freckles away on the first day of May, with the morning dew. Stump water also cures freckles.

For a cold, grease red flannel and wear it on the chest. Or wear a bag of asafetida around the neck.

Put mud on a bee sting, or try a liniment made of St. John's wort and vinegar.

If the throat is sore, tie a piece of pork rind around the neck.

Sassafras tea clears the blood; also sulphur and molasses.

For heartburn, wear a match over the right ear.

If you step on a rusty nail, grease it and carry it in your pocket to prevent lockjaw.

Bury an old dishrag to drive away a wart.

There was a school of thought that put great stock in saliva therapy. Spit on a burn to cure it. Put tobacco juice on cuts and sores; also on a hornet sting. Let your dog lick an infected finger or toe.

Bleeding from a wound could be staunched by reciting or reading a certain verse from the Bible. Unfortunately, information about which verse is lacking.

Such cures and treatments existed for a long list of ills that were visited upon rural people; frostbite, colds, sore throats, nosebleeds, croup, ringworm, kidney trouble, wounds, boils, aches, and burns, 'summer complaint,' the 'flux,' chills, cuts, fits, gallstones, and pneumonia. There were, too, the special and violent experiences of a rough environment which called for emergency treatment — knifings, gougings, gunshot wounds, bear clawings, accidents with axes, scythes, and pitchforks. Felling trees was dangerous work. 'Widow makers,' they called the big timbers that occasionally did not fall where they were supposed to.

Sometimes when a healthy, hearty, normal child of twelve pushed back a piece of apple pie, untouched, her mother would pause, look narrowly, and utter the pronouncement: 'You're bilious.' Down would come a jar from the top of the cupboard and a round of calomel would be given to clear up the condition. A sniffle called for generous doses of castor oil. The chest was rubbed with 'coal oil' and lard, thoroughly 'baked in' by the heat of the kitchen stove. Then a piece of flannel was pinned tightly to the long, scratchy woolen underwear which was worn day and night. After that came a mustard foot bath, 'as hot as you can stand it,' and so to bed in a feather bolster heated with soapstones. Next day a sticky, sweetish syrup of cherry bark was administered every hour on the hour. When the hoarseness continued there was further punishment with a mixture of honey and alum.

'If a coughing spell struck during the night,' a New York state woman recalled, 'Mother invariably administered black pepper. Possibly her belief in the therapeutic value of this remedy was justified since, to forestall a second dose of the fiery mixture, I made a superhuman effort to suppress my bark.'

There were, of course, doctors in the country districts a hundred years ago who practiced medicine in accordance with the Medical Faculty and the state of knowledge existing at the time; but there were also the quacks, eclectics, and itinerant patent-medicine artists who peddled door to door. That sometimes 'simple country people readily detect the ring of false metal' is suggested in a satiric poem about a traveling doctor called 'Medicine Jack.' The first verse:

How do, my friends, How are you all?
I hope you're very ill
For then I know you'll let me sell you
Chust von liddle pill!
De'r made of rhubarb, quills und butter,
Soap und flour und cheese.
De more you dakes, de less you vants,
I know de' vill you blease:

He goes on to tell how he has plasters and pulls teeth.

A real doctor, a 'Philadelphia Doctor,' was called in only for surgery or for the last stages of a desperate illness. The same might be said of a homeopathist or the cayenne-pepper-and-lobelia botanic physician. Home diagnosis and self-administered medicine was generally the only care there was, with such assistance as might be gained from scanning a *Family Physician or Home Book of Health;* or perhaps Nicholas Culpepper's *English Physician Enlarged,* wherein herbs were related to certain ailments 'according to the Doctrine of Signatures or signs on the plants.'

Country people were convinced herbalists, gathering their catnip, spearmint, boneset, tansy, pennyroyal, burdock, and lobelia along field and stream. Our great-grandmothers were high advocates of various infusions: catnip for colic, horehound for coughs, sassafras for a spring tonic, mullein leaf for asthma. They dried the leaves and hung them from the rafters in the back shed, and what a pleasant sight and smell the little bunches made when one opened the door. If not administered as teas, the herbs were steeped in water and enough flour was added to make a ball. The dose was one pill, regardless of the medicament or the size of the bolus.

A certain great-grandmother Brown thought highly of dandelion roots for stomach trouble. She boiled them up in water, strained the solution, and added maple syrup. On one occasion, great-grandfather persuaded her to add some hops to the mixture. Coming across the brew some days later, and wishing to ward off stomach trouble, grandfather drank heartily. As a result he became somewhat unsteady on his legs, and when his wife next saw him he was asleep in a chair and she could not rouse him. She looked at the empty jug and quickly sized up the situation. Snatching up the container with considerable vexation, she brought it down hard on his sore toe until he roared for mercy. No more hops were put in the medicine after that.

The patent-medicine kings were allopaths and there was much talk in their literature of alteratives that altered and restored a *morbid* body to health. Expectorants promoted the secretion of fluid in the respiratory tract. There were sanatives, carminitives, pectorals; and over all a brisk air of science and progress. One old country store ledger pasted full of wholesalers' invoices contains a circular of Dr. D. Jayne, who, 'keeping fully abreast with the advance in Pharmaceutical and Medical Science, has improved his famous Sanative Pills.' They are now — 1890 — 'reduced in size, concentrated, and sugar-coated.' The price was unchanged at twenty-five cents a box; but the quantity was increased to fifty pills instead of thirty. Ed Howe, the Kansas sage, took note of Dr. Jayne's popularity in a characteristic paragraph: 'Every time we see big, fat George Shifflett, we can't help laughing over the fact that when he isn't feeling well, his wife makes him take Jayne's Vermifuge, a worm medicine for children.'

Dyspepsia was widespread and its torments undoubtedly real. 'The disorder of the digestive function is the most frequent and prevailing of the ailments that afflict man in the civilized state,' said the 1830 edition of the *Encyclopedia Americana;* 'all classes and all ages suffer from its attacks.

Few are so happy as to pass through a life of ordinary dura-
tion, without undergoing a protracted struggle with this
malady.'

In *Martin Chuzzlewit*, Dickens portrays the journey from
New York to the western Eden as one long adventure in dyspepsia. The natives of the region were lank, sallow, sick, yet
ever famished. They devoured poultry, pickled oysters, cu-
cumbers, tongue, ham, dried meats, cakes, and preserves,
bolted down in an instant, without conversation, relaxation or
any feeling for the amenities. The heavy farm fare was often
poorly prepared and relied on root crops, white flour, and salt
pork. The tendency toward gluttony of those who were malad-
justed in life provided the patent-medicine agents with a rich
selling opportunity. Dr. J. W. Cooper, playing along with
the high repute of botanicals, met the crisis with a dyspepsia
bitters which was 'Purely Vegetable.' A Dr. J. S. Houghton,
on the other hand, went all out for pepsin. 'If you are miserable from dyspepsia,' said a trade card, 'there is no medicine
on earth that will strengthen debilitated organs as well as
Parker's Tonic.' It also cured consumption, asthma, bron-
chitis, dysentery, cramps, 'and has often saved life.' It did just
that for Mrs. D. Schultz of Louisville, Kansas, she says on the
back of a trade card, the front showing a colored chromo of a
demure young woman toying with a bouquet of small, bright
flowers — harmless, health-giving botanicals, no doubt.

Some of the ills with which the patent medicines were so
urgently concerned have abated or disappeared. Ague, and
with it the reliable anti-periodic, Aguine, have gone the way
of malaria. Female weakness is under control. The skin erup-
tions caused by dirt have been routed by soap and hot water.
The same could be said for most childhood diseases, particularly worms, 'the bane of a child's existence,' though one ir-
reverent skeptic has already been mentioned who suggested

that the worms were in the minds of the patent medicine pro-
moters. Most of the panaceas, if they were good for anything
at all, were good for a good many things, which made it unnecessary to invest too many dollars just for variety's sake.
The versatility of Parker's Tonic was not anything extraordinary, when we consider that Perrin's Fumigator was sold
'for Loss of Voice, Catarrh, Minister's Sore Throat, Deaf-
ness, Rumbling Sounds in the Head, Sounds of Distant
Waterfall,' and so forth.

The memory of Indian times has become so faint that it
may not be immediately clear why Dr. Townsley's Toothache
Anodyne was called 'Indian.' It was 'a purely vegetable
preparation,' of course; but why Indian? Far back in time,
Indian medicine men were believed to have medicines of great
virtue, compounded from the secrets of forest glade and
stream bank; and some of the recipes and ingredients the Indians used passed into the farm kitchen. The patent medicine
men could not afford to miss on a romantic opportunity such
as this. There was a Kickapoo Indian Medicine Company at
Clintonville, Connecticut, whose cough cure would do anything that a solution of sugar, glycerine, salts, water, and alcohol would do.

Mary Ellen Chase, distinguished Professor of English Literature at Smith College, remembers how in Blue Hill, Maine,
in the late 'nineties, her father bought a big bottle of 'Kickapoo Indian Sagwaw' from a real Indian each spring. It was a
mixture made from herbs 'and tested as to its efficacy upon
any number of Indians.' A vintage bottle of Kickapoo Indian
Sagwaw may be viewed by tourists, social historians, the Medical Faculty, and Indians just passing through, at the Grant
Minor Store at Old Sturbridge Village, near Southbridge,
Massachusetts, along with other drugs which demonstrate

that the old general stores carried whole cloves, 'ess. Peppermint,' flaxseed, Rochelle Salts, and dried slippery elm.

The white men who set up as 'Indian Doctors' added to the root and herb decoctions of Indian materia medica whatever might be suggested by a smattering of Greek or Latin and a tour through the pharmacopoeia. None of your simples or yarb teas for them. They elaborated and improved as fancy suggested — a little brimstone and alum, pulverized with gunpowder, made into a potion with vinegar and water. Half a gill was enough. Drunk promptly, this heroic treatment counteracted mortified flesh.

During the closing years of the last century and the early days of this one, the drugstore, the traveling showman-doctor, with his Indian costume, gasoline flares, and minstrel show, and the mail-order catalogues, all competed vigorously with the general store for the patent medicine dollar. It was a bonanza, a Comstock lode, a Spindletop. Every bottle of Black Draught, Wine of Cardui, and Father John's Medicine carried an enormous markup, known in the trade as 'a regular drug store profit.' A mail-order catalogue for 1905 devoted twenty pages to such remedies. There were, in addition, nearly five full pages of trusses and braces for hernia which the skilled technicians in Chicago could fit perfectly by mail. Rupture was cured without, as they said, the use of the knife. If there were rumbling noises, or the sound of distant waterfalls, it must have been the Niagara of liquid, bitter, brown, and mysterious, which flowed down the American gullet. When the store profits from the medicine shelf slowed down, it was not because of competition, but the effects, after 1906, of the federal Food and Drugs Act, and the supplemental Harrison Law of 1911, directed at the indiscriminate sale of opiates.

Meanwhile, it was enough to make a country merchant with any gumption fighting mad to think of the money going through the post-office window right under his nose, for Tanlac, Peruna, 'lithia' waters, and electric belts, all obtained from those catalogue houses. It was not only medicines, but everything else that people ought to buy at the home store — dress goods, button shoes, candy by the pail, all of the thousand-odd articles to be found in a well-run general merchandise store.

'Shears and Sawbuck,' he jeered. 'Monkey Ward.'

THE OLD STORE GETS A NEW LOOK

Different men think of different matters when in church. Some reflect upon the life of the spirit, and some upon their dinner. James Boswell indulged in reveries of beautiful women. Harley Procter of Cincinnati thought about soap.

'All thy garments smell of myrrh,' intoned the minister, following his text from Psalms 45:8, 'and aloes and cassia, out of the ivory palaces whereby they have made thee glad.'

Sweet-smelling garments . . . out of ivory palaces. Ivory . . .

The thriving young company of Procter and Gamble had recently been the victim of an accident; as it turned out, a most happy accident. One day a careless workman permitted a soap-mixing device called a 'crutcher' to run during his lunch hour, with the result that air bubbles were introduced into the mixture. The soap floated — and the customers liked it. For long periods of the year, in the decades after the Civil War, townspeople and villagers along the Ohio River filled their dishpans and tubs with water that was a deep, tawny brown. A soap cake that sank was definitely lost. Procter and

Gamble's floater might have a brilliant future, if it only had a name, a catchy trade name.

And so it was that Harley Procter was glad he had heard the invitation, 'Let us go into the house of the Lord,' for there he found his inspiration, 'Ivory Soap.' Ivory Soap was not the first household article to be mass-produced, identified with its maker's name, and sold in ready-wrapped convenient units of uniform quality and known value; though it did become a notable leader in advancing storekeeping out of the dicker-cut-measure-weigh-wrap era of merchandising. Early beginnings of branding appear long before Ivory, a relative latecomer of 1879.

In its original, precise meaning, a brand was a mark applied with a blacking brush or a hot iron to a bale or cask, showing either where the goods came from or the initials of shipper and consignee. When the Birmingham exporting firm of William Wallis shipped twelve bundles of frying pans to Willets & Seamans in New York, each bundle was marked
$$\frac{W}{W \quad S}$$
$$N$$
W   S, the two W's standing for the shipper, the W and S for the consignee, and the N for the port of New York. Coffee came in grass mats marked to indicate the importer and the district where the beans were grown. The symbol $\frac{C \& S}{M}$ would denote that Chase and Sanborn were the importers, and that the coffee was from Malang.

Another kind of mark which is antecedent to the modern trade-mark was the brand placed on a container as a sign that the contents had been examined and passed by a public inspector; and so, by extension, it came to mean a grade or certain quality, though the definitions were not sharp. Flour, for instance, was known in the trade as 'fine, middling, and common.' A long list of commodities could not be sent from one state to another, or exported, unless they had been inspected, approved, and branded, the barrels 'made of seasoned oak, the cask hooped with at least ten hoops, three of which shall be on each chime, and properly nailed.' The tare — an allowance made by the seller to the buyer for the weight of the chest or hogshead — 'shall be marked on one head with a marking iron.' In the case of barrels of flour, 'they shall likewise be branded with the weight of the flour . . . and with the initials of the Christian name, and the surname of the manufacturers thereof,' plus a mark of the quality.

Pork was graded as 'mess, prime, and cargo.' The staves of the barrels had to be of a certain thickness, of white oak or white ash. There had to be fourteen hoops to a barrel, the barrel itself identified on the bilge with the cooper's initials. A reminder, like the requirement about the manufacturer's Christian and surname initials, that the small businessman and the craftsman preceded the corporation. The barrel of salt pork is a vivid memory of the country stores, with its four-pound chunks of meat floating in the brine. A large salt-encrusted hook hung at the side of the barrel. The merchant would fish out a slab of pork with the hook, cut off a hunk with a sharp knife, and let the rest fall back with a *plop*.

Buyers came to recognize the brand marks and to rely on them, though their faith was not always justified. Complaints about over-salted mackerel blew like a nor'easter on an unfortunate Inspector General of Fisheries in Massachusetts under whose feckless management 'The abuses in the cull and brand of mackerel have been so great, that pickled fish from the United States have suffered much disrepute in foreign ports, where buyers have often been subjected to heavy loss, by giving too much credence to the brand.' Alexander Hamilton, interested in preventing frauds on the home consumer as well as the foreign buyer, was an early advocate of setting up under federal control 'a judicious and uniform system of inspection throughout the ports of the United States.' 'The reputation of the flour and lumber of some States, and of the potash of others,' he wrote, 'has been established by an attention to this point.'

Modern trade-marks have still another branch to their family tree. Early craftsmen and European guilds used producers' marks; not, however, for the purpose of building a reputation with the consumer but to ferret out competitors' wares. This practice led to the general use of the maker's name on durable or luxury goods, such as a silver bowl, a clock, or a rosewood melodeon. But the same thinking was not applied to other kinds of merchandise such as staple commodities or soft goods, which continued until almost the end of the nineteenth century to be anonymous except for an indication of a general geographical origin: Salem rum, New Orleans molasses, dress goods from Lowell, or Laconia sheetings.

By the 1860's a few articles were ready-wrapped in a unit of convenient size for the ultimate buyer, the wrap imprinted as an identifying label. In addition, the name was impressed on the goods when that was possible, such as the words 'American Family' on a bar of soap. Scales came to have 'Fairbanks-Morse' in raised letters on a casting. Some other names which indicate that the manufacturer was beginning to be identified with his product before Civil War days are Babbitt's Lye, which goes back to 1855; Burnett's Vanilla, 1845; Booth as a mark on fish, 1854; Robert Burns as a cigar name — probably 'segars' then — 1857. After that same year, Eagle Brand stood for condensed milk, and there was the self-dating 1847 Rogers Bros. silverware.

The use of trade-mark names slowly picked up speed. In 1870 there were still a mere handful of registered trade-

marks, about one hundred and seventy. Then the names begin
to come along faster. Sometimes the mark was easily carried
through to the consumer because the product needed a certain
kind of packaging to deliver it and the labeling presented no
problem. Chas. H. Fletcher's Castoria had to come in a bottle,
and the bottle carried the name. None-Such Mince Meat was
packed in a labeled jar. When coffee was put into packages,
the trade-mark idea went along with it. Caleb Chase and
James S. Sanborn wanted to change an ancient habit, the
custom of roasting green beans in the family skillet. They
were out to silence the grinder at the country store, too, a fine
idea in the estimation of every grocery 'boy' who ever had to
grind and parcel up 200 pounds of coffee on a Friday for the
Saturday trade.

The old coffee grinders lingered around the country stores
for a long time before they were sold for junk or rescued by
some dealer in roadside antiques. In one respect the bean coffee was handier around the store than the convenient packaged sort. Roasted coffee was considered an invaluable disin-
fecting agent, 'useful to purify any place having an offensive
smell or foul air,' says the *Grocer's Companion.* A customer
who lived intimately with her goats and chickens used to like
to toast herself at the stove in the F. A. Yutzler store at West
Cornwall, Connecticut. After her departure, Mr. Yutzler
made the air 'thoroughly pure and sweet' again by scattering
freshly-ground coffee over the top of the heater and letting it
cook itself out.

As manufacturers began to see that the package was not
only a container but a sales builder, names and designs began
to be evolved out of traditional material. Tobacco appro-
priated the jolly sailor theme, the brawny American mechanic, the happy plowboy, the granger — America's noble-
man. The Indian motif produced not only cigar store sculp-

Perhaps more than any other object the gaily painted, hand-operated coffee grinder recalls the period of the country store.

ture but also gave us the generously proportioned dusky maidens who appeared on the lids of cigar boxes, a remote compliment, perhaps, to Pocahontas.

As industry acquired a sense for publicity, marks were devised to associate merchandise with a great personality, an invention that had excited the public, almost anything that was topical and in the public eye. A hundred years ago, when Hungary was more highly regarded in the United States than is the case now, Kossuth, the Magyar patriot and exile, made a triumphal tour of the country and set off a great wave of popular enthusiasm, which was noted by the advertisers of the day, who rushed upon the market with Kossuth coats, Kossuth oysters, and Kossuth cigars. This was simple, brassy opportunism, and like any nine days' wonder, soon as stale and forgotten as last week's newspapers. Names capable of being promoted with more permanence came along later such as Royal Victoria Queen's Blue in a wooden box, a sound name

for a bluing compound in the days of Britain's great home-
body queen. There was a Dewey Scrap, echoing memories of
our empire-building days, '999 Smoking Tobacco,' a sentimental memory of the New York Central Railroad's famous
locomotive of the 'nineties. The soapmakers, never backward
in sensing a trend, blessed the age of electricity with 'Electric
Light Soap.' It is impossible to know now whether 'Telephone
Headache Tablets' honored Dr. Alexander Graham Bell's invention, or were put forward as the specific for the relief of a
new ailment.

Some of the most successful product names were sheer inventions, easy to pronounce, remember, and protect legally,
but without any previous meaning. They were coined in
strange ways — by a George Eastman, for instance, pushing
the letters of the alphabet around, reacting mysteriously to
their effect upon the eye and the ear, and finally hitting upon
a winner — such as Kodak. At other times it required more
than one mind to whip a trade-mark into shape.

'You need a name,' said George Gair, the paper box manufacturer, meeting with a National Biscuit Company group of
executives on how to put a new cracker before the public.
'Uneeda — Uneeda Biscuit!' exclaimed someone, probably
Henry W. McKinney, the advertising man, who also had
christened Keds, Karo, Meadow Gold Butter, and had been
playing with 'Uneeda Cracker' as an idea. But 'Biscuit' was
thought to be an improvement because it suggested high-
grade goods. For all its elegant name, the product was a soda
cracker, though a good one, with its corners clipped off to
give it more individuality.

Henry D. Seymour turned in desperation to the encyclopedia to help him solve the problems gathering around an oatmeal mill at Ravenna, Ohio. His eyes stopped at the entry on
'Quakers.' Many complimentary things were said about the

sect which affected Seymour powerfully, since all the compliments could also be used to describe his conception of the solid
worth of his oatmeal works and their product. An associate,
William Heston, contributed the fact that he had once seen a
picture of William Penn. And so it was that the kindly figure
of a well-setup gentleman in Quaker garb was materialized,
registered in the U.S. Patent Office on 17 August 1877, and
lithographed on square — yes, square, not the round style of
today — cartons. If not the first, Quaker Oats was certainly
one of the first cereals in the world to move out of the bulk
goods class and into the package.

The new packages and trade-marks might not have trans-
formed storekeeping as they did, had it not been that national
advertising came along at the same time. Like the trade names
themselves, advertising was now new ; but it was used in a new
way and produced astonishing new effects. Colonial and early
Federal advertising dealt with local matters, craftsmen's
cards, notices about stores for sale or rent, auctions, arrivals
and departures of ships. It appeared in newspapers, or as
broadsides, suggesting more than anything else the classified
advertising of today.

When we remember that the nineteenth-century merchant
was the dominant figure in commerce rather than the manufacturer, it is not surprising to find that the retailer, not the
maker, did the advertising. Until deep into the century, most
advertisers were content to announce that certain goods had
arrived, for it was a greater feat to acquire a stock than to sell
it. Often simply a sort of inventory of the store's stock, with no
specific information, no mention of price, the advertisement
made no attempt to persuade beyond some such effort as
'Don't Read This Unless You Want Cheap Goods.' Copy often
appeared for weeks or even months without change. Nobody

minded. There was not anything new to talk about until a new assortment of goods arrived.

Many developments occurred with a most delicate timing in the creation of the United States national market. Transportation became fast, reliable, and cheap. Invention and technology provided new and better goods in vast quantities. The people could be talked to as a whole for the first time. Big and little newspapers proliferated. Steam presses using stereotypes poured out books and directories that were packed full of advertising. Almanacs and recipe books reached a public thirsty for information and diversion. Magazines of polite literature, magazines for ladies only, religious papers catering to every sect, farm magazines such as *The Rural New Yorker* and *The American Agriculturist*, general magazines such as *Comfort* and *Hearth and Home* widened the horizons and the wants of the customers who traded at the country stores.

One novel form of advertising which enjoyed a great vogue was the trade card, a bit of engraved or lithographed pasteboard, illustrated with a scene, a pretty design, a picture that told a story built around the advertiser's goods. These cards, usually printed in color, were distributed by the millions over store counters to help customers remember a bottle of medicine, a can of condensed milk, a nice article of crackers. Storekeepers handed out the cards as a favor to good customers. Some country stores put out cards of their own, imprinted with the store name, such as an advertising card for the soap products of Lautz Bros. & Co., of Buffalo, New York, but passed out by Bostwick & Corwin at Montrose, Pennsylvania. There was no better way for a general store owner to do some advertising on his own account, and put some hurrah into a dull day.

Young and old collected and swapped the cards, and the sale of albums and scrapbooks kept pace with the cards. Animals and babies were the commonest subjects in settings of unabashed sentimentality. Birds, flowers, national sports, costumes of all countries, plants, trees, ball players, famous actresses, and the pretty American girl all came into play. A cologne company perfumed its cards. Some cards folded so as to play some kind of trick. Today all trade cards issued before 1900 have some value and are once again sought by card collectors who assemble them by subjects, such as birds, or by products, such as baking soda, starch, or sewing machines. Cigarettes, as they became socially acceptable, fell in with the craze and little silk flags were placed in their packages, and the girls covered sofa pillows with them — a pretty thought, and as good a conversation piece as a lozenge that said 'Be My Sweetheart.'

The historic change in merchandising methods, from the twilight confusion of the old cracker barrel store to the disciplined brightness and order of the modern shopping center began when factories packed their first consumer units — a 'paper' of coffee, a 'paper' of dry yeast — and shipped them, twenty-four or thirty-six to the case, in wooden boxes. Babbitt put his potash in tin cans and advertised it 'at about the same price as that in casks, with full directions for use printed on each can, being in a much more portable condition for retailing.' Babbitt also had 'the best SALERATUS in pound papers, 60 in a case.' The units were large, but so were the families and houses.

Between the 'sixties and the 'eighties many products came to be 'papered.' The papers acted as a transportation device and indicated the later role of the folding carton as a means of building good will. There is a preview of the future in a trade-paper advertisement read by grocers offering 'Fancy

Pasteboard Caddies' printed 'in rich colors' with the retailer's 'business card' on the faces of the boxes: 'As an advertising medium alone they will repay you their cost.' The container, the box, demonstrated that among its many advantages was that of being an advertisement. One of the most candid of these was printed on a corset box by a manufacturer who said: 'I do not advise any woman to wear a corset, but if she *will* do so — and she generally will — I advise her to use one of Ball's Health Preserving Corsets as it is less likely to do her injury than any with which I am acquainted.'

As recently as the early 1900's, when a factory manager pushed back his kelly and picked up his trade paper, *Packages*, he could find in it a modest department called 'Paper Box News.' That meant the modern consumer-unit package. Mostly he read of barrels and boxes, hoops and shooks, fruit baskets and tub stock; articles and advertisements about stave saws, machines for crozing, dovetailing, and nailing, new barrel heaters, and the price of good Michigan timber, the market for twines, burlap, and sisal rope. But the modern package was coming fast. The consumers had given a clear signal. They wanted to buy in smaller quantities and more frequently. Goods had to be endowed with more personality than formerly, and packed more conveniently and more attractively.

It was held as self-evident in the days of McKinley that no nation could go backward so long as its men wore derby hats. The inventors and mechanics set their stiff lids at a jaunty angle and went to work on new methods of making consumer packages and new equipment to fill and close them. Boots and shoes used to be tumbled all helter-skelter in a wooden bin at the country store. Later they came twelve pairs to a carton. Finally, each pair had a nice box of its own, the now familiar shoe box. Before the Civil War the only paper boxes in use were pill boxes and band boxes for 'bunnets.' Then came the rage for paper collars. Each dozen collars was packed in a paper box. After the Centennial Exhibition in Philadelphia in 1876, where merchants and manufacturers found conclusive evidence that goods neatly packaged caught the eye of the buyer and held his confidence, the use of boxes and cartons developed rapidly.

Generally speaking, the packaged article was of high quality and there was little variation one from the other; but it would be an exaggeration to say that the package immediately put an end to substandard goods. A 'paper' of coffee could contain skimmings as well as a burlap bag. Tea fannings or re-colored leaves could go into a caddy as well as a bale. If, however, tea and coffee were packaged, given a trade-mark, sold over the maker's name and on his responsibility, it was certainly much more probable that the company would provide its customers with a good beverage. What finally set the new system of selling to spinning at a fast rate was the improvement in transportation, the railroad train's flanged wheel rolling on the steel rail.

Hires, when he began, could peddle only so much root beer. Wrigley, as a young man, could carry only one basket of his chewing gum. Heinz could trundle only a limited number of wheelbarrow loads of his horseradishes or pickles. But the railroad could haul the drummer who found the merchant who stocked the goods in unlimited quantities. It spread the influence of magazine and newspaper advertising across the face of the land. The advertising itself tells a good deal about the lives of the rural customers. Brokers who dealt in mailing lists accumulated thousands of names by the appeal 'Get Lots of Mail.' It was like cutting a picture window on the world for a lonely resident of Hard Times or Skunk's Misery to know that all he had to do was send in his name to the list

broker and it would soon go 'whirling all over America,'
bringing back free samples of magazines and papers, as well
as news of astonishing discoveries in the field of patent medicines. Black type jumped at the reader, talking an exciting
telegraphese: Weak Men . . . Liquor and Opium Habit
Cured . . . Marriage Papers Free . . . Busts Developed
. . . the W. L. Douglas $3 Shoe . . . Grand Commandery
March and Two Step, 2½¢ per copy . . . Free Land in
California . . . I Cure Fits . . . Fortunes in Old Coins
. . . Ruptured? . . . Burnt Cork Comicalities, the Best of
Darkey Wit and Humor.

Ladies were promised clear complexions, bright eyes, long
lashes, offered hair switches and lace curtains, employment
without unpleasant convassing. Gentlemen were asked how
they would like to raise some ready cash — '$100 in Gold,'
'How Can I Get $300?' 'Grasp a Fortune,' urged one adver-
tiser; 'Own a Gold Mine.' And then, coming down to earth
with a somber thump, there was the medical advertiser always
at hand to introduce the theme of the tired, exhausted heart.
'Feel your pulse . . . see if your heart beats regularly and
steadily,' commanded Dr. Albro of Augusta, Maine. 'No doctor,' said Albro, who sold heart tablets, 'can tell better than
you if your heart is out of order.'

There was something bracing in the air of an economy that
was doubling itself every third decade. Slowly the merchant
class gave up the old mercantilist philosophy of buy low and
sell high, and turned to the idea of selling the largest possible
volume of goods, doing it faster than had ever been thought of
before, and at lower margins of profit. The package idea
fitted in with these concepts like a nesting of Chinese baskets.
Some merchants were skeptical, fearing 'a species of serfdom
which holds them in the power of great advertisers and forces
them to sell "Called For" goods without adequate compensa-

tion.' But the bandwagon rolled on. 'American housewives,' observed an early twentieth-century businessman, 'take kindly to the pasteboard carton.'

The change from the barrel to the carton was especially noticeable in general stores that had a good grocery trade. The oatmeal barrel, for instance, traditionally stood in front of the counter, the top loose or gone. Imagine the surprise of a customer, when he came into the store with oatmeal on his mind, to find for the first time that the old barrel had clean disappeared. Instead, there were rows of paperboard cartons, with names and pictures printed on them. The packages were all lined up on new shelving behind the counter — weighed, ready-wrapped, and Untouched by Human Hands. Even the whittlers gaped when they heard the storekeeper explain another new wrinkle, how if the customer bought by the brand name thereafter, the tops of the boxes could eventually be turned in for a whole set of ironstone dishes.

Oatmeal had had a curious history in the United States. Known in America for two hundred and fifty years as suitable food for invalids, but never accepted as a staple, oatmeal came into general favor only after Ferdinand Schumacher, 'the father of oatmeal,' emigrated from Hanover and started grinding oats in a twenty-barrel mill near Akron, Ohio, in 1856. It was largely because of Schumacher's efforts that the oatmeal barrel became such a familiar feature of the general store. As the market expanded, competition increased even faster. The jobber and the retailer controlled the industry, and their pressure on prices forced one crisis after another on the hungry mills. The trade-marked package and national advertising turned out to be their way of escape from the tyranny of cheap goods and poor quality.

The modern Quaker Oats Company emerged in the 'nineties, firmly committed to the package system of merchandising, and using methods that were new and spectacular — free samples for housewives, cooking schools, recipe books, trade cards. The Quaker made personal appearances at fairs and expositions. He was on display in the magazines and newspapers. He turned up on walls and poster panels. Even the white cliffs of Dover were once adorned with Quaker's vigorous propaganda for oatmeal, until an Act of Parliament put a stop to *that*. When polar regions were to be explored, Quaker Oats was there, too, with men such as Peary and Amundsen ; and with Hedin, Quaker Oats penetrated mysterious Tibet.

As a result, the name and face of the respectable Quaker became associated in the public mind with oatmeal. Everybody knew the old gentleman, his long hair falling to his shoulders, and looking as Heston vaguely remembered William Penn, dressed in knee breeches, waistcoat, stock, and broad-brimmed hat. With the scroll in his hand labeled 'Pure,' he remained for many years a familiar sight where he had been painted on barns and the walls of stores. The signs were a part of the rural landscape, lending a helpful, steadying hand to the sale of an A-1 article of crushed groats, partially cooked in steam chambers, and rolled into flakes under heavy pressure.

The new look in the country stores was carried still farther with the invention of the ready-to-eat or dry cereals, which were packed in the modern style right from their beginnings in the late '90s and early 1900's. Lengthen the shelves. Clear the counter space. Get the goods up off the floor. Farm diet was fast losing its monotony !

Henry D. Perky, the Shredded Wheat man, C. W. Post, the originator of Grape Nuts and Postum, and the two Kelloggs of Battle Creek — Dr. John and his younger brother, W. K. — added ingenious processing, new flavors, forms, and textures to the cereal seeds — and plenty of mass psychology.

They found that the cereal grains could be flaked, rolled, extruded in filaments through orifices, baked and ground up, exploded, and shredded. The new cereal foods, which one storekeeper said 'looked like dog biscuit but tasted more like sawdust,' had the entrancing flavor of dextrinized starch. To the public the new products became distinct personalities. This 'product personality' was something new in the world, a composite of the way the food tasted, the dietary preachments of the advertising, those jolly package faces, and the whimsical names, Granola, Zest, Malta-Vita, Triabita, Egg-O-See, Force, Elijah's Manna, and Post Toasties.

The cracker barrel followed the oatmeal barrel out of the general store as a consequence of the formation of the National Biscuit Company in 1898. In that year the new concern put out Uneeda Biscuit as a consumer-unit, five-cent package of soda crackers in an airtight, patented, moisture-proof package, which stayed fresh — the first soda cracker ever sold nationally under a single brand name. 'The idea was novel, and we soon found we had struck the taste of the people,' the president recalled later in an annual report. Advertising was used lavishly to launch the new crackers. A mysterious new word appeared in bold, black type in the newspapers, the single word UNEEDA. Next day it was UNEEDA BISCUIT. The day after that 'Do you know Uneeda Biscuit?' Next 'Do YOU know Uneeda Biscuit?' Next: 'Do you KNOW Uneeda Biscuit?' And finally, 'Of course, Uneeda Biscuit, Certainly!!!'

The veteran country merchant did not give up easily on his bulk crackers. The old cracker barrel was a familiar friend with its hoops of wood, the circle of cardboard under the head, the serried layers of common or prime crackers. Crackers were cheaper by the barrel, the margin of profit greater too. Yet the store owner gradually came to reckon on his loss from spoilage, theft, scrounging, and breakage ; and he liked to feel consumer demand. There was no doubt about it — the preference had shifted to the boxed article. It did work out, astonishing though it seemed, that fresh goods, selling rapidly, with only that puny little markup of twenty per cent, brought a man more dollar profit than the bulk article.

There was something so dramatic about the sudden establishment of a name-brand soda cracker in the market at a monthly sales level of ten million packages, that it was the Uneeda merchandising plan, more than any other, which lead the way to similar schemes for coffee, tea, butter, lard, rice, molasses — even sugar and flour.

The cracker drummer appeared at every back settlement and crossroads, decorated with Uneeda emblems, watch fobs, cuff links, and stickpins, the In-er-Seal button in his lapel. He was an enthusiastic missionary of the package method of selling, the man who interpreted N.B.C. to mean 'No Bad Crackers.' Commercial laureates wrote poems apostrophizing the idea of the sanitary package :

> *I am Uneeda, I defy*
> *The roaming dust, the busy fly,*
> *For in my package, sealed and tight,*
> *My makers keep me pure and white.*

At least one minister found a modern parable in the new way of selling groceries. The Reverend Oliver C. Horsman, pastor of the First Baptist Church, Williamsport, Pennsylvania, preached on the subject of 'Uneeda Biscuit' at one of his evening services. His text was from the seventh chapter of Hosea, part of the eighth verse : 'Ephraim is a cake unturned.' As he preached he held aloft a package of the crisp, clean crackers before a congregation of more than four hundred people, including all the National Biscuit Company's local employees, who attended in a body, but without insignia. Reverend Horsman paid his compliments to the excellent quality of the crackers and developed the metaphor that a churchman who does not carry his religion into every department of life is like a half-baked biscuit.

As times changed and the pace of merchandising quickened, there was less leisure to whittle, chew Dewey Scrap, and enjoy the pranks and devilment of the store sitters. It was as though backwoods character and the old cracker barrel faded away together. With the barrel went the other forms of cooperage; piggins, noggins, pails and tubs, firkins and tierces. It was just as well, too, from the point of view of our forest resources, considering the depleted state of the remaining stands of white oak.

A big change was under way and the country merchant felt it. His business was developing in new directions. No longer could he hand out salt, sugar, and tea to grateful customers, desperate for such necessities. Now the merchant had to exercise salesmanship to expand his business. A novelty such as ground coffee in a tin can called for explanation. The new idea of premiums as a reward for buying goods needed the store owner's active backing and authority before the ladies of the neighborhood would accept the exhilarating notion that they would get a set of free dishes just by asking for one brand by name and saving the coupons.

There were more customers; but the clerks could handle more sales because it took less time to wait on trade and put up an order. There was more cash around, so that a prudent merchant was able to add some $200 a year to his profits just by discounting his bills when due. The inventory was larger but the turnover was faster and the labor less. It was necessary to think sharply about display and store arrangement, and to show as much ingenuity as a six-hole mousetrap.

Clerks were still a hard nation, but even the slouchy ones produced better yearly sales. At least they did not streak as much lard and butter from the tubs to the scales, now that the manufacturers and processors were turning to the new sanitary packages. Used to be, a merchant would look at the floor between the canisters filled with the bean coffee and the place where the grinder stood, and he would think it 'paved with coffee and enough grounds on the floor to banquet all the Socialists in Rochester,' as one merchant grumbled. The slipcover can had cleaned up that situation. Customers came from a larger area and the dealer did not know them all as well as he used to. They expected better service and had not only trade-name loyalties but new-fangled ideas about health and diet. They liked a wide choice in everything from dry goods to wallpaper and casket fixtures. That posed questions of capital and inventory.

Once again the country dealer had to adjust himself to new conditions. Everything was easier, in a way — but so much faster! There were fewer two-hundred-pound packages to push, heave, and tilt. The next generation of merchants would not be wearing trusses before they were forty. The store itself looked brighter, neater, more inviting. Everyone was happier except the checkerboard strategists, no longer granted the solace of a free cracker, the dog who could not get at the Leaf Lard, and perhaps the owner himself. He could not help but notice that the situation did not settle down but kept right on changing. There were fewer of those big Saturday night orders to be put up for the farm families and their hired men. A smaller farm population was producing larger crops, and buying their supplies where stocks were larger and prices lower.

The post office window seemed to be less of a drawing card. A storekeeper who had gone before a magistrate and solemnly sworn that he would support the Constitution of the United States, faithfully perform his duties as postmaster, and abstain from everything forbidden by the laws in relation to post offices and post roads within the United States; a man in whose Ability, Integrity, and Prudence the President of the United States had reposed special confidence — a man once accustomed to such responsibilities and honors, could not look on unmoved when he saw a diminishment in his stamp sales and the dignity of his position. He yearned to hear the comfortable, genial post office jokes, such as the standard query: 'What's your price on three-cent stamps today?' And then deliver the expected reply: 'Ten for thirty cents today, John.' Perhaps the Post Office Department had had a bad idea when it put in that rural free delivery system. Some fourth-class offices were even being closed up, disturbing news indeed to any general store owner who liked the taste of a postmastership.

The merchant-postmaster watched moodily as a farmer filled in a money-order form. Out in front he heard a man furiously cranking a Model T Ford. 'She's on magneto now,' said a voice. 'Pull on the wire and spin her hard.'

Had he done right, he wondered, in putting that red gas pump out in front? Maybe the trouble with country store-keeping was spelled a-u-t-o.

YOU CAN'T GO TO TOWN IN A BATHTUB

AN OLD INSTITUTION does not customarily come to its end through some sudden sickness, or the onset of a catastrophe such as a cyclone or the fall of a dull axe on the neck of a luckless fowl. So it was with the passing of the general store. It just slowly dried up, like a farm pond in the August heat, scarcely changing from one day to the next, until it was gone. Thousands of store buildings were boarded up, moved away, abandoned to other uses. Other thousands transformed themselves into convenience stores, such as can be found anywhere in the Loop in Chicago, or under the Third Avenue 'El' in New York, handy places to fill in with small purchases which got overlooked on the serious shopping expeditions to the large stores.

One might, if he wished, choose almost any year between 1891 and 1921 as the critical year for the general store, and make out a good case for his choice. In 1891, one could say, Frank Duryea made his homemade automobile run successfully on the streets of Springfield, Massachusetts, and see in that event the beginning of the end for the small retail store carrying multiple lines of unrelated goods. Or the same year could be pointed out as crucial for a different reason, the laying of the first rural, brick road, in Cuyahoga County, Ohio. A just date for closing one age and opening up another might be 1909, when Henry Ford's first Model T rolled off the assembly line — basic transportation for the masses, which 'got you there and got you back!' By 1918, when the effects of the Federal Aid Road Act were beginning to show, state by state, and car registrations had reached a sensational 6,146,617, it was clear enough that the American people had fallen in love with the automobile. In 1920, Studebaker, the old wagon firm, stopped all production of horse-drawn vehicles. There was a feeling almost of today about 1921, with 10 per cent of the road traffic interstate, the General Staff of the Army taking a respectful interest in the country's highway system, and the ordinary reader of newspapers becoming educated in concepts such as Death Toll, Unsightly Road Signs, The Parking Problem.

And so we might take a date, any date, and it would reinforce the point, each date a route marker pointing in the same general direction. The essential truth involved was that the car brought the paved road and the paved road took away the country store's customers. Of course it all happened gradually. The country merchant kept right on dusting his cases and sweeping out and wondering, sometimes, where all the drummers were. He did not know that he was a casualty of a transportation revolution.

Like the railroad, which in an earlier day gave life to one village and took it away from another, the auto and motor highways upset the old ways of living, shook up each neighborhood, its church and lodge, shifted the location of the school and the pattern of trade. Thousands of little valley and hill localities, which once had place names of their own, lost their identities. Others flourished, drawing new strength from a larger hinterland.

For nearly a hundred years long-haul traffic had moved by train or waterway. While the steel rails, polished by use, shimmered in the sun, the wagon road dwindled to a rutted track of weeds and grass. Local in use, local in supervision, the roads of the United States were so poor in 1903 that it took Dr. Nelson Jackson seventy-three days to drive across the country in his sturdy Winton. On this pioneer venture the Doctor had to open gates, run down dry stream beds, and confess himself lost innumerable times, for no one had ever thought to mark the way.

Once a year the farmers gathered to work out their road tax, a public improvement which lasted until the next rain. 'No taxpayer would pay a dollar,' said Bill Nye, 'when he could come and make mud pies on the road all day and visit and gossip with the neighbors and save his dollar too.'

In 1920 the teacher of a Bible class wound up her account of the Creation by asking the class whether there was any animal man could have done without. 'The horse,' said one boy, and the class agreed. 'Horse geography' had gone. The boy of 1890 dreamed of owning a pony. The boy of the 'twenties wanted a Stutz Bearcat.

What the railroad did to the buffalo, the automobile did to the country merchandiser. Going to town came to mean riding to the nearest big community, twenty to forty miles away, where there were full stocks of goods in all lines, better prices for eggs and chickens, as well as movies, barbers, dentists, lawyers, beauty shops, service stations — not just one facility, but all the conveniences of urban life.

'You have a car, I see, but no bathroom?' remarked a Department of Agriculture investigator to a farm wife.

'You can't go to town in a bathtub,' the lady replied.

The country store had been feeling the pressures of competition, as a matter of fact, even before the automobile reached the farms. The city department store, a grouping of some twenty departments, each a store in itself, was simply a logical extension of the general merchant's idea of all-goods-under-one-roof and one-stop shopping. After the 1870's, the big stores drew more and more rural customers into the large towns with their quantity buying and lower prices, orderly departments, better display, quick service, and 'One Price to All.'

The country cousin found another alternative where the power of the consumer was recognized and catered to — the mail-order catalogues. 'Parcel post, rural free delivery and the mail order houses are ruining business,' was the analysis of one country merchant. The mail-order catalogues spoke with condescension of the general store. Sometimes they referred with severity to the 'tyrrany of the village' over the country customers, a shrewd cut at the monopolistic features of country trading during the years when the United States was unable to pull itself out of the mud.

The general storekeepers had their stock of arguments, too, and hard-hitting propaganda, with no holds barred. In the South they circulated the rumor that Richard W. Sears was a Negro, so that Sears, Roebuck & Company distributed millions of photographs of Sears with their catalogues to refute the allegation and make more friends for 'The Great Price Maker,' as they called the catalogue. The local man mentioned also the disadvantages of the mail-order method of buying goods, such as freight charges, damage in transit, cheap merchandise masquerading under the appearance of a bargain price, and long delays in the arrival of the order.

'Did you hear the one about the mail-order go-cart?' the

store owner would say easily to a customer suspected of sending a money order off now and then to Chicago or Kansas City.

' "Stop shipment on that baby carriage I've been waiting for," the man wrote, "Substitute shot gun and a plug of tobacco — our boy is growing up." '

'Send No Money,' replied Sears, Roebuck. When the mail-order catalogue houses were willing to ship a Morris chair or a steel windmill C.O.D. they were talking a powerful brand of 'Farmer English.' 'No name and address shows on any box, package, wrapper, tag or envelope,' they went on, 'to save customers, *including merchants*, from embarrassment.'

The home-town merchant had the country press on his side. It was able to whip up a considerable measure of social disapproval of 'sending money off to the Chicago millionaires.' This mood is reflected in an aphorism of Ed Howe's, the great paragrapher of the Atchison *Globe*, who wrote during the years when the catalogues were getting fatter each year:

'Ben Bradford, known to be a little gay, says the first time he kissed a woman other than his wife, he felt as sneaking as he did when he first began buying of Montgomery Ward and Co. But Ben gradually became hardened, and many say he now trades with Sears-Roebuck, too.'

Even the most flourishing general store could not carry everything that people wanted when they wanted so many things. Each store was known to be strong in certain lines, but it was never true that every store had wallpaper, or buggies and wagons, or dining room furniture. Not every store owner was an embalmer, with a line of coffins and tombstones. The tendency, indeed, was to contract rather than to expand existing stocks. Ladies' ready-to-wear dresses cut into the old piece goods business; but the little stores could not handle such a stock of dresses as hung on the racks in the dress shops and in

the department stores, luring the label-conscious country ma-
trons to the larger centers. So the merchant gave up on
dresses. Shoes had always been a headache, including the
pesky machine for adjusting shoe buttons. The ladies wanted
a high-button shoe with a medium high heel that gave a dressy
appearance, made on an opera last with a narrow toe, a turned
sole with thin bevel edge, and they would not pay above three
dollars to get it. That was pretty near the local dealer's cost
price. Sadly he watched the money orders go off to Montgomery Ward and Co. for Number 52003. There just was not
enough capital available in a crossroads operation to spread
over fashionable French kid shoes, common sense ladies' Fat
Ankle shoes, the Old Ladies' Serge Congress, and on down to
the $1.85 'Housekeepers' Delight.' So, many a general store
got out of the shoe line too.

The U-shaped counter, which Butler Brothers urged the
country storekeeper to put in, featuring low-priced novelty
goods, was all the rage — for a while. 'Keep in touch with the
masses,' Butler Brothers had said, 'Get all the high-toned
trade you can, but never forget that in the long run the store
that succeeds must get the trade of the common people.' There
still seemed to be a lot of the common people around; but
Woolworth gathered in more and more of their nickels and
dimes.

As farming grew more mechanized, the farm machinery
business was taken over by the implement stores, equipped to
finance big-ticket purchases, carry stocks of parts and accessories, and render repair service. The farmers and the drummers who used to pick up a quick lunch at the store — sar-
dines, bread and cheese, an apple and milk — rode on to town
and victualed at the Court House Cafe. Some general stores
tried putting in a meat counter and some did not. Either way,
the salt provisions, great staple of the nineteenth century,

Butler Brothers, the catalogue wholesalers selling only to the trade, brought the joys of catalogue shopping to the little store back in the hills — and told the owner to put in racket store merchandise, to buy a cash register, and to keep up with the procession.

gave way to the variety of refrigerated, fresh meat which knew no season and was frequently peddled right up to the farmer's dooryard by the meat markets. If a countryman needed money it was likely he would need a lot of it, more, certainly, than he could get from the country merchant. So he did his banking at the nearest commercial bank, or got a farm loan through state or federal agencies.

It was a very solemn and personal moment when a prosperous farmer wrote 'January 1st, 1901' in his farm account book, and realized that he was Twentieth-Century Man. Though he had not at that time ever seen a horseless carriage, a self-service store, or a short-haired woman, it was only natural that he and his family should wish to embrace the opportunities for a fuller life which were predicted for the new century. The ordinary man's access to material goods exceeded anything that had ever been known before. At this point the country storekeeper, that old neighborhood friend, was at an acute disadvantage. He could not, but Sears, Roebuck and the department stores could, provide the country homestead with 100,000 articles of merchandise, including such symbols of a

new and better day as embossed dining room pictures of game
subjects or a high-grade guitar. Country people wanted a
talking machine that would be the envy of all on their road,
with records of Sousa's Band doing the 'Coon Band Contest,'
'End Man Stories,' and the 'Trip to the County Fair.' There
was a demand for hand-painted cornucopias made of translu-
cent celluloid, with a cord for hanging, outfits for the practice
of pyrography, 'the art of wood etching,' and magic lanterns.
'Wish books' indeed ('Wish I had a Daisy Air Rifle'), the
catalogues were the stuff that dreams are made of. Evidences
of their authority pop up in the most unexpected ways, such
as the case of the schoolgirl who passed up the dictionary in
preference to telephoning her mother to ask her to look up the
spelling of 'khaki' in the catalogue.

The old country trader found himself between wind and
water, left with a shrinking business of low-profit necessities,
the sugar, the salt, and the flour, and convenience goods such
as a pocket tin of smoking tobacco, a deck of Camels, cola
drinks, and the overalls that did not get on the shopping list
when the family last visited the city. He could not stand up to
the big stocks of the big retailers. The country store was still
classified as a general store. The old, weathered sign might
say it dealt in groceries, boots, shoes, dry goods, hardware,
and so forth. The merchant might, if he liked reminiscences,
dwell upon his thriving trade in earlier times, and overlook
the dwindling stock of 1920. The concrete road brought business as well as took it away, but always took away more than
it brought.

A strong influence in this change was the country doctor,
not because he was opposed to country stores but because of
his enthusiastic leadership in popularizing the motor car.
Early in the 1900's, the doctors debated searchingly such
questions as 'Are automobiles practical?' 'Are they econom-

The surrey with the fringe on top furnished first-class transportation in the day of the rutted road, when a store visit was made memorable by a package of cubebs, a taste of Sen-Sen, or an old Edison cylinder record that scratched out 'I Love My Wife, But Oh, You Kid!'

ical?' 'Are they better than horses?' They compared costs and tinkered with their machines when they had 'attacks of indigestion.' The doctors went thoroughly into questions of solid *vs.* pneumatic tires, two-cycle as against four-cycle engines, the gasoline machine compared with the steamer, or the specifications for an 'automobile house' as a shelter for the new conveyance. Doctor W. P. Hartford, of Cassville, Wisconsin, made a prediction: 'The country doctor who could buy an automobile for $500 that would go through anything and go sure every time, make fifteen miles per hour and last ten years, would sell his horse and buy one tomorrow.'

An automobile that came very close to the doctor's specifications, and exceeded them in some respects, appeared in 1909. It was the Model T Ford, a high, spidery, drab, austerely functional machine, devoid of all graces. Nevertheless it got the doctor out to the hill farms faster than he had ever

The Ford car, the car 'built to run without bother' (1919 Model T, above), symbolizes the beginning of the end of the old system of country merchandising. The auto gave country folks a new option, and they chose the chain store, the department store, and Woolworth's.

made it before, usually in good time to diagnose an inflamed appendix and to order the cook stove stoked up with dry hardwood, water put on to boil, and the barn lantern hung over the kitchen table.

What rural American who was alive in the years before the First World War does not have vivid and personal recollections of the Model T, that 'car for the people, and at a price they can afford to pay'? Each has his own memories, of measuring the gas supply with a dirty old ruler, straining the gasoline through a chamois into the tank under the front seat, of the hard buggy springs, the mysteries of the old planetary transmission. He can still remember how the hand levers for spark and throttle were set before cranking, like the hands of a clock at ten minutes before three o'clock.

This Ford automobile was no luxurious plaything for rich people and city sports in linen dusters. The Model T was spirited and temperamental, no two alike, and called for as much individual pampering as a blooded horse. On each car the choke worked a little bit differently, the rattles broke out in some new, obscure place. Uniform firing in all cylinders was the ideal. But there was always something that needed doing about the timer. It was continually necessary to lift out the front seat, and the floor boards, too, were always being taken up and then juggled back into place. No matter — the fun and exhilaration of rolling on rubber at thirty miles an hour was worth all the pains. You knew it *was* thirty miles because you got a friend whose car had a speedometer to pace your Ford. Mr. Ford did not consider the speedometer a necessary accessory on the car for the people.

The Ford was whatever the owner wanted it to be, the nearest thing to a magic carpet men had yet seen — 'the family car of pleasure, the fast car for the busy business man, the reliable car for the doctor, the dependable car on the farm.' Light enough so the average man could lift it up, with or without the aid of a fence rail, the Ford seldom got stuck, even on clay hill roads. If it did, the driver threw it into reverse and usually could back out of the situation. Jacked up, the Model T sawed wood, ran a churn or a hay baler. On a nice summer evening it provided a new sense of release, a delightful feeling of personal power as the family drove out the farm gateway to get cooled off, look over the state of the neighbors' crops, and drop in for a visit with a distant cousin. People quoted joyfully, unbelievingly:

> *The calamity howlers put up a great spiel*
> *The country's going to hell in an automobile.*

Neither weather nor sand hills nor gumbo mud could keep a farm family with a Model T from hauling butter, milk cans, poultry, and eggs to the market of their choice and bringing back in record time bags of feed, spray materials, an astonishing number of board feet of lumber lashed on to the running board, or a hundred-pound cake of ice roped to the bumper. The Ford hauled farm implements to a new site, rounded up

stock or day labor at harvest time, gave people a new freedom of choice about what they would buy and where. The
country store lost its monopoly based on nearness to the consumer. Statisticians worked it out that the farm buyer would
travel on the average six to eight miles for hardware, fourteen
for furniture, and twenty for women's fashions.

Those Model T owners who yearned for beauty, gadgets, or
more social prestige than Marse Henry thought needful, supported a whole sub-industry engaged in making fancy radiator caps with wings springing out on each side, wire wheels,
special mudguards. There was a Jericho exhaust horn, with
an 'attractive penetrating tone'; so named, one supposes, because it was loud enough to bring down the walls of a city. For
those who felt the piecemeal addition of reflectors, rubber
floor mats and pedal pads, anti-rattle devices and hand klax-
ons did not go far enough, there was a concern in Detroit that
went the whole hog. For $260 it would transform the homely
Ford with 'a beautiful, luxuriously upholstered Beau Brum-
mel Body to fit any Ford chassis.'

As country folk pushed the clutch down to the floorboard,
and disappeared with a roar and a rattle, there was indubitably a loss of ruralism and picturesqueness. Distinctions of
speech and clothing disappeared. Country people were no
longer 'countrified.' There was a new sense of unity, of belong-
ing, as the countryside drew nearer to urban patterns.

Traditional ceremonies such as those of Memorial Day and
Independence Day slipped in importance. Tom shows, even
when accompanied by a pack of genuine, live bloodhounds and
a band, needed more tack signs and street parading than
formerly to fill their tents. Interest declined among the young
in a corn popping or a candy pull. It was more exciting to go
to a show at the nickelodeon, which had moved into an empty
store building, the old stand where the general store used to

be. Big farm families no longer gathered around the cottage organ with everybody singing 'Tenting Tonight' or 'Her Golden Hair Was Hanging Down Her Back.' The time-spirit was better represented in the lyrics of 'How're You Gonna Keep 'Em Down on the Farm, After They've Seen Paree?'

As the farmers bowled along the hard road in their tin liz-zies, elements of urban life were borne out along the main motor arteries to meet them; city newspapers, department store deliveries, string-along-the-road settlements made up of homes and businesses dependent on the road and the car, owned by people who were in the country, but were not coun-try people. Nor were they customers for country stores of the older type. They liked the new stores without counters or clerks, many stores run by one efficient management, which sold standard goods at low prices and advertised heavily, under fanciful, alliterative names like Piggly Wiggly, Handy Andy, and Helpy Selfy.

The catalogue business slowed down and for the same rea-sons as did the business of the country merchant — rural mo-bility. The county *Clarion* stopped harping on 'the mail order evil,' being more concerned about whether the city was about to gobble up the village completely. The catalogue houses saved themselves by a fast transformation in the early 1920's into retail chain store systems. The country store, for all its rugged will to live, its many previous successful muta-tions, could not make this final adaptation. For a while, it looked as though the village, too, faced a future of decline and coma. Magazines were filled with retrospective articles on the old spirit of the village and intimations of a declining virtue and muscle in American life. 'Are Small Towns Doomed?' asked the Village Trustee, assuming that the battle was lost.

But the flight of trade from the country to the city was not without its exceptions, and out of the exceptions came a new day for the small, rural community. Certain businesses and services could stay small and local and still prosper — the shoe repair shop, the dry cleaner, the laundry, the insurance agency, the gasoline filling station. The automobile was repaired, fueled, and shoed as near home as possible. It became an American credo that the family car, as well as home electrical appliances, should be purchased from a local dealer, 'where you expect to get your service.'

The specialized country dealers discovered that they had certain solid advantages over the city retailer. Rents and taxes were lower. Parking was easy, service more personal. By concentrating on groceries, hardware, or men's clothing, country merchandisers could maintain stocks which would stand comparison with those of a medium-sized city store. And they were a lot nearer. But these new evidences of business vitality in the country towns did not extend to the old-fashioned type of country store.

A signal that trade was shifting to new patterns was given by the drummers. The hardware man began to space out his calls on the general store. The visits of the 'detail men,' the missionaries of the big manufacturers who replaced old stock and set up special floor displays, became infrequent. There came a year when the toy and confectionery commercial traveler skipped the general store; so there was little display of Christmas goods that year or thereafter. The canned goods man was too busy cultivating chain store headquarters to swing around through the sticks as he once did; and so it went through many lines. The salesmen knew that the customers had already disappeared, never to return, down the feeder roads that joined the concrete slab that sped like an arrow to the Big Town.

As the lights burned for the last time, then winked out in

the hanging lamps over the scarred, battered counters, the country store retired before forces that could not be diverted or stayed. As the world grew smaller, the community became larger, too large for the simple mechanism of the general store. The institution of the old, cluttered, redolent, leisurely general merchandise store is now a memory and a tradition, recalled with affection and humor and that wistfulness which is often attached to the remembrance of things past. Starting as an American improvisation to meet new conditions, serving a scattered population which had no other facilities for buying its necessities, or disposing of its little surpluses from home-use farming, the country store took on the local need, whatever it was, and tried to meet it; 'so many wants supplied on the same spot.'

Behind the counter, the general store provided for countless thousands of bright young men a first taste of the zest and adventure of business. It was a training school in the art, if not the science, of commercial affairs, graduating a continual stream of young men who found that what they had learned as crossroads clerks had its application for a banker, an automobile dealer, the sales manager of a factory, a salesman on the road, or the operator of a chain of food stores.

Other methods of distributing goods came along to serve better the needs of the motor age. None ever equaled the original Pa and Ma store as a social as well as a commercial institution.

Can the modern matron enjoy the relaxed talk-fest that her grandmother knew along country store counters, while pushing a little wire wagon in a super-market? Will the check-out girl deliver a telegram or a baby, stamp your letters, and keep an eye out for your niece who is supposed to get off the down train? Where can the stove-side congress of democratic males hold their deliberations now? Not at the livery stable, for it too has slipped off into the shadows of the past. Not at the barber shop, for it is filled with short-haired women. Not at the busy garage, reverberating with the crashing decibels and dissonances of dyspeptic engines; not at the filling station, with its grease, vapors, and cramped quarters; not at the teeming teen-age soda fountain. There are still times when a man feels the need to convene with those others of his acquaintance who also like to sit on the sunny side of life. Where is he to do it?

With the departure of the country store — counter, stove, and settle — there is no longer any point of assembly.

The congress has adjourned, sine die.

APPENDIX

Some Museum Country Stores

IN RECENT YEARS, the country store museum has come into prominence as an attractive development in the movement to bring history closer to the people generally. Often a part of a large-scale restoration or 'outdoor' museum, visited by increasing numbers of American families each year, these museums of the old crafts and trades appear to have a bright future with the assurance of able management, permanence, and continuous collecting. Among such museums are the following:

Allaire, New Jersey, restoration (projected), Department of Conservation and Economic Development, State of New Jersey.

The Brick Store Museum, Kennebunk, Maine. A general collection housed in an old store building.

Chester County Historical Society, 225 North High Street, West Chester, Pennsylvania.

Country Store of 1880, Hastings Museum, Hastings, Nebraska.

Country Store and Post Office of 1875, Rochester Museum of Arts and Sciences, Rochester, New York.

The Farmers' Museum of the New York State Historical Association, Cooperstown, New York.

General Store, part of the restoration of Virginia City, Montana.

Greenfield Village, Dearborn, Michigan.

New Salem State Park, New Salem, Illinois.

Old Country Store, 1114 S. Salina Street, Syracuse, New York. A reproduction, in a corner of Lawrence A. Johnson's supermarket.

Old Museum Village of Smith's Clove, Inc., Monroe, New York.

Old Sturbridge Village, Sturbridge, Massachusetts.

The Country Store, The Ohio State Museum, Columbus. An exhibit.

Country Store Exhibit, Chicago Historical Society, Chicago, Illinois.

Pennsylvania State Museum, Harrisburg, Pennsylvania.

Pony Express Museum, Arcadia, California.

Shelburne Museum, Shelburne, Vermont.

The Sheldon Museum, Middlebury, Vermont.

The Southampton Historical Museum, Southampton, New York. Old Country Store (projected).

Storrowtown, West Springfield, Massachusetts.

Warp's Pioneer Village, Minden, Nebraska.

Those who enjoy 'collecting' old-time stores may wish to take note of another kind, where a modern business is conducted in an old-fashioned setting. The past and the present are combined in the celebrated country store of Vrest Orton at Weston, Vermont. Milton and Miriam Sunderland run an active 'Crossroads Store' at Waterbury, also in Vermont. F. H. Trumbull's Country Store at Concord, Massachusetts and Larry Freeman's at Watkins Glen, New York, are random examples of a flourishing group which carries on today's business in the traditional type of building, equipped with old fixtures. All of these modern country merchants also carry on a mail-order catalogue business.

Various individuals have found a personal hobby in re-creating the nineteenth-century world of shelves and counters, coffee grinders, paper collars, and high button shoes; among them, Major A. Erland Goyette, Peterborough, New Hampshire, Dr. Herbert W. Kuhn, Milwaukee, Wisconsin, and George H. Stone, North Stonington, Connecticut. Henry Ford restored a 1798 building in 1930, which is now operated as part-store, part-museum by Milt and Edna Swanson, at South Sudbury, Massachusetts. During the summer months Janet Harkin Massopust, Route 1, New Ulm, Minnesota, shows visitors around her grandfather Harkin's store, which is not a restoration but consists of the original stock and fixtures in an 1871 building.

Notes on Sources and Authorities and Chapter References

QUOTATIONS AND SPECIFIC FACTS taken directly from a document, contemporary source, or modern work are cited under the chapter references that follow.

In addition, the writer wishes to acknowledge a broad obligation to numerous publications not cited, but which were drawn on for the re-creation of the social or economic situation in earlier times. A list, necessarily incomplete, follows:

Percy Wells Bidwell's 'Rural Economy in New England at the Beginning of the Nineteenth Century,' *Transactions of the Connecticut Academy of Arts and Sciences* (Vol. 20, Apr. 1916) was frequently consulted for information on agriculture and farm marketing, commercial and social life in New England. Another regional account of rural life, David Maldwyn Ellis's *Landlords and Farmers in the Hudson-Mohawk Region,* 1790–1850 (Ithaca, 1946) covers much the same period for portions of New York state; and Ulysses Prentiss Hedrick's *A History of Agriculture in the State of New York* (Albany, 1933) brings its account down to the 1900's. A valuable social and agricultural history for Pennsylvania is Stevenson Whitcomb Fletcher's *Pennsylvania Agriculture and Country Life* (Harrisburg, 1950).

Chapters IV, V, and VII of *The Rise of the Common Man,* 1830–1850, by Carl Russell Fish (New York, 1927), in the *History of American Life* series, are excellent for summarizing farm life during the period, the development of industry, manners and customs, and the intellectual atmosphere. The critical essay on authorities is invaluable. *Robert Gair: a study,* by H. Allen Smith (New York, 1939) contains material on the change-over in consumer goods from bulk commodities to small-unit, branded shelf goods, with special reference to the paper board industry and the folding carton.

Personal narratives consulted, other than those cited in the chapter references, include *The Diary of Philip Hone,* 1828–1851, edited with an introduction by Allan Nevins (2 vols., New York, 1927); Frances Trollope's *Domestic Manners of the Americans,* edited by Donald Smalley (New York, 1949); *Nailer Tom's Diary,* with an introduction by Caroline Hazard (Boston, 1930); and *A Tour Through Indiana in* 1840, by John Parsons, edited by Kate Milner Rabb (New York, 1920).

Local histories provide a rich source of anecdote and detail, such as M. M. Baldwin's *Historical Sketch of the Town of Groton, Tompkins County, New York* (Groton, 1868); Charles R. Baker's *Philadelphia in the Late 'Forties* (2 vols., Philadelphia, 1931); *City Cries* (Philadelphia, 1850); *Annals of Philadelphia and Pennsylvania,* by John F. Watson (3 vols., Philadelphia, 1900); James H. Smith's *History of Livingston County, New York* (Syracuse, 1881);

Cries of New-York, by Frances S. Osgood (New York, 1846); *They Broke the Prairie,* by Earnest Elmo Calkins (New York, 1937); *Connecticut, a Guide to Its Roads, Lore, and People,* written by Workers of the Federal Writers' Project of the Works Progress Administration (Cambridge, 1938); *Chronicles of Kennebunk,* by William Edward Barry (New York, 1923); and by the same author, *A Stroll Thro' the Past* (Portland, 1933); and Edward E. Bourne's *The History of Wells and Kennebunk from the Earliest Settlements to the Year* 1820 (Portland, 1875).

Pamphlets not referred to in the chapter notes, issued by the sponsors of various 'museum stores,' contain a variety of useful material:

The Farmers' Museum (Cooperstown, 1948); *Greenfield Village Guide Book* (Dearborn, n.d.); *A Guide Book for the Museum of the Edison Institute* (Dearborn, 1941); *New Salem State Park* (Springfield, Ill., n.d.); *The Old Country Store* (Cooperstown, n.d.); *Storrowtown* (West Springfield, Mass., 1930).

A considerable amount of pamphlet literature exists on the auction method of selling goods at wholesale. Pamphlets used as background for the portion of Chapter VII which discusses this subject are: *Auctions Inconsistent with Regular Trade and Injurious to the City: Address to the People of New-York* (New York, 1817); *Auctioneering, the Beneficial Tendency of, and the Danger of Restraining It,* by a Friend to Trade (New York, 1817); *Reasons Why the Present System of Auctions Ought to be Abolished* (New York, 1828). See also letter from Richard Peters of Philadelphia, Speaker of the Pennsylvania Assembly, written 9 Mar. 1790, to Thomas Fitzsimmons in New York (*The Pennsylvania Magazine of History and Biography,* 1883, Vol. VII, No. 1: 110); *American Agriculturist* (Vol. XIX, No. 1, New Series No. 166: 357, Nov. 1860); 'Jacob Peabody and Company, Auctioneers,' (*Bulletin of the Business Historical Society,* Vol. VIII, No. 3, May 1934).

The age of cottage industry is admirably chronicled in *Household Manufactures in the United States* 1640–1860, by Rolla Milton Tryon (Chicago, 1917). For the later development of manufacturing and industry, Victor S. Clark's *History of Manufactures in the United States* (3 vols., New York, 1929); *U.S. Census. 10th. 1880. Manufactures,* Vol. 2; Carl Crow's readable *The Great American Customer* (New York, 1943).

The following works were consulted in connection with the

development of trade and commerce: *One Hundred Years of Ameri-*
can Commerce 1795–1895 (2 vols., New York, 1895); *One Hundred*
Years' Progress of the United States (Hartford, 1871); Kenneth
Wiggins Porter's *The Jacksons and the Lees, Two Generations of*
Massachusetts Merchants, 1765–1844 (Cambridge, 1937); *History*
of Domestic and Foreign Commerce of the United States, by Emory
R. Johnson and others (2 vols., Washington, 1915).

Business handbooks, catalogues and price lists, circulars,
trade cards, advertising, and other ephemeral printed matter helped
to fill out details on country retailing; such as *McCready's Credit*
Register for Retail Dealers and Country Merchants (Boston, 1884);
Weekly Price Current of Arbuckle & Co. (25 Jan. 1886); *Brad-*
street's Weekly Market Quotations in Dry Goods with Index to First
Hands (Vol. III, No. 6, New York, 8 Feb. 1877); a circular of
H. Crouse's Notion and Variety Store, Reading, Pa., *c.*1870; cata-
logue of Thomas Dana and Co., wholesale grocers (Boston, 1879);
J. Montfiore's *The American Trader's Compendium* (Philadelphia,
1811); Parker's *American Citizen's Sure Guide, or Ready Reckoner*
(Sag Harbor, 1808); *Price List of Groceries, Jan. & Feb.* 1902, No.
473, Montgomery Ward & Co. (Chicago, 1902); 'Things Ain't What
They Used to Be,' mimeographed (Dayton, 1941); *Origin of the*
Cash Register, National Cash Register Company, mimeographed
(n.p., n.d.); *Food Merchandising in America* (Dayton, n.d.); *Bicar-*
bonotes, Vol. I, No. 1, March 1946, internal company publication of
Church & Dwight (New York, 1946); *Only a Drummer,* by Wilbur
Elijah Castelow (n.p., 1903).

Many articles have appeared in periodicals over the years
dealing with the country store and related subjects, written from a
personal, reminiscent, or anecdotal point of view, or as a contribution
to sociology or business history. The writer found the following useful: Earnest Elmo Calkins, 'The Changing Face of Main Street,'
The Rotarian, 54: 14–17, Apr. 1939; Don Marquis, 'My Memories
of the Old-Fashioned Drummer,' *American Magazine,* 107: 20–21,
Feb. 1929; Phyllis Fenner, 'Grandfather's Country Store,' *American*
Mercury, 61: 672–7, Dec. 1945; Margaret Dana, 'Elegy of the Country Storekeeper,' *The Atlantic Monthly,* 153: 285–94, Mar. 1934;
Charles Moreau Harger, 'The Country Store,' *The Atlantic*
Monthly, 95: 91–8, Jan. 1905; 'Counter Irritants,' by the Proprie-
tor's Daughter, *Canadian Magazine,* 62: 331–9, Mar. 1924.

For material used in Chapter IV on penmanship and writing
accessories, the writer drew upon 'American Penmanship,' by Stanley Morrison, *The Colophon,* Vol. V, Part 17, June 1934. In *Food*

Marketing in New England, Sept. 1950, and Jan. 1951, are scattered articles, pictures, and captions regarding 'period' stores, old-time merchandise, and store equipment. *Harper's Magazine,* Centennial Issue, Oct. 1950, contains retrospective material about life and society in the century 1850–1950. An excellent summary of the social significance of the general store by Professor Thomas D. Clark appeared in the *Ohio State Archeological and Historical Quarterly,* Vol. 60, No. 2, Apr. 1951, under the title 'The Country Store in American Social History.'

Other serial publications which were useful were 'The Country Store,' by Ellen C. (Hobbs) Rollins, *Old-Time New England,* Vol. xx, No. 3, Serial No. 59, Jan. 1930; 'Kim's Store,' by Sarah Endicott Ober, edited by Augustus Peabody Loring, Jr., *Old-Time New England,* Vol. xli, July 1950–Apr. 1951; Will Rose's 'The Passing of the Country Store,' *Scribner's Magazine,* 80: 362–7, Oct. 1926; *The Rural New-Yorker,* 7 Jan. 1950, 100th Anniversary issue, dealing with country life over the century; Charlotte Curtis' 'My Grandfather's General Store,' *Yankee,* May 1949; 'The Country Store Survives,' by Charles Morrow Wilson, *Outlook and Independent,* 157: 142–3, 28 Jan. 1931; 'Who Said Eheu Fugaces?' by Henry Tetlow, *Commonweal,* 29: 294–5, 6 Jan. 1939; 'Are Small Towns Doomed?' by a Village Trustee, *American Mercury,* 32: 74–9, May 1934.

In addition to the sources referred to in the references on Chapter xiii the following were consulted during the preparation of this chapter: David I. Cohn's *Informal History of the Automobile Age* (Boston, 1944), and 'The Automobile and the Village Merchant,' *University of Illinois Bulletin, Bureau of Business Research,* #19, Vol. xxv, No. 41, Urbana, 1928; and 'Farewell, My Lovely,' by Lee Strout White, *New Yorker,* 16 May 1936.

A specialized dictionary of great usefulness was the *Dictionary of Folklore, Mythology and Legend,* edited by Marie Leach (New York, 1949). Among bibliographical works that opened up avenues for investigation were William Matthews' *American Diaries, An Annotated Bibliography of American Diaries Written Prior to the Year* 1861 (Berkeley and Los Angeles, 1945); Henrietta M. Larson's monumental *Guide to Business History* (Cambridge, 1948), a work absolutely essential to this study; and the check-lists to the manuscript collections of the New-York Historical Society, the Historical Society of Pennsylvania, and the second edition of the *List of Business Manuscripts in Baker Library,* compiled by Robert W. Lovett (Boston, 1951).

CHAPTER REFERENCES

LOCATION OF MANUSCRIPT MATERIAL is given the first time the item is cited. Key: (B) = Baker Library, Harvard University; (C) = Columbia University Library; (Ill) = Archives of the University of Illinois Library; (MHC) = Michigan Historical Collections of the University of Michigan; (NYHS) = New-York Historical Society; (NYPL) = New York Public Library; (NYSHA) = New York State Historical Association Library; (NYSL) = New York Library; (P) = privately owned; (W) = Library, Williams College.

Preface
'Coles County in the 1840's,' *Journal of the Illinois State Historical Society, Summer,* 1952, Vol. XLV, No. 2.

News Release. Text of the remarks made by President Dwight D. Eisenhower to the American Retail Federation, at the Statler Hotel, Washington, D.C., 5 March 1953.

The language used by Governor Thomas Dongan in setting up a manorial patent appears repeatedly in *The Documentary History of the State of New York,* 4 vols., Albany, 1850, III.

Chapter One
The anecdote about Eddie, the dispensable man, is from Walter Hard's *The Connecticut,* New York, 1947. Grandma Crumbaker's listening technique on the telephone was described in *The Chicago Tribune,* 6 November 1952.

For the financial situation following the Revolution, the following authorities were consulted: William B. Weedon, *Economic and Social History of New England* 1620–1789, 2 vols., Boston, 1891; and John Bach McMaster, *A History of the People of the United States,* 8 vols., New York, 1900–1920. The characterization of the spirit of inquiry and invention in the 1790's was suggested by a passage in Edwin G. Conklin's *Brief History of the American Philosophical Society,* separate from *Year Book* of The American Philosophical Society for 1950, Philadelphia, 1950.

The verses are from the *Connecticut Courant,* 27 Apr. 1795, quoted in Margaret E. Martin's, 'Merchants and Trade of the Connecticut River Valley 1750–1820,' *Smith College Studies in History,* Vol. xxiv, Nos. 1–4, Oct. 1938–July 1939.

Chapter Two

Olive Butland appears in the Personal Account Book of William Wise, Kennebunk, Me. (NYHS); A. H. French in the store ledger of Lyman C. Scott, Rockport, Ill. (P). Milo Milton Quaife edited the edition of *A True Picture of Emigration* (Rebecca Burlend), Chicago, 1936. George Walker was a general merchant at Lenox, Mass. References are to his personal papers (W).

The country merchant's role in developing manufactures is developed in Harry A. Wooster's essay, 'A Forgotten Factor in Industrial History,' *American Economic Review,* Vol. xvi, No. 1, 1926. The saying about cider apples was collected by Edith E. Cutting for *Whistling Girls and Jumping Sheep,* Cooperstown, 1951. The recollection of Jedediah Barber is found in Herbert Barber Howe's *Jedediah Barber,* 1787–1876, New York, 1939.

Charles Morrow Wilson tells how back hills whiskey was extended in *Backwoods America,* Chapel Hill, 1934. Tom Haines told me what the farmers' wives did when a mouse fell into the cream. The merchant-diarist who bought a load of frozen apples will be found in James W. Silver, ed., 'Diary of a One-Horse Enterpriser: Fifty Years Ago in Up-state New York,' *New York History,* Vol. xxxiii, No. 2, Apr. 1952.

P. T. Barnum's account of sharp practices is from *Barnum's Own Story,* New York, 1927. The brush between the storekeeper and the weaver is from Alice Brayton's *Trading in Scrabbletown,* Newport, n.d. Crevecoeur's remark appears in St. John de Crevecoeur, *Sketches of Eighteenth Century America: More 'Letters from an American Farmer,'* edited by Henri L. Bourin, Ralph H. Gabriel, and Stanley T. Williams, New Haven, 1925. Helen Hartness Flanders found the versified inventory in 'The Cobb Manuscript of Reading, Vermont,' *Vermont Quarterly,* Vol. xx, No. 3, July 1952.

For the attitude of countrymen toward the businessman I am indebted to the material developed by Kenneth Wiggins Porter in 'The Business Man in American Folklore,' *Bulletin of the Business His-*

torical Society, Vol. xvii, No. 5, Whole Number 110, Nov. 1944. Data on the mail-order catalogue business was gathered from Montgomery Ward and Company's *Fall & Winter Catalogue & Buyers Guide, No. 63,* 1894–5, Chicago, 1894; and from *Send No Money,* by Louis E. Asher and Edith Heal, Chicago, 1942.

Chapter Three

The Skowhegan peddler appears in *Southern Folklore Quarterly,* Vol. xii, No. 3, Sept. 1948. The Newark *Advertiser's* description of the Yankee peddler was reprinted in the *Vermont Quarterly,* Vol. xix, No. 2, Apr. 1951. Information on the scope of peddling appears in *U.S. Census,* 1850: *Statistics,* lxxiv; *U.S. Census,* 1860: *Population;* and Fred Mitchell Jones, 'Middlemen in the Domestic Trade of the United States 1800–1860,' *Illinois Studies in the Social Sciences,* Vol. xxi, No. 3, Urbana, 1937. The poetic treatment of the same theme appears in Richardson Wright's *Hawkers & Walkers in Early America,* Philadelphia, 1927.

For the licensing of peddlers, and the difficulties involved in their occupation, I relied on Fred Mitchell Jones, op. cit.; Lewis E. Atherton, 'Itinerant Merchandising in the Ante-Bellum South,' *Bulletin of the Business Historical Society,* Vol. xix, No. 2, Whole Number 113, Apr. 1945; and *Peddlers' Licenses,* 4 vols., 1840–86, Secretary's Office, New York State (NYSL).

I met the peddler who outwitted the sheriff in Frazar Kirkland, (pseud.), R. M. Devens, *Cyclopaedia of Commercial and Business Anecdotes,* 2 vols., New York, 1864. The quotation from Timothy Flint appears in *Recollections of the Last Ten Years,* Boston, 1826. J. L. McConnel sketched the clock peddler in *Western Characters, or Types of Border Life in the Western States,* New York, 1853; and President Dwight's pronouncement on the morals of peddling will be found in his *Travels in New England and New-York,* 4 vols., New Haven, 1821; also quoted in George Lyman Kittredge's *The Old Farmer and his Almanack,* Cambridge, 1924. Gouverneur Morris's views on Connecticut will be found in *Yankees and Yorkers,* by Dixon Ryan Fox, New York, 1940. Bernard's remark is in *Retrospections of America,* 1797–1811, edited by Mrs. Bernard Bayle, New York, 1887.

A credit report is the basis for the estimate of peddler Samson's net worth, from Roy A. Foulke, *The Sinews of American Commerce,* New York, 1941. The sketch of the peddler at Williams College is from Nathaniel Hawthorne, *Passages from the American Note-Books,* in *The Complete Works of Nathaniel Hawthorne,* 12 vols.,

Cambridge, 1886. James Guild's picaresque adventures are taken from his journal 'From Tunbridge, Vermont to London, England — The Journal of James Guild,' *Proceedings of the Vermont Historical Society,* Vol. v, No. 3, New Series, Sept. 1937. Information about William Holbrook comes from his MS. Diaries and Journals, Jan.-Dec. 1834 (NYSL).

Morillo Noyes, the master peddler, appears in the annotated *List of Business Manuscripts in Baker Library,* compiled by Margaret Ronzone Cusick, Boston, 1932. I also used a collection of Noyes's records, 1859–77 (B). Fred Ellis, the Missouri peddler, was the subject of a feature article in *The Gazette,* St. Joseph, Mo., 28 Sept. 1950; quoted in Hallie Burrow's 'The Travelling Sears & Roebuck,' *Missouri Historical Review,* Vol. XLV, No. 3, Apr. 1951. Oren Wiley's journal was published in *The Ohio State Archeological and Historical Quarterly,* Vol. 60, No. 2, Apr. 1951.

I found details on women peddlers in 'Early Peddlers Around Wilmington,' by Elizabeth Covey, *Green Mountain Whittlin's,* Vol. II, Burlington, n.d.; and Mary Ellen Chase's *A Goodly Heritage,* New York, 1934. Arthur N. Hall described the 'Carter teams,' in 'The Old Wholesale Peddler and his Teams,' *New England Magazine,* Aug. 1900. Barnum's peddler story is from the work by him already cited. Details of the equipment and cost of Jared Warner's venture in peddling are taken from Fred Mitchell Jones, op. cit.; of Dexter Knowlton's rise in the world from Addison L. Fulwider, *History of Stephenson County, Illinois,* 2 vols., Chicago, 1910. The old merchant's prayer for his son is quoted from James W. Silver, ed., op. cit.

Chapter Four

The contemporary estimates of keeping store as an occupation are from *The Perils of Pearl Street, including a taste of the Dangers of Wall Street,* by a late Merchant (Asa Greene), New York, 1834; and Barnum, op. cit. Lincoln's experience in a pioneer country store is the subject of *Berry and Lincoln Frontier Merchants,* by Zarel C. Spears and Robert S. Barton, New York, 1947. I have followed their account. Solomon Aines's store sign may still be seen at the Sheldon Museum, Middlebury, Vt. *Willard's Troy Almanac* is the 1852 issue. Dr. Rutherford's letter about prices and store credit appears in 'Coles County in the 1840's,' *Journal of the Illinois State Historical Society,* op. cit. The names of Boston wholesalers and the lines they handled were found in an old barrel by Alice Brayton, op. cit. The marketing of Ohio produce in New Orleans is told with particular grace by Harriet Connor Brown in *Grandmother Brown's Hundred Years*, 1827–1927, Boston, 1929. My account of the financial operations of Burrows in early Davenport, Iowa, is taken from *The Early Day of Rock Island and Davenport: The Narratives of J. W. Spencer and J. M. D. Burrows,* edited by Milo Milton Quaife, Chicago, 1942.

The aphorism about misleading with the truth is in *Yankee Drummer,* by R. E. Gould, New York, 1948. Mrs. Stephen K. Perry (Alice Cone) wrote to me about the patience of the general storekeeper, with Mark Cone (1819–85), of Hartford, Vt., especially in mind. James W. Silver, ed., op. cit., records the belief that grocers are born, not made. Barber was the merchant who had the law on 42 delinquents, all at once — Howe, op. cit. Gould's comment on the credit customer appears in *Yankee Storekeeper,* New York, 1946, and Fulwider, op. cit., tells how Knowlton collected his debt from Charlie Hall.

Stories of George Clark's ham and Hiram Bissell's peephole were told to me by Sidney O. Cowles. The dealer who offered his customer his money back and later regretted it appears in Frank Farrington's *Talks by the Old Storekeeper,* Delhi, New York, 1906. The tale of the stolen barrel of pork is authentic folklore. I got it from Charles W. Brewster, *Rambles About Portsmouth,* Second Series, Portsmouth, N.H., 1869; and Howe, op. cit. Clarence Stotts and Tom Haines each told me about the use of the cane in petty thievery. Howe, op. cit., has the anecdote of the Wisconsin judge. Tom Haines tells of the turnip deal in Illinois.

The tale of Tubbydub was a memory of Wilbur Cross's, told in *Connecticut Yankee,* New Haven, 1943. Sophronie, the slow-witted girl with the fast answer, was 'collected' by Harold W. Thompson, op. cit. I drew material from a story of Sylvanus Cobb, Jr., 'The Crossed Dollar: or The Country Dealer and his Clerk,' *Gleason's Pictorial,* Vol. v, No. 23, Whole No. 75, 18 Feb. 1854. The description of rustic shoppers was suggested by a scene in *Rural Hours,* by a Lady (Susan Fenimore Cooper), New York, 1850. The incident in the store at Arrow Rock, Missouri, is retold from T. C. Rainey, *Along the Old Trail: Pioneer Sketches of Arrow Rock and Vicinity,* Marshall, Mo., 1914. Brown, op. cit., tells how Dan'l Brown found the good life in a country general store.

Chapter Five

Allyn Fuller told me about storekeeper Bragg and his unconventional accounting system. How to make ink? See Henry Dean, *Dean's Analytical Guide to the Art of Penmanship,* Salem, 1805. Information on pricing and storekeeping in the early Middle West rests on John Beauchamp Jones ('Luke Shortfield,' pseud.), *The Western Merchant,* Philadelphia, 1849; and Samuel H. Terry, *How to Keep a Store,* New York, 1887. For the description of country store accounting, various books on mid-nineteenth-century methods were consulted, but primarily John H. Shea's *Bookkeeping, by Single and Double Entry: simplified and arranged, according to the present practise of Well Regulated Counting Houses in the United States,* 2nd ed., Baltimore, 1841.

The 'chore boy' supplied me with a most useful MS. memoir, 'The Rapp Store at Geff, Illinois, in the Eighties,' by S. S. Lappin. The year of the *Farmer's Almanack* to which I referred is 1806, quoted in Kittredge, op. cit. Asa Greene, op. cit., gives a summary of the educational equipment a country clerk was supposed to have in the early 1800's. Professor Megonegal and his advertising contemporaries live — or are buried? — in *Paulson's American Daily Advertiser,* Philadelphia, 24 Dec. 1836. The cry of the charcoal man, with many others, too, is printed in Mrs. A. J. Rowland's *Street Cries of Philadelphia,* 2 vols., Philadelphia, 1922. All that we are ever likely to know about Fred Hall is in his MS. Bookkeeping Study Book, Birmingham, Conn., n.d. (C). The form letter for sending an order to a jobber is given in *The Letter Writer's Own Book, or, the Art of Polite Correspondence,* Philadelphia, 1850.

The letter describing the opportunity at Jackson, Mich., appears in David T. McCollum's Scrapbook, letter of 18 Aug. 1853 (MHC). Higinbotham, op. cit., was consulted generally for details on how clerks were managed. For the early history of the cash register I used John H. Patterson's *Report to the Stockholders of the National Cash Register Company,* June 1906. The critical account of cash register sales methods in the 'eighties and 'nineties is that of T. C. Henry, *Tricks of the Cash Register Trust,* Winchester, Ky., 1913. The description of the competitive machine comes from *Our Drummer: Unabridged Catalogue No. 494, Spring,* 1904, Butler Brothers, New York, 1904. The honesty of the rural dealers, based upon a study of store records, is affirmed by Jacqueline P. Bull, 'The General Merchant in the Economic History of the New South,' *The Journal of Southern History,* Vol. xviii, No. 1, Feb. 1952.

The old daybook with the 'well' cut out of its center was Chauncey M. Brewer's, Battle Creek, Mich., Day Book I (MHC). The mid-nineteenth-century joke was found among the George Walker papers (W).

Chapter Six

'Cash given,' etc. — advertisement of Ebenezer Hunt, *Hampshire Gazette,* 9 Nov. 1797. 'Anything eatable, drinkable' — advertisement in the *Weekly Visitor,* Kennebunk, Me., 1809; quoted without day or month, in Daniel Remich, *History of Kennebunk from its Earliest Settlement to* 1890, Portland, 1911.

For cobbling as a side line, see Sewell Dearborn, Deerfield, N.H. Mercantile Account Book, 1811–34 (NYPL). John Bigelow tells about lumbering and tan bark as side ventures of his father, Asa, a general merchant at Bristol, now Malden, N.Y., in *Retrospections of an Active Life,* 5 vols., New York, 1909–13.

The Battels, father and son, appear in *History of Litchfield County, Connecticut,* Philadelphia, 1881. The storekeeper who also manufactured pot ashes was probably the commonest example of petty capitalism in industry. Jared Van Wagenen, Jr., has estimated that there were over 700 asheries in New York state alone in the early nineteenth century. The versatile Stephen Thacher appears in Remich, op. cit. The comparison of country trader and city merchant is developed from Martin, op. cit. John Beauchamp Jones gives the characterization of the merchant as a general *locum tenens.*

The account of how Lincoln acquired his Blackstone, as given here, is supported by Ida Tarbell, and by Zarel C. Spears and Robert S. Barton in their work previously cited. Other authorities affirm that Lincoln got his *Commentaries* at an auction in Springfield. Brayton, op. cit., prints the schoolmaster's letter of application. The story of Dote Thompson was given to me by Mrs. Paul Eager, in the MS. recollections of James Theodore Budrow, 'Adventures of a Boy in the Sixties,' n.p., *c.*1932 (P). Mrs. Post's exploit is taken from Pomroy Jones, *Annals and Recollections of Oneida County,* Rome, 1851. The pretty exchange between Miss Grant and storekeeper Palmer occurs in Edward E. Bourne, *The History of Wells and Kennebunk from the Earliest Settlement to the Year* 1820, Portland, 1875.

For the account of militia doings the following works were consulted: William Oliver, *Eight Months in Illinois,* Chicago, 1924; Frances Manwaring Caulkins, *History of New London, Connecticut,* New London, 1852; Timothy W. Robinson, *History of the Town of Morrill in the County of Waldo and State of Maine,* edited by Theora Mears Morse, Belfast, 1944; Howe, op. cit.; *Hoosier Folklore,* Vol. IX, No. 4, Oct.–Dec. 1950; *The Berkshire Hills,* Vol. II, No. 5, Jan.

1902, Kittredge, op. cit.; and *Green Mountain Whittlin's,* op. cit. Paul Eager told me about Frank Bailey, Dr. Arthur W. Peach about the dealer at Marlborough, Vt. 'Butch' Carr's funeral is based on the obituary in *The Patriot,* Carrollton, Ill., 8 Feb. 1895.

Chapter Seven

My portrayal of lower Manhattan a hundred years ago is based on *The New York City Directory for* 1851–52, Doggett & Rode, New York, 1851; E. Porter Belden, *New York: Past, Present & Future,* New York, 1849; I. N. P. Stokes, *Iconography of Manhattan Island,* 1498–1909, 6 vols., New York, 1926. See also Asa Greene, *A Glance at New York,* New York, 1837. Foulke, op. cit., gives a detailed account of the origins of the mercantile credit agency.

For the atmosphere of the New York wholesale markets: Kirkland, op. cit., John Beauchamp Jones, op. cit., and Edwin T. Freedley's *U.S. Mercantile Guide,* Philadelphia, 1856; and Paul H. Nystrom's *Economics of Retailing,* 2 vols., New York, 1930. The newspaper quip about the jobber's salesman being a 'borer' appeared in the *Public Ledger,* Philadelphia, Pa., Thursday, 23 Aug. 1836.

The bibliographical essay in the preceding section makes acknowledgment of sources used generally for describing the struggle between the wholesalers and auctioneers, an early outbreak of the 'middleman' issue. Specifically, I used the MS. Papers, 'Deeds, Letters 1807–1841' of Jacob Peabody & Company, Vol. 11, Salem, Mass. (B); Ray Bert Westerfield, 'Early History of American Auctions — a Chapter in Commercial History,' *Transactions of the Connecticut Academy of Arts and Sciences,* Vol. 23, May 1920; *New York Assembly Journal,* 1816, quoted in Westerfield, op. cit.; and Kirkland, op. cit. See also Gerald Carson, 'The Great Auction Controversy,' *Journal of the National Society of Autograph Collectors,* Spring 1953.

The episode of the country merchant venturing out upon New York to taste the town is imagined. Details were gathered from *The New York City Directory,* op. cit.; the *New York Herald,* 9 Mar. 1852; and Lewis E. Atherton's *The Southern Country Store,* 1800–1860, Baton Rouge, 1949. The agricultural machinery of the period is described in Hamlin Garland's *A Son of the Middle Border,* New York, 1917, and U. P. Hedrick's *The Land of the Crooked Tree,* New York, 1948. Edwin T. Freedley, in *Leading Pursuits and Leading Men,* Philadelphia, 1856, emphasizes the obligation upon the merchant to bring home ideas as well as a stock of goods.

The line about Hubard Smith's discomfiture is quoted from the

MS. diary of Mark Cone (P). Israel Brayton's misfortune comes from Brayton, op. cit. For the Scovil Manufacturing Company's experiment with traveling salesmen, I am indebted to Theodore F. Marburg's 'Manufacturer's Drummer — 1832,' *Bulletin of the Business Historical Society*, Vol. xxii, No. 2, Whole No. 131, Apr. 1948. The canny youth who decided that $600 in Battle Creek was as good as $1000 in New York was McCollum, op. cit. Farwell's exuberant way of announcing the arrival of his drummers is taken from Lloyd Wendt and Herman Kogan, *Give the Lady What She Wants*, Chicago, 1952. One day's list of new inventions is given as it appeared in the *Public Ledger*, Philadelphia, 24 Dec. 1851. The little book the merchant carried with him was by Charles P. Forbes, compiler, *The Merchant's Memorandum and PRICE BOOK: adapted to the Principal Branches of Mercantile Business, Designed as a General Memorandum for Country Traders*, 5th ed., Boston, 1828.

The advertising splurge which, it is suggested, the country dealer planned in order to signal his return home, is modeled on the advertisement of William H. Kelly, Milledgeville, Carroll County, Ill., 1855, reproduced in Marshall Davidson, *Life in America*, 2 vols., Boston, 1951.

Chapter Eight

Data for the account given of the local licensing of traveling salesmen comes from: *The System of Commercial Travelling in Europe and the United States; its History, Customs, and Laws*, New York, 1869, and Edward P. Briggs, *Fifty Years on the Road: The Autobiography of a Travelling Salesman*, Philadelphia, 1911. For the transition from stay-at-home to *traveling* salesman, I consulted Isaac Holmes, *An Account of the United States of America*, London, 1823; Nystrom, op. cit. 1915 ed.; William H. Baldwin, *Travelling Salesmen: Their Opportunities and their Dangers, An Address Delivered before the Boston Young Men's Christian Union, November 22, 1874*, Boston, 1874; Charles S. Plummer's *Leaves from a Drummer's Diary, or Twenty-five Years on the Road*, Chicago, 1889; Briggs, op. cit.; *The System*, etc., op. cit.; Scrapbook of the Commercial Travellers Association of the State of New York, c.1872–3 (NYSL); and *New York Herald*, 19 Feb. 1877.

For the traveler's view of himself, I am indebted to L. P. Brockett's *The Commercial Traveller's Guide Book*, New York, 1871; Plummer, op. cit.; *What I Know About Commercial Travelling*, by A. Emerson Belcher, Toronto, 1883; and the *National Magazine*, Vol. 19: 645. Biographies of early salesmen who later made a stir in the world were found in *Modern Packaging,* Vol. 22, No. 12, Aug. 1949; and in *Pills, Petticoats and Plows,* by Thomas D. Clark, Indianapolis, 1944.

The whiskey salesman's joke on the D.A.R. is told in *News and Notes,* Vermont Historical Society, Vol. III, No. 6, Feb. 1952. The hatching out of a young drummer is based on Charles N. Crewdson's *Tales of the Road,* Chicago, 1905. Mrs. Roy Runka told me many stories about Charles Nuffer, and I wish I could have used them all. The comment of the hotel stenographer on drummers is from *The Travelling Man as I Found Him,* by a Hotel Stenographer (Mabel Hoster), Indianapolis, 1904. The idyll of the Arm and Hammer Soda man in New York state has two sources, a letter from W. Ford Haviland, and the MS. diary of Foster L. Haviland, Sept. 1897 (P). The samples of drummers' advance notices of arrivals are from Mrs. J. Q. Rapp, General Store Invoice Book, Jeffersonville, Ill. (Ill).

The date of the quotation from *The Daily Freeman,* Kingston, N.Y. is Thursday, 13 Jan. 1876. The Scrapbook of the Commercial Travellers Association, op. cit., contains the *New York World* item, n.d. The poem from which I used four lines is Lena Hertzberg's, 'A Letter from Home,' quoted in Plummer, op. cit. Advice on what the well-dressed drummer should wear is from Brockett, op. cit. The moral strictures appear in Baldwin, op. cit., and the *New York Herald,* op. cit., reported the Rev. Talmadge's sermon. The social doings of the drummers in Syracuse are preserved in the Scrapbook, op. cit. Efforts of Butler Brothers to promote the five-and-ten-cent counter idea among rural stores are described in *A Man of Samples,* by William H. Maher, Chicago, 1888.

Donald Sears told me about Henry Hull and his goose-poke. The pulpit story is in *Green Mountain Whittlin's,* Vol. II, op. cit., and is also told of the Grant Minor store, which was moved in 1938 from Stafford Springs, Conn., to become part of Old Sturbridge Village, in Mass. Howe, op. cit., has the tale of the toad.

Chapter Nine

The passage 'An Omnibus Store' appeared in *Philadelphia Merchant,* n.d., quoted in *Hunt's Merchants' Magazine and Commercial Review,* Vol. 32, Jan.–June 1855. A thread cabinet still stands on the counter of the old C. L. Adams river-front store at Quincy, Ill. Another is part of the exhibit at the Waterford Store, Greenfield Village, Dearborn, Mich., and William Medders, who is very much in business at Still Pond, Md., has several tucked around in one corner or another.

Information on country store candies comes from Louis Unter-meyer, *A Century of Candymaking: 1847–1947. The Story of the Origin and Growth of New England Confectionery Company*, Cambridge, 1947. Estimates of the value of general store stocks are based on specific stores; Hedrick, op. cit., and the Inventory Book of Fuller and Peet, Canaan, Conn., 1865–70 inclusive (P). James A. Carson told me about the smell of Mason's Blacking. Clark, op. cit., develops the importance of mourning goods. Clarence F. Stotts has a counter railing in his store at Colebrook, Conn. Cross, op. cit., tells about the room behind the store. The shift in the manufacture of tinware from artisan's shop to factory is one of many instances given of industrialization in J. Leander Bishop, *A History of American Manufactures*, 2 vols., Philadelphia, 1864.

For the discussion of the beginnings of the paper bag and folding carton I used *The Folding Carton*, Folding Carton Paper Box Association of America, Chicago, 1950; *the American Grocer and Dry Goods Chronicle*, No. 14, 4 Oct. 1883; article on 'The Paper Bag,' in *Modern Packaging Encyclopedia*, New York, 1946–7. Also *Modern Packaging*, Vol. 19, No. 10, June 1946; and *The Grocer's Companion and Merchant's Hand-book*, Boston, 1883.

About flies and screens: Bishop, op. cit., does not mention door or window screens, nor does Edwin T. Freedley when he discusses the metal-working industry in *Philadelphia and its Manufactures*, Philadelphia, 1858. The effort to establish the date of door and window screening was based on a study of the *Subject-matter Index of Patents for Inventions Issued . . . 1790–1873*, U.S. Patent Office, 3 vols., Washington, 1874.

Donald Sears told me about Dean's windlass. William Lord's may still be seen at the Brick Store Museum, Kennebunk, Me. Dote Thompson's storage arrangement is given in detail in the Budrow MS., op. cit. The figure of 5400 varieties of 'the queer' is from Ernest Ludlow Bogart's *Economic History of the American People*, 2nd ed., New York, 1937. The credit policy of the Portland, Indiana, general merchant is from *American Grocer*, 27 Mar. 1884.

Chapter Ten

Incident at a Methodist camp meeting: *Vermont Quarterly*, Vol. xix, No. 2, Apr. 1951. Fred Barnes, who used to drum for a New Haven cigar firm, told me the Bill Freeland story. Country sayings, such as those quoted, pop up in many places. I leafed through Thompson, op. cit., for the ones I chose; also *New York Folklore Quarterly*, Vol. iii, No. 2, 1947; B. A. Botkin, ed., *A Treasury of New*

England Folklore, op. cit.; *Vermont Quarterly,* Vol. xx, No. 1, Jan.
1952; and *Southern Folklore Quarterly,* Vol. xi, No. 1, Mar. 1947.
The Missouri Republican, St. Louis, Mo., 12 Sept. 1825, carried the
advertising notice to loafers; Charles Morrow Wilson tells of Uncle
Homer's encounter with the general store telephone in the work previously cited. Miz Esty appears all too briefly in *Country Kitchen,* by
Della T. Lutes. The language used around the store stove is described
by Cross, op. cit.

Stories come so thick and fast in this chapter that I can only brief
the sources: The horse trader, Perkins, appears in Botkin, op. cit.;
the Hartwell cow, from Cutting, op. cit.; the elder's horse, Botkin,
op. cit.; also the tale of the watered milk and the quaint custom of
'deaconing' the apples; the 'stove piped' potatoes were contributed
by Tom Haines: I retold the anecdote of the johnnycake from Botkin, op. cit. The redoubtable McDowell brothers appear in *The Chicago Tribune,* 6 Nov. 1952.

The store dog, Jim Pug, was a personal acquaintance of Tom
Haines's. For Mr. Taylor's odd cigarette papers, see J. Evetts Haley,
*Charles Schreiner, General Merchandise: The Story of a Country
Store,* Austin, 1944; how Ezra fished up a lighted lantern, *Vermont
Quarterly,* Vol. xx, No. 1, Jan. 1952; Abe's fast team, *Green Moun-
tain Whittlin's,* Vol. i, op. cit.; the Bill and Abner Greenfield stories,
Thompson, op. cit.

Memories of weather and natural phenomena: the year of the big
snow in Illinois, *History of Pike County, Illinois,* Chicago, 1880;
the Yellow Day and the Dark Days, Kittredge, op. cit.; the hot summer of 1865, *The Berkshire Hills,* Vol. i, No. 11, July 1901; the
aurora borealis in 1811, Robinson, op. cit.

More country proverbs: Clifton Johnson, *What They Say in New
England,* Boston, 1896; Cutting, op. cit., and Thompson, op. cit.

Chapter Eleven

The discussion of stomach bitters is indebted to Arthur J. Cramp,
M.D., *Nostrums and Quackery,* 2 vols., Chicago, 1912, 1921; and to
Frank Presbrey, *The History and Development of Advertising,* Garden City, 1929. Kirkland, op. cit., goes into the matter of fashions in
patent medications. My paragraph of generalizations about patent
medicines was developed from material in Madge E. Pickard and
R. Carlyle Buley, *The Midwest Pioneer, his ills, cures & doctors,*
Crawfordsville, Ind., 1945. McNeil appears in the Rapp invoice
book, op. cit. Milton Silverman gives data I used on the presence of

narcotics in patent medicine formulas in his *Magic in a Bottle,* New York, 1941.

Robert P. Letcher depicts the cure-all artists as a type in *Annals of Congress, 18 Congress, I Session,* 2325, quoted in R. Carlyle Buley, *The Old Northwest, Pioneer Period,* 1815–1840, 2 vols., Indianapolis, 1950. Thomas Dyott, who needed medicine bottles in vast quantities, is the subject of several biographical paragraphs in Rhea Mansfield Knittle's *Early American Glass,* New York, 1935. 'Doctor' Chism is from Pickard, op. cit., and Joe B. Frantz has published a monograph, which I used for Borden data — *Gail Borden,* Norman, 1951. The phrase epitomizing the 1840's was taken from *The Columbian Lady's and Gentleman's Magazine,* Jan. 1844, quoted in 'Portrait of a Popular Journal,' by Mentor L. Williams, *The Bulletin of the New York Public Library,* Vol. 56, No. 1, Jan. 1952.

The importance of Philadelphia as a medical center is treated in Pickard, op. cit., and in Freedley, *Philadelphia and its Manufactures,* op. cit. Dr. Merriam's advertisement may be read and his face seen in the *Gazetteer of Berkshire County, Massachusetts,* Syracuse, 1885. Medical advertisements are quoted from *United States Commercial Register,* George Prior, Publisher, New York, 1852; the *Public Ledger,* Philadelphia, 25 Dec. 1851; *The Albany Argus,* Albany, N.Y., Vol. vii, No. 635, 23 Feb. 1819; *The Fabulous Forties,* by Meade Minnegerode, New York, 1924, and *To the Veteran,* Dr. Williams Medicine Company, Schenectady, New York, c.1895.

Mrs. Roy Runka told me about the time Hannah Lefevre backed into the store stove. The two Michigan anecdotes are retold from Richard M. Dorson, 'Folk Traditions of the Upper Peninsula,' *Michigan History,* Vol. 31, No. 1, Mar. 1947. The posthumous career of Lydia E. Pinkham is given in considerable detail by David L. Cohn, *The Good Old Days,* New York, 1940. Presbrey, op. cit., tells of the lady's confusion between Helmhold and von Humboldt. Mrs. Winslow's Soothing Syrup figures prominently in *Farmers and Mechanics Almanac,* A. L. Scovill & Co., New York, 1868, and in Cramp, op. cit.

For folk beliefs about medicines and cures, I used *Green Mountain Whittlin's,* Vol. i, op. cit., and *Southern Folklore Quarterly,* Vol. xiv, No. 4, Dec. 1950; *Journal of American Folklore,* Vol. 63, No. 249, July–Sept. 1950; and 'Oldtime Remedies,' by Lulu Walker, *The Rural New Yorker,* 100th Anniversary, 7 Jan. 1950. The poem about 'Medicine Jack,' of which I cited only the first verse, is quoted from an article by Ruth Conrad Henry Murray, in *New York Folk-*

lore Quarterly, Vol. vii, No. 4, 1951. For country wives as herbalists, I drew upon *Grandfather Was Queer,* by Richardson Wright, Philadelphia, 1939, and *Green Mountain Whittlin's,* Vol. ii, op. cit. Ed Howe's aphorism about Dr. Jayne is in his *Country Town Sayings,* Topeka, 1911. R. E. Banta tells in *The Ohio,* New York, 1944, how the white 'Indian doctors' elaborated on the natives' simples.

Chapter Twelve
The origin of the name Ivory Soap is given in *Into a Second Century with Proctor & Gamble,* Cincinnati, 1944. For the section on the precise meaning of 'branding' I consulted Willets & Seaman Order Book, 25 Feb. 1800 to 20 June 1801 (NYPL); *The Grocer's Companion,* op. cit.; *The Revised Statutes of the State of New-York,* 3rd ed., Albany, 1846; *Hunt's Merchants' Magazine,* op. cit. Vol. xxvi, No. 3, Mar. 1852; and Alexander Hamilton's 'Report to the House of Representatives, December 5, 1791,' *The Works of Alexander Hamilton,* New York, 1885.

The portion of this chapter dealing with brands in the modern sense of the word is derived from *The Story of Selling,* op. cit.; the article on 'Uneeda Biscuit,' *Modern Packaging,* Vol. 22, No. 6, Feb. 1949; 'Quaker Oats Modernizes a Sixty-Nine Year Old Character,' ibid. Vol. 19, No. 7, Mar. 1946; advertisement of P. T. Babbitt in *American Portrait Gallery,* 3 vols., New York, 1855; *The American Grocer,* op. cit. 9 Jan. 1879; *Packages,* Vol. v, No. 6, June 1902; 'The Great Breakfast-Food Industry,' by Frank Fayant, *Review of Reviews,* Vol. 77: 613–14; John Harrison Thornton's *The History of the Quaker Oats Company,* Chicago, 1933; Gerald Carson, 'Early Days in the Breakfast Food Industry,' *Advertising and Selling,* Sept. and Oct. 1945; the *N.B.C.,* Vol. i, No. 2, Mar. 1914; and ibid. No. 1, Feb. 1914.

Chapter Thirteen
The opening section of this chapter is based on an examination by Jean Labatut and Wheaton J. Lane, eds. *Highways in our National Life: A Symposium,* Princeton, 1950; *Public Roads,* Vol. i, No. 12, Apr. 1918; *Good Roads,* Vol. lxi, No. 1, 6 July 1921; and *Studebaker Centennial Report,* The Studebaker Corporation, South Bend, 1952.

Bill Nye's 'saying' about farmers working on the roads is quoted in *The Road Policy of Pennsylvania,* by Wilbur C. Plummer, Philadelphia, 1925. Robert S. and Helen Merrell Lynd tell the anecdote of the modern boy's view of the horse in *Middletown,* New York, 1929. The story that gives this chapter its title is recounted by Franklin M. Reck, in *A Car Travelling People*, Detroit, 1945. For the treatment of the general storekeeper and the mail-order houses, the following materials were used: Louis E. Asher and Edith Heal, op. cit.; E. W. Howe, *The Anthology of Another Town*, New York, 1920; *Catalogue*, 1894–95, Montgomery Ward & Co., op. cit.; *Our Drummer*, op. cit.; Mark Sullivan's *Our Times*, 6 vols., New York, 1926–35; and *Catalogue* #113, Sears Roebuck & Co., Chicago, 1903.

The role of the country doctor in popularizing the automobile is indicated in 'Automobiles for Physicians' Use.' *The Journal of the American Medical Association*, Vol. XLVI, No. 16, 21 Apr. 1906. Information on the Model T Ford comes from the files of *Ford Times* and *Made in America*, by John A. Kouwenhoven, Garden City, 1948. The shopping habits of the motorized farm family are reported in *Recent Social Trends in the United States*, 2 vols., New York, 1933. President Eisenhower's question addressed to retailers of today occurs in *Remarks of President Dwight D. Eisenhower*, op. cit.

PICTURE CREDITS

FRONTISPIECE: *Good Housekeeping Magazine.* TAIL PIECE: *Our Drummer,* Spring 1904, Butler Brothers, Chicago, author's collection. CHAPTER HEADINGS: *Specimens of Printing Types,* Mac-Kellar, Smiths and Jordan, Philadelphia, 1873, The New York Public Library. CHAPTER ILLUSTRATIONS: 1, Trade card, William B. Bradford, Jr., Boston, n.d., American Antiquarian Society; *Geography for Beginners,* by Emma Willard, Hartford, 1826, The New York Public Library. 2, 'Fresh Goods,' handbill from The Bella C. Landauer Collection in The New-York Historical Society; Store interior, wood engraving by Alexander Anderson, The New York Public Library. 3, Peddler's cart, wood engraving by Alexander Anderson, The New York Public Library; Bill head, from The Bella C. Landauer Collection in The New-York Historical Society. 4, Wall motto, *Yankee Magazine* and Arthur F. Lear; Crossroads store, *Hearth and Home,* Vol. i, No. 27, 26 June 1869, The New York Public Library. 5, Ledger page, Lincoln Life Foundation; Hand and quill pen, wood engraving by Alexander Anderson, The New York Public Library. 6, General store post office, *Hearth and Home,* Vol. i, No. 38, 11 Sept. 1869, The New York Public Library. 7, Auction scene, *American Agriculturist,* Dec. 1860, author's collection; Handbill of an assignee's sale, Susan Reed and James Karen. 8, Commercial traveler's post card, author's collection; Group in hotel lobby, 'That Reminds Me! New Crop of Drummers' Yarns,' New York, 1894, author's collection; Tobacco cutter, *Our Drummer,* op. cit. 9, Broadside of Francis Conkling Huyck, Edna L. Jacobsen; Wall motto, from The Bella C. Landauer Collection in The New-York Historical Society; Advertisement of Abel Smith, Winslow, Illinois, in *Prairie Democrat,* Vol. i, No. 10, 26 Jan. 1848, Freeport, (Ill.) Public Library. 10, Old store chair, *Our Drummer,* op. cit. 11, Patent medicine broadside, from The Bella C. Landauer Collection in The New-York Historical Society. 12, Coffee mill, *Our Drummer,* op. cit. 13, Train carrying U.S. mail, *Our Drummer,* op. cit.; Surrey, *Our Drummer,* op. cit.; Model T Ford, 1919, Ford Motor Company.

INDEX

Candy, conversation, 194
Canned goods, 196
Card, trade, 13, 255, 267-8
Carpenter, Amos, 111
Carr, Robert W., 133-4
Carter, Henry W., 57-8
Carter team, 58
'Carting gentleman,' 38-9
Carton, see Package
Cash, and credit, 211-13; discount for, 153
Cash register, 107-9, 211
Cassia bark, 201
Cassville, Wis., 287
Castle Garden, N.Y., 139
Castoria, 263
Catalogues, mail-order, 156, 184, 257, 282
Cedar Street, N.Y., 141
Censuses, 18, 165
Chair, sitters', 219
Chamber pots, 196
Chambers Street, N.Y., 147
Chambersburg, Pa., 250
Chase, Mary Ellen, 256
Chase and Sanborn, 260
Cheese safe, 204-5
Chelsea, Vt., 58
Chewing gum, 197
Chicago, Ill., 153, 175, 180, 279
Chicago Jokes and Anecdotes for Railroad Travellers and Fun Lovers, 171
China trade, opening of, 9
Chism, Dr., 240
Chore boy, 96
Cigar cutter, 194
Cigarettes, 194, 226, 268
Cigars, 264
Cincinnati, Ohio, 150, 152, 180, 249, 259
Clark, George (Pennfield, Mich.), 205
Clark, George (Salisbury, Conn.), 79
Clark, George A., 193
Cleaning store, 98-9

Clerk, 7, 15, 65-6, 276-7
Clintonville, Conn., 256
Coalton, Ohio, 107
Coat livery, 178
Cobb, Sylvanus, Jr., 86
Cobbler, 199
Cockles, 194
Codes, cost price, 94-5; selling price, 93-5
Coffee, 20, 263; mill, 205, 263-4; roaster, 207, 263
Coffin & Landell, 100
Coffins, 196
Coinage, need for, 8-9
Cole, George W., 170
Colebrook, Conn., 82, 155
Coleman & Stetson, 135
Collection letters, 78
Comfort magazine, 267
Commentaries (Blackstone), 121
Commercial Advertiser, New York, 135
Commercials, see Salesmen
Commercial Traveller's Guide Book, The, 169
Committee of the Society of Commercial Travellers, 161-2, 165
Complete-stock motif, 189-90
Condensed milk, 196
Cone, Mark, 98, 151
Conestoga wagon, 203
Congress of the Confederation, 5-8
Connersville, Ind., 240
Constitution, U.S., 8, 278
Consumer packaging, 203
Conversation candy, 194
Cook, William, 58, 60
Cooper, Dr. J. W., 255
Cooperage, see Barrels
Cooperstown, N.Y., 39
Cost symbol, 30
Cottolene, 170
Counterfeiters, 7-8, 71, 211
Country pay, 20
Country store, 12, 117, 121, 123, 137, 202, 207, 211, 277, 279, 283, 286,